STORIES *of* JEWISH LIFE

STORIES *of* JEWISH LIFE

CASALE MONFERRATO-ROME-JERUSALEM, 1876–1985

AUGUSTO SEGRE

Translated and with an Introduction by Steve Siporin
Foreword by Tamar Segre and Daniel Segre

WAYNE STATE UNIVERSITY PRESS

DETROIT

ISBN 978-0-8143-4765-2 (hardback); ISBN 978-0-8143-4766-9 (ebook)

Library of Congress Control Number: 2019952506

Wayne State University Press
Leonard N. Simons Building
4809 Woodward Avenue
Detroit, Michigan 48201-1309

Visit us online at wsupress.wayne.edu

Published with support from the fund for the Raphael Patai Series in Jewish Folklore and Anthropology.

To Augusto and Iris's children,

grandchildren, great grandchildren,

and all the generations to come.

CONTENTS

STORIES OF JEWISH LIFE

MAPS

FOREWORD

Our father's short stories cover a period of more than one hundred years, from 1876 to 1985. They begin in Casale Monferrato, where he was born, and end in Jerusalem. People, situations, moments, values, and experiences blend in the stories in a dynamic mixture that intrigues the reader throughout the course of the book.

The stories bring to life moments that have had a deep influence on our lives. Like little drops of time crystallized in our memory, these moments are full of values, teachings, reflections. They come from the world in which we were educated and make it possible for us to establish rapid and meaningful connections. These little drops, atoms of life captured in a bubble of time, protect and maintain their freshness. They are sleeping moments awakened by a word, a look, a feeling, a color, a light, a smile, a hug, a push, a sound, a place, or anything that has enough strength to create the sufficient and positive energy of memory.

The stories our father wrote are suspended forever in a timeless reality. These drops of time behave like the rain, not melting into each other to create huge drops, which would be unbearable. Each drop falls on its own, leaving our lives as time goes by, yet still, at the same time, remaining locked in our memories independently.

Most of the stories arise from a world that existed before we were born, but in reproducing moments, dialogues, and situations, our father gave the stories a specific new function: to show us, through his experience, the multicolored ways that life offers challenges and experiences.

Perhaps the most unusual and unexpected element in this book is what our father wrote in his dedication: "To myself and to all those who openly and without compromising always fought, at a dear price, against everything and everybody, for freedom and for living according to humanity and justice." Our father dedicated this book to himself and to people like him. He passed away the day after the book was published, just a few hours before it was officially presented to the public. Thus, a dedication, in a mere second, became an epitaph that could have been written on his headstone. In a split second, our father's words gained prophetic depth.

Changes occur, the stories seem to say, sometimes with no warning. We ask ourselves how: How did such changes occur? How were they allowed? The journey our father describes in these short snapshots of life give us remarkable insight into some of the difficult moments in his life and in the life of his family and community. His journey allows us to reflect and understand that each moment in one's life has an almost eternal value and that in each moment we can find a positive, vital reinforcement that allows us to carry on and look at the future with expectations and hopes.

These stories have accompanied us throughout our years. First, they were a curiosity, a window opening on the reality that our father lived and that we were slowly discovering. With time, they became part of our heritage, the comfortable feeling that our family has a firm background of experiences from which to receive guidance and reassurance.

For us today, two scenes come to life every time we read these short stories. The first is each story itself, each with its own touch of magic, keeping the reader alert to the end. The second scene is made of the images and the sounds of our father actually telling these stories, often to guests and friends in our home in Rome. His voice, his ability to keep an audience attracted, focused, and almost hypnotized through his precise diction and well-timed pauses created tension, excitement, and expectations. His capacity and energy were no doubt the result of a life often lived on the edge, which by necessity forged his sharp awareness. But perhaps our father's willpower and stamina were also fueled by our mother, who was a living example of how to overcome adversity by concentrating on the future while dealing with daily obligations and tasks. Our mother and father complemented each other and produced a firm, secure harbor where we could take shelter, charge our batteries, and learn.

Through the amazing work done by Professor Steve Siporin, whose translation is a work of art, coming as it does from an enormous love and respect for our father and from an outstanding professionalism, you will be transported in a sequence of moments that actually happened in real life and marked our father, our family, and us. Thank you, Steve.

Readers, enjoy these unique moments. We are sure that at the end of the book, you will look at your own crystallized drops of time from a different perspective.

Tamar and Daniel Segre

ACKNOWLEDGMENTS

I feel a deep sense of gratitude toward Augusto Segre for writing this book and for telling me his stories. When I met him, I was in the midst of a long quest to find "the small Italian Jewish world." He opened that world to me from the inside as no one else could. A nearly equal sense of thanks goes to Tamar Segre and Dani Segre: They trusted me with their father's precious legacy. I also thank Dani's wife, Ruth, and their children, who warmly welcomed my family and me into their family.

Professor Dario Calimani was unfailing in his generosity when I had questions about Italian language, especially dialects. He also shared his profound knowledge of Italian Jewish culture.

I began this translation as a Lady Davis Fellow at the Hebrew University of Jerusalem in 2010, and I am grateful to the Lady Davis Foundation for giving me that opportunity and support.

The staff at Wayne State University Press combined enthusiasm with patience to make my dream of publishing Augusto Segre's *Stories* in English a reality. I especially want to thank Annie Martin, Kristin Harpster, Emily Nowak, Kristina Stonehill, and Jamie Jones for their fine work.

Mimi Braverman edited my translation and introduction not only with professional skill but with insight. I will always be grateful for all the improvements she made.

Ona, my wife, you are also my irreplaceable editor and patient ear. You listen and respond and help me when I am frustrated and in despair over the challenge to be articulate, and you join me when I am overjoyed with discovery and beauty.

My translations of two of the stories from *Stories of Jewish Life* appeared previously in literary journals. "Jachetu's Ring" was published in *Metamorphoses* (23 [2015]: 241–50) and "Purchase of Goods of Dubious Origin" in JewishFiction .net (issue 16 [fall 2015]).

A NOTE ON THE TRANSLATION

Part of a word's meaning lies in its history and its cultural associations. Even when a translator finds a precise equivalent in another language, these subliminal dimensions usually fall away because, like a good local wine, they do not travel well. I want to provide two examples of such words, because these two words are critical and recur regularly in my translation. With these examples I lay out what gets lost in translation. The English words are *Jew* and *community*, but it is the Italian words that stand behind them that need to be explicated.

Italian supplies three different words for *Jew*: *ebreo*, *giudeo*, and *israelita*. Segre uses the first and the last but not the second.

Ebreo (feminine *ebrea*) literally means "Hebrew" (a person, not the language) and is the most common term used to denote Jews in Italian today. Thus I translate *ebreo* as *Jew* because in English we do not commonly call Jews "Hebrews." *Ebreo* is generally considered "unmarked" or neutral, as is *Jew*. Segre writes *ebreo* most of the time, unless he is quoting historical texts verbatim. Still, it should be noted that *ebreo* is not always neutral and can be used negatively to mean "miser" or "skinflint," just as *Jew* in English is usually neutral but can also be used as an insult. (See Dario Calimani's observations about *ebreo* when I discuss *israelita*, after my brief remarks about *giudeo*.)

Giudeo (feminine *giudea*) literally means "Judean" or Jew. Historically, *giudeo* became the most pejorative of the three Italian terms and was used as a slur.[1] It could also mean "usurer," "Judas," or "traitor." Its similarity to the name Judas (*Giuda*) has been noted and exploited. Both *ebreo* and *giudeo* appear in a taunt I collected in Venice in 1978.[2] Segre does not use *giudeo*.

Israelita (masculine and feminine) literally means "Israelite," but it can be translated as "Israelite" or "Jew." Of the three terms, *israelita* is the most interesting for the historical period of Segre's stories. By the late nineteenth century, the term *Israelita* had been adopted as a polite way to refer to Jews because, as Calimani writes, "the term *ebreo* had come to be considered derogatory, often used in disparaging contexts, as in the phrase *sporco ebreo* ('dirty Jew')."[3] The need to find a polite term seems ultimately to mean that being a Jew was in itself not polite or respectable and that a euphemism was required. Nineteenth-century Jews embraced the term *israelita* (a noun) and the adjective *israelitico* and applied them to their institutions, such as synagogues (Tempio Israelitico, Israelite Temple) and communities (Comunità Israelitica, Israelite Community).[4] Ephraim Nissan writes that in "the late 1980s . . . the *Unione delle Comunità* Israelitiche *Italiane* [Union of the Italian *Israelite* Communities] changed its name to *Unione delle Comunità* Ebraiche *Italiane* [Union of the Italian *Jewish* Communities]. This was a restoration of the dignity of the term *ebreo*."[5] By that point, the late 1980s, the term *israelita* was "felt to be prudish and obsolete."[6] To preserve the self-conscious assertion of respectability that *israelita* represented for middle- and upper-class Jews in the post-ghetto, pre-Holocaust era, I usually translate *israelita* as "Israelite," especially when it appears in the documents from the late nineteenth and early twentieth century that Segre quotes.

The second word considered here is *community*, the translation of *comunità*. When *comunità* is used in conjunction with a particular city, as in la Comunità ebraica di Venezia or la Comunità ebraica di Casale, it seems, at first, that the best English equivalent would be *congregation*, because *congregation* refers to "a group of people assembled for religious worship."[7] But the Italian word *comunità*, in a Jewish context, is more encompassing than the English word *congregation* because Italian Jewish Communities evolved out of self-governing entities with extensive internal communal ties beyond assembling for religious worship. To be counted and defined as Jewish in Italy, one must be enrolled as such in a particular *comunità*. Furthermore, in the United States several congregations might be established in a given city, but in Italy, until recently in Milan and Rome, only one official *comunità* existed per city. Thus there is the Comunità di Venezia, the Comunità di Casale, and so on, each of which consists of the enrolled Jewish population of the city in its entirety. The literal translation *community* seems better at communicating the Italian Jewish corporate sense than *congregation*.

Given this context and following the Italian, I capitalize *Community* in English to distinguish the proper name of a legal, Jewish, communal entity from the generic community.

It is also worth noting that until roughly the beginning of the twentieth century, Italian Jewish Communities were called "Universities" (*Università*): thus l'Università israelitica di Venezia or l'Università israelitica di Casale. This older usage of *university* to refer to a Jewish Community was based on and paralleled the use of the term to refer to guilds or other corporations. Occasionally, translators have mistakenly translated *università* in this context as "university," with humorous outcomes, such as "the Jewish University of Pitigliano" (a town of a few thousand inhabitants). I have anachronistically "updated" these earlier references by translating *università* as "community" when *università* occurred in Segre's nineteenth-century texts.

INTRODUCTION

Stories of Jewish Life is a chronologically ordered series of short stories, sketches, vignettes, and personal essays. Taken together, this spectrum of prose genres creates a subjective history (in the best sense) of the Italian Jews from the last quarter of the nineteenth century to the late twentieth century. A number of recent historical studies cover part or all of this period,[1] but Augusto Segre's book does something these books cannot do. He lived through a large part of the era in Italy and knew it firsthand and intimately, which made him a witness and his writing a testimony. The result is a collection of stories but also an unconventional history told through revealing moments in the lives of ordinary people and communities, not through a history of leaders' decisions, critical moments, precise data, and confirmable facts, even though that kind of history is essential and irreplaceable. In reading Segre's stories, we zoom in on individuals and scenes to observe small yet telling episodes that uncover the inner life of Jews in Italy during the dramatic period from 1876 on. We progress chronologically, focusing story by story on new characters and episodes yet realizing that the issues and dilemmas Italian Jews faced remained constant. We move from the exultation of liberation from the ghettos, national unification, and full citizenship to the dark era of fascism, anti-Semitic racial laws, the retraction of citizenship, and the ultimate betrayal, the Holocaust. In sketches from the postwar period we catch glimpses of how Italian Jews tried to return to a normal life and how Moshè, the protagonist of the latter part of the book, fulfilled his lifelong dream of immigrating to Israel. The "unimportant," the "minor," and the everyday yield a strong sense of the texture of life in the oldest yet relatively unfamiliar community of European Jews during the period 1876–1985.

Map 1. Italy and Israel

Segre's stories resonate most fully when read with awareness of their historical and cultural background. Thus in the first of the three parts that make up this introduction I provide a short summary of Italian Jewish history, focusing on the past two centuries, one of the most critical periods of change during the more than 2,000 years of Italian Jewish history and the period most relevant to *Stories*. In the second section I present observations about the place of the stories in Jewish literature. In the final section I examine *Stories of Jewish Life* as Augusto Segre's personal life review.

★ ★ ★

To begin with the earliest hard knowledge we have of a Jewish presence in Italy, we know that Jews were living in Rome in the time of Julius Caesar, and probably before. (And their presence is continuous to the present day.) Several Roman authors mention Jews. Graves of Jews, visible today in catacombs beneath the city, display images of seven-stemmed candelabras (*menorot*), one of the most important ancient Jewish symbols, verifying the Jewish provenance of these ancient burials and the permanent residence of Jews in the Eternal City. Jews also lived in dozens of towns and cities in Sicily and Sardinia and throughout southern Italy from Roman times until the sixteenth century. Rephrasing a famous biblical passage, a twelfth-century scholar wrote, "From Bari comes forth the Law, and the word of God from Otranto,"[2] placing southern Italy on par with ancient Israel for its learning and holiness. In other words, southern Italy's Jews participated fully in the Jewish culture of the Middle Ages.[3]

In the early sixteenth century, when southern Italy came under Spanish dominion, Jews were expelled (1541), as they had been earlier from Sardinia

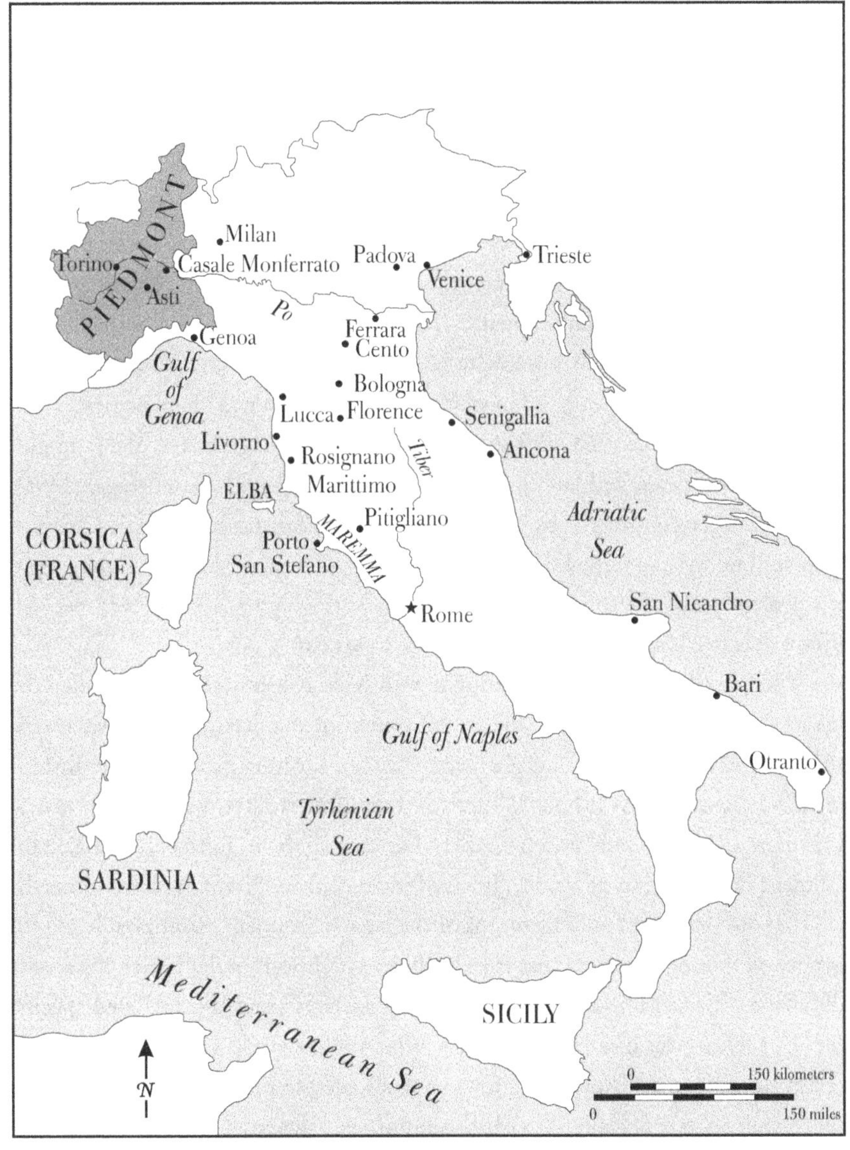

Map 2. Italy

(1492) and Sicily (1493). Some found refuge in the Muslim world, especially the Ottoman Empire, and others traveled to central and northern Italy to join Jewish communities that had existed since the Middle Ages or later in towns and cities such as Florence, Ferrara, Padova, and Venice.

This great sixteenth-century shift of the Jewish population from southern Italy to central and northern Italy had enormous ramifications immediately and for centuries to come. For instance, in the nineteenth century, when industrial development and economic growth accelerated dramatically in Italy, it was in the north where it all happened. Jews, by then long settled there, were in the right part of the country to take part in this economic boom, both benefiting from it and contributing to it. On the negative side, during World War II, central and northern Italy were the wrong parts of the country in which to live, especially for Jews. Because the battlefront moved slowly up the peninsula from south to north over the course of nearly two years, the farther north one lived, the longer one was subject to the German occupation and its brutality. Jews were vulnerable to capture and deportation to Auschwitz by German soldiers much longer than they would have been had they lived in southern Italy, which was liberated first.

The sixteenth-century shift to northern Italy was magnified by the immigration of recently expelled Jewish refugees from Spain (1492) and Portugal (1496), either directly or indirectly, by way of places such as Amsterdam and the Ottoman Empire. This influx swelled the Italian Jewish population in absolute numbers and as a percentage of the total Italian population to the highest level it ever reached, although it was still quite small, only about 1 percent.[4]

This population shift also coincided with what has sometimes been called the age of the ghettos, from 1516 (the establishment of the first ghetto, in Venice) to 1870 (the liberation of the last ghetto, in Rome). Loaning money (an act forbidden Christians by the Catholic Church) at low interest rates was the main reason Christian rulers allowed "unbelievers" to live among them. Even before the establishment of the ghetto of Venice, Jewish residence throughout central and northern Italy was tolerated only by means of the legal instrument of renewable ten- to twenty-year-long contracts that stipulated the conditions under which Jews were allowed to live within a given city. These contracts (*condotte*), included specific details, such as the interest rates under which loans could be made and which occupations besides loan banking Jews were allowed to practice. Local authorities also levied special taxes on Jewish communities, stipulated that Jews wear particular items of clothing (a red or yellow hat or badge), and maintained travel restrictions. Once ghettos were established, Jews were required to remain inside them from sunset to sunrise and during Christian holy days.

Despite these restrictive, repressive conditions, Jewish life in Italy generally thrived during the sixteenth and early seventeenth centuries, at least compared to Jewish life elsewhere in Europe. This is not the place to describe the many remarkable achievements of what was a vital, creative Jewish society. Suffice it to say that, despite the restrictions under which they lived, Jews achieved a great deal. They not only wrote significant, enduring works on the traditional topics of religious scholarship; they were also innovators. They developed printing, especially the printing of religious texts, for example, the Talmud. They participated in and contributed to the Renaissance arts, particularly music, dance, literature, and theater. They were valued as doctors, and exceptions to the law that Jews could not leave the ghetto at night were allowed when non-Jews needed a doctor. Jewish folk culture also flourished, as Italian Jews developed local holiday customs, dialects, and cuisines that varied according to the Italian regions in which they lived. Jewish women created textiles with which to adorn the synagogue, its holy objects, and their homes. Some of these textiles have come down to us today and are still used in Italian synagogues; others are conserved in museums and private collections. Historian Attilio Milano asserted that, though the cost was great, the ghetto strengthened Jewish religious identity because the synagogue took on the role of unifying the community and raising spirits: "[The synagogue] succeeded in imposing on Italian Judaism, through the centuries of seclusion, this precept: everything in the synagogue, nothing outside the synagogue."[5]

Nevertheless, the longer Jews lived in ghettos, the more their economic lives deteriorated. A census undertaken immediately after Napoleon's troops conquered Venice and liberated the ghetto in 1797 revealed that this Jewish community, which once featured wealthy international merchants, had become extremely impoverished.[6] Even 140 years later, in 1937, almost one-fourth of all Venetian Jews still remained poor.[7] The ghetto of Rome was equally impoverished and extremely unhealthy as well, partly because of the annual floods from the Tiber River, which flows through the center of Rome, next to the low-lying ghetto.

The liberation of Italy's ghettos did not happen nationwide in one fell swoop, because Italy was not yet a unified country capable of passing laws for the entire peninsula. In fact, at the dawn of the nineteenth century Italy was merely a "geographical expression," as Austrian chancellor Count Metternich, Europe's preeminent statesman of the era, famously called it—a puzzle of different kingdoms and principalities, each with its own laws. The termination of these separate states and the unification of the country, which was accomplished through the canny politics and patriotic wars of the Risorgimento (the "resurgence" or "resurrection") was the most important political development for nineteenth-century Italy. The Risorgimento also meant everything to Italian Jews, both because they were patriotic Italians and because part of Italy's liberal, enlightened Risorgimento agenda was brotherhood and equality of citizenship for everyone, regardless of religion. That meant ending the ghetto system.

Segre's *Stories of Jewish Life* begins in the wake of the Risorgimento. "Love of Country," the opening account, anchors its events with a date, "the year of grace 1876," only six years after the liberation of Italy's last ghetto, in Rome, and a generation after the major emancipation of the Jews of Piedmont in 1848, which closed many ghettos and granted Jews citizenship. "Love of Country" frames the entire book by introducing the major questions that remained with Italian Jews, in one form or another, from then on: Did the wonders of equality and citizenship also bring dangers to the Jewish way of life? Were Jews required to sacrifice their Jewish identity if they wanted to be good Italians? In "Love of Country" Segre shows that these worries were already present, active, and recognized by some members of the older generation by 1876.

In "Love of Country" Segre portrays the mentality of the time through the single-minded patriotic career of Rabbi Sabato Graziadio Treves and the language of the equally patriotic Jewish press. Rabbi Treves's words are even more disturbing for what they leave out than for what they promote, for they leave out Jewish content. The rabbi himself seems to regard Judaism mainly as a useful tool for the support of Italian patriotism. "Love of Country" implies that this attitude and leadership will undermine Italian Judaism and contribute to its decline. The results will be Jewish cultural illiteracy and assimilation, what Segre's father called the "fine fruits of emancipation."[8] Rabbi Treves is important, Segre makes clear, because he was not unique: "From the many possibilities, here is one 'edifying example,'" as Segre puts it. In other words, Rabbi Treves's values and style of rabbinic leadership were widespread among Italian rabbis. Another was Chief Rabbi Giuseppe Foà of Torino, who said, "We feel ourselves to be firstly Italians rather than Jews."[9] An even earlier and yet more extreme example from 1848 was "Rabbi Salomone Olper . . . [who] publicly kissed the cross in Piazza San Marco in Venice in the name of Italian unity."[10] Olper became chief rabbi in Casale Monferrato, Segre's hometown.

It is no wonder that besides the gratitude Jews felt toward King Carlo Alberto, they also felt pride in their new status because they themselves had done much to gain it. They made up only one-tenth of 1% of the Italian population in the early 1800s, a minuscule minority by any standard. Yet they had taken part in the Risorgimento as soldiers[11] in numbers far out of proportion to their tiny percentage of the population.[12] Napoleon's conquest and the resulting legacy and diffusion of the ideals of the French Revolution excited Jews as well as Christians. If Jews, like many others, saw realistic benefits to themselves in Italian unification, they were also sincere, ardent patriots, caught up in the fervor and hope that swept north and central Italy, especially among the literate, urban middle-class population, which included many of Italy's Jews.

★ ★ ★

The Italian Jewish historical context yields a richer reading experience of Segre's stories, sketches, and essays, but the stories, in turn, enrich the historical context by giving the reader a feel for traditional Jewish life in Italy in modern times. There are few other places to which we can turn to get this sense. Significant and celebrated Italian Jewish authors exist—Giorgio Bassani, Natalia Ginzburg, Carlo Levi, Primo Levi, Alberto Moravia, and Italo Svevo, to mention a few. But these best known Italian Jewish authors have written little about the traditional dimensions of twentieth-century Italian Jewish life. In their writings, glimpses of Italian Jewish culture, let alone Italian Jewish *traditional* culture, are rare. Segre brings to light what his contemporary compatriots have missed, what they were unable or chose not to describe: the "small Italian Jewish world" (Segre's phrase). In *Stories of Jewish Life* Segre does not just recreate that world; he makes it the center of attention. Through characters, issues, and events that resonate profoundly with Jewish culture and experience in other times and places, he evokes the "small Italian Jewish world" during one of the most critical periods in its long history.[13]

There is, for instance, the literary sketch "A Shrinking Violet," in which a poor woman who, through no fault of her own, lives the life of an uncomplaining martyr, misused by her community. Segre lifts this anonymous protagonist from the pages of a newspaper column written in 1877, gives her story life, and describes the hypocritical, unjust way in which the community exploited her. This woman's life and attitude may elicit thoughts of another downtrodden, poverty-stricken figure, Bontsha the Silent, one of the most famous characters in Yiddish literature. The words the judge in the heavenly court addresses to Bontsha after his death could easily have been addressed to the shrinking violet: "You have always suffered and you have always kept silent. . . . Your silence was never rewarded."[14] Segre gives us an Italian Jewish version of this Jewish archetype, a version with the particular nuances of the post-ghetto era in Italy.

Other of Segre's stories allude to other important Jewish texts, whether by design or simply because Segre tapped the shared underground roots of Jewish culture. He could do so because, unlike other Italian Jewish writers of his time, he was in touch with the core of traditional Jewish expression. The son of the rabbi of the small Jewish community of Casale Monferrato, Segre studied and became a rabbi too, although, after witnessing his father's sometimes humiliating experience, he never accepted a congregational post himself. His interest in Jewish culture went beyond traditional religious texts, and in his reading and personal encounters he also explored Jewish history and culture in societies beyond Italy, making direct and indirect use of foreign and historical religious and secular Jewish texts in his own writing. In "Chronicle of a Journey," for instance, Segre reconstructs the 1878 travels of Flaminio Servi, a rabbi who traveled to several of Italy's Jewish communities less than a decade after Italian national unification. The connection to another Jewish text in this case lies in the way Servi's journey recalls the famous medieval-era journey of Benjamin of Tudela. Beginning in Spain, Tudela traveled through the northern Mediterranean (including Italy) and the Middle East in the late twelfth century, visiting and describing the Jewish communities of his time. His writing remains a landmark of Jewish history and ethnography.[15] In the summer of 1878, Servi—newspaper editor, publisher, as well as rabbi in Casale Monferrato—visited Jewish communities in Alessandria, Bologna, Cento, Ancona, Senigallia, and Parma. In his newspaper, *The Israelite Banner* (*Il Vessillo Israelitico*), he wrote a quasi-ethnographic account of his journey, which Segre excerpts and comments on in "Chronicle of a Journey." In this story the reader gets a sense of the vitality of these Jewish communities, although they were actually on the eve of their decline. Like Benjamin of Tudela, Servi provides us with information about Jewish communities that is difficult to come by and thus echoes his illustrious model's voice. Thanks to Segre, this rare ethnographic travelogue from an obscure Italian Jewish newspaper comes to our attention today.

In other passages Segre also portrays post-ghetto individuals who retain something of the ghetto world in their character, behavior, and speech. These characters may also remind us of figures from other small Jewish worlds, especially Ashkenazic Eastern Europe, who we have learned about from folklore and literature. They sometimes feel like stage characters from the commedia dell'arte (or, maybe better, the *commedia del ghetto*), and their very names (Jachetu, Giuseppin, Rusin, Duardo, Polda), some of which are vernacular splicings of Piedmontese dialect and Hebrew,[16] evoke the small world of the Italian Jews.

Among these memorable characters is an old, unnamed Jewish railway porter who reveres Hebrew so much that he responds to a shipping tag written in Hebrew on Segre's suitcases as he would to the holy Torah itself. In "A Railway Porter in Venice" Moshè's

> astonishment knew no limits when he saw the porter move his fingers along the edge of the suitcases, and then to his eyes first and afterward to his mouth, to kiss them. In short, something like what happens in the synagogue when any of the faithful kiss the *Séfer Torà* (Scroll of the Torah).
>
> More and more surprised, Moshè asked him, "May I know what you're doing?"
>
> "What? Don't you see?" the old man asked, somewhat vexed. "Don't you see that it's Torah?"[17]
>
> Moshè drew nearer and read. Written in Hebrew on the small tags glued to each suitcase, was simply, "Tel Aviv–Haifa!"

The porter's sincere, un-self-conscious sanctification of the mundane, finding the holy in the ordinary, fulfills a Jewish religious ideal to perfection. That ideal finds expression in the theme of the unlearned but authentic worshiper whose prayer, because of its sincerity and utter lack of affectation, is more beloved by God than the prayers of the learned, no matter how knowledgeable and adept they may be. This theme is well known from Hasidic stories set in the woods, fields, and small towns of Eastern Europe in times long past. Segre discovers the same theme and finds it to be at home in Italy, in the modern railway station of Venice, in his own experience with a Venetian Jew in 1948.

The dramatic tragedies of "Jachetu's Ring," "Purchase of Goods of Dubious Origin," and "A Forbidden Marriage," each a small masterpiece, bring the reader into a Jewish world that no living person remembers from firsthand experience and that few, if any, have ever described. In several of Segre's other literary sketches ("The Small Winter Temple," "Unexpected Death Notice," and "Occupational Hazards"), we are privileged to observe the experiences of a rabbi in that world, in a small Italian Jewish community in the 1920s and 1930s—privileged, because, once again, no one else has described this world and experience intimately, from the inside.

Segre's treatment of this vanished world is affectionate but not romanticized. For instance, "Occupational Hazards" reveals the abject poverty, unsanitary conditions, and ignorance of an aging Jewish family in Casale in the 1920s and 1930s. Taken together, the stories treat the major concerns of Segre's activist life and meditative writings; they are not upbeat, at least not most of them. Their themes include the seductiveness of modern life, the betrayal of tradition, the attraction of fashionable political movements, and the effects of totalitarianism. More positive are the stories of national rebirth and renewal in the Land of Israel. All these themes, positive or not, have lost none of their relevance with the passage of time, nor are they limited to the Italian Jewish experience. Segre, who lived with these concerns in real life in twentieth-century Italy, is the reader's guide. And the reader is Segre's confidant.

★ ★ ★

As a literary interpretation of Italian Jewish everyday life and history during the period 1876–1985, *Stories of Jewish Life* gradually spins another thread as the narratives follow one after the other, gliding imperceptibly from stories of Italian Jews in the late nineteenth and early twentieth centuries to the story of one Italian Jew, Moshè. He first appears in "A Bar Mitzvah," actually Moshè's own bar mitzvah, toward the end of the 1920s. The subject of the story is not religious ritual or responsibility; rather, it is the boy's main concern—his first suit. Making that purchase is a ritual too, and it becomes an extraordinary vehicle for conveying the normal concerns and emotions that were part of Jewish life, even under fascism.

Initially, the reader may not recognize the writer's shift to a single central character. Even when the reader realizes that this character, Moshè, reappears in episode after episode, it may not be evident that Moshè is Segre himself, the author, and that he has made himself the central figure of the narrative throughout the rest of the book. But fairly soon the reader probably realizes that *Stories of Jewish Life* is autobiography and memoir as well as stories of a particular time and place. Segre disguises himself slightly (Moshè was Augusto Segre's Hebrew name) by writing about himself in the third person. The chronological thread of Italian Jewish history continues, but the trail of the narrative passes to Moshè's personal experiences as he grows up, learns what it means to live in a fascist society,

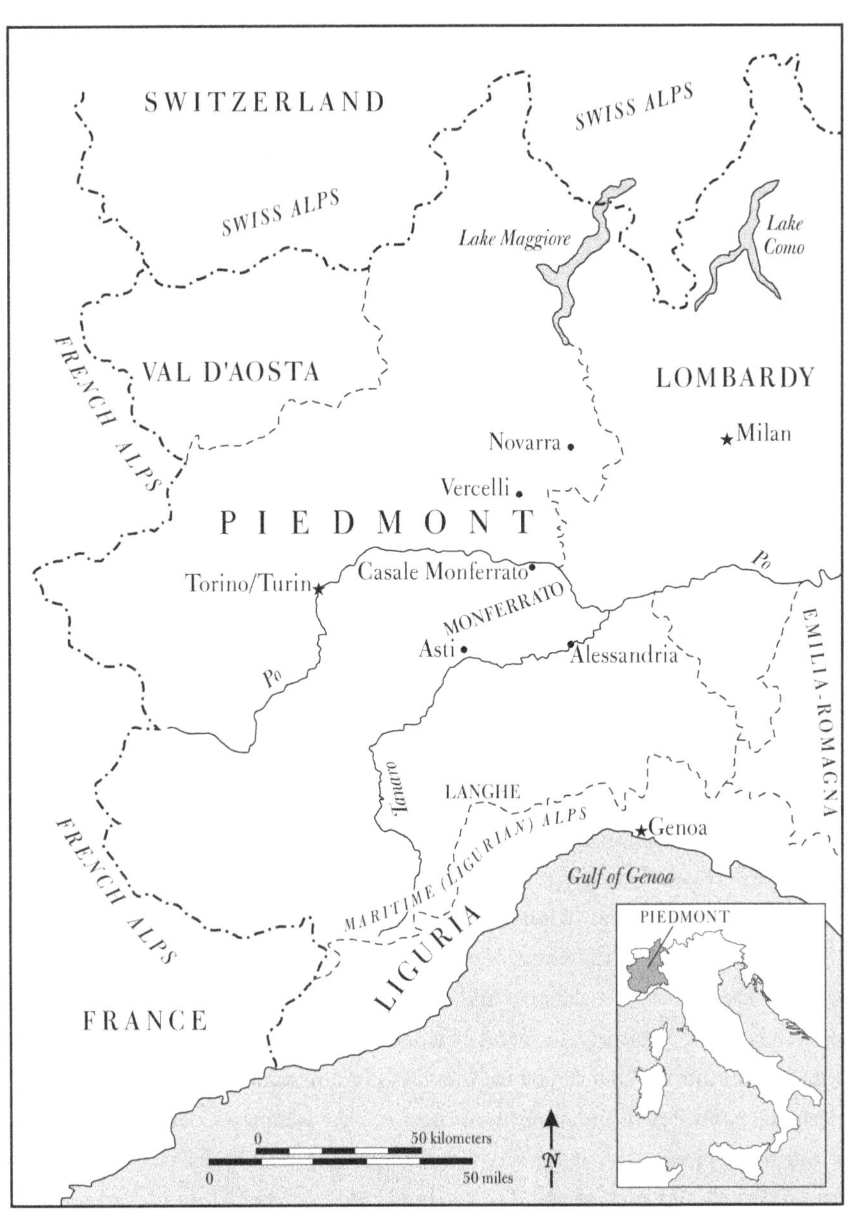

Map 3. Piedmont

and later, what it means to fight in a war in which Jews like him, his family, and his friends are hunted down. Moshè becomes a partisan in the countryside near Casale. In 1948, three years after World War II ends, he travels to Israel for three months during the War of Independence and then returns to Rome to carry out a career in Jewish education and cultural affairs. When he retires, in the late 1970s, he immigrates to Israel, and his emigration/immigration narratives and meditations form the substance of the final part of *Stories of Jewish Life*.

That Moshè is actually the same person as the author is never acknowledged by Segre. Why this transparent artifice and why the third person? Why create an indirect kind of memoir from a series of stories and anecdotes, and why, after already publishing one memoir (*Memories of Jewish Life*),[18] write a second one?

There is more than one puzzle here. Perhaps the concept of life review provides some answers to these questions, or at least a fruitful way to approach, appreciate, and enjoy *Stories of Jewish Life*. The life review concept asserts that as we age, especially as we reach our 60s, 70s, 80s, and 90s, we tend to look back and evaluate our lives as the end approaches. Memories may become sharper and clearer as they return to consciousness and thus aid in a normal developmental stage of life. Hence reminiscence is not pathological; rather, it is a kind of self-administered therapy that we may even be "programmed" to undertake. Resolution of past conflicts and problems—learning to accept the life one has lived—appears to be the goal of a process that takes place consciously or unconsciously. Thus the phrase "life review" simply refers to the developmental task of making sense of one's life retrospectively, a kind of debriefing during one's final years.[19]

Much happens in the course of a long life, and sometimes the connections between the countless events big and small, people past and present, and places, seem to be weak, arbitrary, or merely chronological, without meaningful connections or continuity. One can be haunted by one's mistakes, harm one has caused, harm one has suffered, and unresolved conflicts. We ask questions about the whole of our lives: How can I, at age 75 (or whatever age), possibly be the same person who did such and such at age 21? Yet how can I not be? How is that younger self connected to the person I am today? Somehow s/he must be! And perhaps less consciously, how can I integrate these different versions of myself and all my experiences, not to mention my private mental life, that unceasing internal monologue, into something that makes sense? The answer for some may be through art, in one form or another. In other words, life review need not be merely contemplative. It can be actively manifested, usually through the production of various kinds of art, especially art based in memories of the past. A person's life review can make connections through artistic expression, bringing the seemingly disparate parts of a life together into a significant whole. In the work of art, the aging person creates the meaning of their life.

Examples are plentiful. Some people, for instance, begin to paint in their 60s and 70s, although they may never have painted before. Their paintings represent scenes, events, places, and people from their childhood or significant events in loved ones' lives. Mayer Kirshenblatt is a good example; he began to paint for the first time at age 73 and went on to recreate the world of his youth in pre-Holocaust Poland through hundreds of paintings.[20] Unconventional as well as conventional art objects emerge: Retired men whittle and sometimes build miniature models of the tools and equipment they worked with at their jobs; women sew patches of discarded clothing into their quilts, reminders of times and people now gone. Some collect objects, anything from barbed wire to thimbles, recalling more active eras in their lives. Literally dozens of artistic activities emerge not merely to pass the time but to find and create the meaning of one's life and to try to resolve the enigmas that remain.

Maybe the most common way to engage in life review is through verbal art, especially telling stories about earlier times. And foremost among these stories are one's own life experiences, ideally told to family members and/or peers. Whereas it was once thought that oral reminiscence was a forewarning of oncoming senility, today we are more likely to see reminiscing as a sign of health. Such storytelling is commonly oral, but sometimes these stories are written—in journals, letters, poems, and memoirs. Today we might include blogs or other electronic forms that provide new platforms for reviewing one's life. Whatever the format and whatever the genre, life reviewers revisit certain episodes repeatedly—turning points, losses, victories, good and bad luck, grievous errors, and more. Stories may try to get at the essence of a character who mattered in the teller's life or at an unresolved quandary, an unanswered question, or the memory of a simple joy that stays in the teller's consciousness, important to their sense of what their life, or life itself, was all about. Although many of an aging person's powers are ebbing, certain creative powers may be at their height.

Stories of Jewish Life, which covers the period 1876–1985, can be considered just such a life review, perhaps a continuation of the process that began with Segre's previous memoir, *Memories of Jewish Life*, which covered the period 1918–1960. Segre intended his first memoir to be a gift for his children, a record not only of his own life, maybe not even primarily that, but a record of the times in which he had lived and the harsh realities his Italian Jewish community had endured. As autobiography it was also a life review. But finishing that book did not necessarily mean he had finished his life review.

Segre's creative gift lies partly in ensuring that *Stories of Jewish Life* was not just "more of the same" (as welcome as that would be), nor simply a continuation of *Memories of Jewish Life*, because it does not start where the previous book ended, which was 1960. This second memoir actually begins at an earlier date than the first (1875 in *Stories* versus 1918 in *Memories*), the opposite of what one would conventionally expect in the second volume of a memoir. Instead, we see Segre make an innovative move with *Stories*. Bearing in mind the idea of life review as well as the dates 1876–1985, how does it make sense to begin one's life review forty-two years before one's birth, for Augusto Segre was born in 1915, not 1876? Could it be that he considered 1876–1985 his *full* life span, at least for the sake of life review? Perhaps as Segre looked back over his life, he saw that the years that made the world he was born into were as crucial to his understanding of who he was as were the years he was actually alive. From this point of view, his life span (and all our life spans) could be considered longer than the years we are on this earth. Our own lives might be said to begin with the world of our parents' or even our grandparents' generation.

For a Jew, this sense of connection to the past, emphasizing the ties between generations, rings true to a Jewish sense of history. For instance, the Hebrew words *zakhor* (memory) and *dorot* (generations) loom large in Jewish religion and culture. The idea that the individual cannot be understood separately from their family, community, and from earlier generations of the Jewish people is familiar. But this feeling and idea is not limited to Jews; it is also familiar to anyone who has a strong sense of belonging to a national, ethnic, or religious group. By placing his social and cultural "birth" in the world of his grandparents' youth, two generations before he was born, Segre finds a universal way of emphasizing that the individual's fate cannot be separated from the fate of their nation—which seems to me to be the central theme of this book. Whether or not Segre consciously thought of this time span in this way is not as important as something else: his commitment to the idea of the indissolubility of the Jews and their community, a core theme not only of his writing but of his life's work.

There is also something to be learned from Segre's shift from the first person in his first memoir to the third person in his second. It appears that after writing *Memories*, Segre reached a later stage in the life review process in which the desire to be objective about himself had grown, and so he adopted a third-person point of view. The third-person perspective may have allowed Segre an objective distance, as a painter might paint a self-portrait more objectively by looking in a mirror rather than by just imagining how s/he looks. In the first memoir, Segre recorded what he saw *as he looked out upon the world*; in the second memoir, *he looks at himself acting in the world*. Segre observes Moshè. In keeping with this logic, he turned to less overtly personal genres—to short stories, vignettes, sketches, and essays—that nonetheless mirrored himself by mirroring his concerns.

What else does Augusto Segre's life review show us about him? What was important to him beyond what we have already learned? He spends a good deal of time describing and honoring those whom we might call his life teachers. Those teachers were not the conventional instructors of skills and technical knowledge—not the law professors in Rome, who are never mentioned in *Stories*, and not the rabbinic college teachers of Hebrew, the Bible, and Judaism, who figure prominently in *Memories* but not in *Stories*. Rather, in his second memoir, Segre evokes teachers who were not formally educated: working-class figures, peasants, and fishermen, like Pinin, the boatman on the Po River in "The Head Physician and the Boatman." Part of Moshè's political education comes from another singular, mysterious figure who actually was well educated but who dropped out of society. Unnamed, he lives the life of a hermit in a shack near the Po, and his sage words are recalled in "The Philosopher of the Po." Then there are the fishermen, who Moshè and his son, Dani, join for several days and nights off the Tuscan coast ("Midrashim at Sea"). The fishermen do not stigmatize Judaism in any way, and they even learn the principles of kashrut regarding fish (from Moshè) so well that they correct Moshè's choice and help him select kosher fish from the catch for his and Dani's meals. The fishermen are sincerely engaged by the biblical and midrashic stories Moshè tells them, and they invite him to tell the same stories to their families when they are on shore (which he does).

Moshè's relationships with the fishermen and their families are reminiscent of the relationships with the Italian peasants who hid Segre and his family in the Piedmontese countryside during World War II.[21] In vignettes such as "Midrashim at Sea," the reader recognizes Moshè's sense of fulfillment when he is involved with Italian working-class culture, with fishermen and peasants; he sees them as practicing not only true human solidarity but also biblical ethical behavior.[22] Thus, when a member of a small community of "spontaneous converts" to Judaism from San Nicandro in southern Italy ("A Voice Told Him") comes to his office to ask for help immigrating to Israel, Moshè does not dismiss him or scoff at the man's claim, "I heard a voice, and I don't know where it came from, that said to me, 'Sell your house and your field and go to Eretz Israel.'" On the contrary. Moshè associates the words the peasant heard with the words God spoke to Abraham, the founder of monotheism and Judaism: "Go forth from your native land and from your father's house to the land that I will show you" (Genesis 12:1). It is remarkable for an observant Jew, let alone a rabbi, to regard these circumstances as similar and to perceive the echo of an ancient, defining moment in Judaism in the words of a contemporary convert. Moshè acts without hesitation: "The request, naturally, was granted immediately, and the papers for his and his family's trip were promptly completed."[23]

The San Nicandro story also has a particular significance for Segre's life review. One of Segre's personal life review tasks appears to have been the challenge of reconciling two important yet ostensibly separate parts of his life and world—that is, his love of the Jewish people and their (his) religion and struggle to return to the Land of Israel, and his love for the world of the Italian peasants and fishermen and their way of life, which he admired and which he was drawn to. He was attracted to two outwardly different worlds. No figure mediates these two seemingly unrelated cultural complexes better than the Jewish convert from San Nicandro. He really is both an Italian peasant and a Jew—and, he is headed for Israel. He symbolizes what Segre may have felt himself to be, though in the opposite order: a Jew who empathized completely and identified with the Italian peasantry. And he too is headed for Israel.

Augusto/Moshè, who initially sought to immigrate to Israel in the late 1930s, accomplished this lifelong dream in 1978, after he retired. In writing about his aliyah (immigration to Israel), he satisfied the mandate of life review with an act of fulfillment and completion—a sense of wholeness for having arrived in "the land of the ancestors." The process of leaving Italy leads to a series of mainly humorous anecdotes, matched symmetrically in humor and epiphanies by the episodes that take place in Israel over the course of the book's last three chapters. In Israel the anecdotes are about new immigrant encounters with the implausibilities of Israeli bureaucracy, the wonders of modern Hebrew as a revitalized

Map 4. Israel 1949

language of everyday life, and an original tongue-in-cheek interpretation of the patriarch Jacob's famous dream ("Jacob's Ladder").

Humorous as it is, the final portion of *Stories* also has a serious side. Augusto/Moshè articulates the values that have guided his life. He frames these values indirectly by responding to current issues, such as changes in editorial policies at the *Rassegna Mensile di Israel*, the major Italian Jewish intellectual journal, which he edited until departing for Israel. With even greater passion, he takes on the vast contemporary question of who is a Jew, the title of the final essay. His sympathies, as always, are with the marginal, such as the Bené Israèl (Jews from India) and Ethiopian Jews, whom he sees as being subjected to a double standard compared with European Jews, whose background does not receive the same scrutiny by the religious authorities.

Segre is inclusive but not unquestioning. In a "kidding-on-the-square" type of answer to the chapter's question, "Who is a Jew?" he offers a solution as he turns to an item of Italian Jewish folklore from his youth.

> With people whom one didn't know, there was a certain system for finding out if they were or weren't Jews. A system, of course, that was not scientific, nor inspired by the usual rabbinic acumen but by that simple common sense of the people that more than once resolved so many ostensibly complicated questions in the best possible way. To illustrate this curious manner of identification there is a story: One day the local rabbi had sent his own son to the station to welcome a guest—of course he was a Jew, but one whom that boy had not yet met. When he asked his father how he would be able to identity him, he heard his father say, "There are only a few passengers arriving on this train. As soon as they leave the station, follow behind them and in a soft voice but in such a way that you can be understood, sing, in any tune, 'Lekà dodì liqrath kallà; se l'é un judì si volterà,'[24] that is, 'Come, my friend, to meet the bride (the Sabbath).' If he is a Jew, he'll turn around . . . You can't go wrong. You'll find our man!"

In other words, it's not genetics, history, complex scholarly argument, or even knowledge derived from official religious belief and theology that makes one a Jew. In the end, as a practical test of who is a Jew, no matter if he or she is Sephardic, Yemenite, Italian, Ethiopian, or Ashkenazic, nothing surpasses familiarity with and competency in Jewish expressive culture. In this, the folk practice of singing a line in Hebrew from a familiar liturgical song accords well with the findings of the academic disciplines of folklore and anthropology. I don't imagine Augusto Segre would be all that surprised to learn this, but he might be glad to know that scholars have caught up with the common knowledge of the small world in which he was born.

STORIES *of* JEWISH LIFE

To myself

and to all those who

openly and without compromising,

always fought,

at a dear price,

against everything and everybody,

for freedom

and for living

according to humanity and justice

LOVE OF COUNTRY

With these iconic words, the chronicles of the era render due homage to one of the many rabbis who, following the Emancipation,[1] committed themselves to educating the faithful entrusted to their care to love of country. They did so from the lectern and from the pulpit of the holy temple with great self-sacrifice and a zeal often superior to that which a Jewish teacher is supposed to devote to the study and the practice of the Torah. Trying to read between the lines, one might want to ask a number of questions regarding the specific duties that were incumbent upon such a rabbi and about his numerous and detailed responsibilities. But that would run the risk of not taking into account that special atmosphere, rich with ferment, that moved within the walls of the ghetto, in the halls of the Council of the "Israelite Universities"[2] (as the Jewish Communities were then called), and even in the private homes of the Jews of that era, when it seemed that at last the sun of liberty was about to rise. Freedom—longed for and prayed for with great faith, amid tears, blood, and hope for centuries—still seemed like a dream that would be realized only in the Messianic era. And yet here it was: Suddenly the walls of that sad prison had collapsed—and by a miracle no doubt. Hadn't Jewish history always been a series of extraordinary, miraculous events? Whoever didn't believe in those wonders, starting with the Bible, couldn't understand Jewish history either. Well, then, was the Messiah himself about to arrive this time? Even that might be—who could know? But in the meantime Jews, too, had to bestir themselves, try to understand these extraordinary events, and do their best to affirm this new proof of divine compassion.

---

1   That is, 1848. For this watershed moment in Italian Jewish history, see the Introduction.

2   See A Note on the Translation.

Although they shared in the anxieties and the expectations, the old generation—sustained day by day as always by a deep, lived faith—did not hide their worries and feared that with the Emancipation they would end up losing all that an authentically Jewish life could give them. Distraught, they asked themselves if accepting the proclamation of equality would not also mean putting the entire future of the Jewish people in danger. The new generation, on the other hand, more attuned to the new developments, were convinced that with freedom they would be able to gain every possible good and therefore were disposed even to sacrifice to the new times all the ancient traditions that had come into being for the defense of the Jewish body and spirit. One exaggeration triggered the other, and that disagreement, which in a short time would throw open the gates of assimilation, was already taking shape and deepening.[3] One might say that this quarrel was to continue in the following generations, although in different forms. But that is a story that deserves to be treated separately.

What mattered at that moment was not to lose sight of the reality of the facts. For one thing, Jews had become "Israelites," and the difference was enormous and incontrovertible.[4] And then the yellow badge, the sign of humiliation for so many centuries, had disappeared from their clothing, and they could live the life (even outside the old ghetto walls) of every other citizen, at least formally, equal to everyone else in almost all duties and rights. Who had been the cherished instrument of this emancipation? Clearly, pending the arrival of the Messiah—the real, true one, who at any rate would arrive one day—it had been King Carlo Alberto, no less, and thus with the king there was the entire homeland, which opened its arms to its children, like a loving mother. And that was nothing to sneeze at!

Now, however, urgent new problems were being faced by every Israelite, without distinction, rabbis included. For the other citizens, the *goìm* (non-Jews),[5] being born outside the ghetto walls was a natural fact of birth, like being Italian,

---

3   Cf. Dante Lattes, *Felice Momigliano: il suo pensiero religioso ed ebraico* [Felice Momigliano: His Religious and Jewish Thought] (Florence: Israel editore, 1924). [Segre's note.]

4   See A Note on the Translation.

5   Segre's translations of Hebrew and Jewish-Piedmontese words appear in parentheses immediately following each word. Segre, of course, translated the words into Italian, and I have supplied the English here. For the rare cases in which I provide a translation or clarification, my text appears in brackets. The glossary at the end of this book supplies translations for words that were not translated in the text as well as fuller explanations for Hebrew and Jewish-Piedmontese words that are translated in the text.

without the need to produce evidence of their loyalty to the House of Savoy and their love of country at every turn. But for the Israelites, reborn to new life, specific new duties were also imposed: a sacred pledge of continuous gratitude toward the House of Savoy (so generous and farsighted, so rich in humanity and justice), the moral obligation of demonstrating, at even the most seemingly modest event, that the trust freely given them was well deserved. Thus, one had to be very careful not to allow any misunderstanding or to raise any doubts about the complete loyalty of the new citizens. If here and there some *sonè jeudì*, some anti-Semite, started up again with the old themes of anti-Jewish hatred, in public or in private, you didn't have to let yourself get pulled into the trap. In cases like these it was best to let it go, act like it was nothing, and above all, not react in any way. After all, it was a matter of isolated instances, and besides, one should never forget, in any case, that the new freedom was still a small plant just flowering and that it needed to be cared for with a great deal of attention and solicitude so that its tender roots would not dry up, with all the easily foreseeable consequences. The ghetto district was still there, a mute testimony to ancient tragedies. Now then, more than anyone else, who, if not the rabbis, could dedicate themselves to this delicate and lofty educational task? Torah in hand, they were able to educate the faithful in the holy religion and love of country at the same time. As time passed, the holy religion kept getting weaker, even taking on, in its outward decorum, characteristics closer to those of the dominant religion in order to make room for a patriotism that seemed exceedingly exhibitionistic, kindling new doubts. But this, too, is hardly a minor page of history, which, however, deserves to be treated separately.

The rabbis didn't lack firsthand historical sources to which they could turn. Everything was in the Bible—one needed only to know how to read the text and interpret it correctly. For example, there were the words of Jeremiah, the holy prophet who exhorted the fellow Jews of his time "to seek the welfare of the city"[6] where they lived. Weren't these words a precise and invaluable reference to a teaching that came from on high? To try to dig too deeply into these words was simply to go astray. And if someone ventured to point out that the same prophet had also exclaimed, with aching nostalgia, "and let Jerusalem return in

---

6   Jeremiah 29:7.

your heart,"[7] he would immediately have attracted the predictable rebukes of the "pastor," as the *rabbi* was already called. And in fact, the text says "in your heart," but what does that mean?

Nothing other than the "celestial Jerusalem!" This conception was much more far-reaching and nobler than the "terrestrial Jerusalem," which by then history had superseded for centuries and the "celestial Jerusalem" fit perfectly within Jewish theology, so rich in universal ferment!

Even today, when one leafs through the yellowed pages of that distant and forgotten world so brutally obliterated by modern anti-Semitism (which spared neither "Israelites" nor "pastor-rabbis," who were sincerely patriotic and Italian), one must try to understand these ancient dreamers of the ghetto, these romantics of liberty. And as far as possible, one must try to understand how the sudden light of the Emancipation had blinded everyone somewhat, even great souls, making them lose every Jewish orientation, and how everyone, to some degree, abandoned themselves, most of them in good faith, to a general intoxication that lasted until the fasces and the swastika appeared over their sky. And it is certainly worth noting that unfortunately not even during those years, which are still quite near to us, did everyone grasp the terrible new lesson.

From the many possibilities, here is one "edifying example," as the Jews of the era would have written—they who always wrote out of the most refined imagination with words that were highly esteemed for their bold and lofty patriotism. Rabbi Sabato Graziadio Treves had been rabbi in Vercelli, Asti, and Torino—at least as much as he needed to be to carry out his mission of patriotic faith at his best. What could have been more inspiring for a rabbi than to live in these cities, especially Torino, where the first glimmer of freedom had appeared, where His Majesty the King had declared on March 29, 1848, that from that moment on the Jews would be *tolerated*? These and other Piedmontese cities, at all times, from Emancipation on, had always established a certain atmosphere around their individual Jewish Communities, which changed in intensity and subtlety over the course of the years but which can be defined without hesitation as an atmosphere of robust assimilation—which still thrives as if nothing had happened.

The fame of Treves, patriotically speaking, must have been quite great, because he was called on to be in charge of the spiritual destiny of the Israelite Community of Trieste, the city that always caused every true Italian to shed

---

7   Jeremiah 51:50.

rivers of tears because of its irredentist status.[8] Arriving there, he felt it his duty to redouble his mission as a patriotic rabbi. Among the many episodes that eloquently illustrate his commitment in ideas and actions, it was duly recorded in the newspapers of the era that, on the occasion of the wedding of a "distinguished" lady (the bride of a philologist of European fame), Treves took the bride aside a few minutes before the celebration of the wedding and said to her, "I hope, my child, that you will remember the duty of educating your children in the love of our country, Italy. Don't neglect this if you want God to protect you."

The quotation was highlighted in the press of the era. It is not reported whether at that moment the rabbi also called the attention of the future mother of the family to the value and the importance of the Torah, which her children would have to be taught as well. Maybe such advice wasn't necessary, it being understood. The reporter, at any rate, doesn't speak of it but instead feels the duty to gloss Treves's words with this note: "These were words that the kind lady repeated many years later with deep emotion."

Certain things—what can one say?—can never be forgotten!

Years of an enlightening patriotic mission had passed by in that still unredeemed city when Rabbi Treves, by then extremely old, returned to visit his beloved homeland. The Community of Torino prepared a triumphal welcome for the "always beloved pastor." A formal meeting took place in the council hall, festively decked-out, as was fitting. "Nor did it lack the ornament of every Italic solemnity, the tricolor flag." Entering, that "venerable man" saw the flag, trembled, and moved to the point of tears, "kissed it, repeating loudly those words of Lamentations (1:16): 'for these things I weep; my eyes, my eyes send forth a flood.'"

But even great joys can sometimes be dangerous, and in fact, two days later, "perhaps not being able to withstand the excess of emotion from again seeing the homeland so happily transformed, he suddenly expired."

In reporting the news of those final hours of intense patriotic fervor and the sudden end of Rabbi Treves, the solicitous journalist, with unconcealed emotion,

---

8   Italian patriots regarded Trieste as part of the Italian cultural map, but the city had not been successfully incorporated into the Italian political map during the Risorgimento (resurgence, 1815–1871), the movement for national unification and independence. By 1871 most of Italy was unified as the Kingdom of Italy. *Irredentist* means "unredeemed," which was considered the status of those Italian-speaking areas, like Trieste, that were not yet part of the Kingdom of Italy. Trieste was the most important goal of the irredentist movement and was finally added after World War I, in 1920.

felt obliged to add more lines that would characterize the long, active life of the illustrious Israelite pastor. "Treves," he wrote, left a reputation for being "extremely learned in casuistical theology and in sacred literature." He had been an "eloquent preacher, an ardent Italian, and a fervent friend of liberty"; nor was advanced old age of any avail in extinguishing "or dampening such sentiments in him." And then, living in Trieste, where "Austrian rule was stronger and more envious, with his mind and heart he kept abreast of the rebellions in Italy, sorrowful to be far away from them." The conclusion of these moving comments that praise the virtues of Rabbi Treves is this: "Thus we deem such an example worthy of everlasting remembrance because the present and future generations are reflected in him."

It was the year of grace 1876.

A SHRINKING VIOLET

This poetic expression, delicate even if not free of rhetoric, is perfectly in keeping with the style of that era, more than 100 years ago, of bourgeois respectability and marked puritanism. According to a Jewish newspaper column from 1877 that carries the signature of Bettina Levi, this expression dramatizes the moral character of a woman abounding in exceptional virtues. The name of this true angel of goodness does not appear. But one should not regard this fact as an artistic touch of the writer to render the merits of the unnamed lady even greater, or to emphasize that her goodness, her altruism, and her sacrifice have no names and that certain actions inscribe themselves in the history of peoples anonymously, even in a small Community like Casale Monferrato. Woman, the ancients said, can be compared to a garden. And when the garden is beautiful, no one asks who planted it; they admire the flowers for the richness of their colors and their fragrances. But it's not always like that.

The curiosity to know who this rare example of virtue was does not get satisfied. But for quite different reasons, neither can one claim to know. The writer of the column, in fact, asks herself, "But who among her Jewish fellow citizens knew her?" Here, truly, even though the rhetoric is used with a light hand, it triumphs—and how. If you read this piece of writing carefully, there's actually no doubt at all that this greatly praised woman was well known and in fact had often fueled both good and evil tongues and had been the object of those comments that women, especially, whisper when they want everything to be known and in the most minute detail but that everyone is supposed to ignore in the name of a very vague and abstract morality. Note well: the woman's name does not appear even in this final eulogy because it is simply a death notice, which concludes with these words: "She had no name." And on her modest grave is the more fitting praise, "What every woman should yearn for: She was good and charitable."

Is there a mystery here? Hardly. It's a simple matter, one of many that come with human experience but that may upset certain social circles and certain delicate consciences that try to block it from their fragile morality, abstract and senseless. Even if we faithfully follow the thread of this rather elevated funeral eulogy, we still will not be able to bring the name of this woman out of obscurity; we will only succeed in explaining why there was such obstinate and useless silence. The hyperbolic praise with which the author begins to sketch the profile of this woman borders on the ridiculous. The starting point is nothing less than a comparison between heroes, scientists, men of letters, philosophers, pioneers from every period, and champions of progress, and the singular, modest, unrecognized, hard-working, and courageous virtue that exceptional people are able to practice throughout the course of their lives. Levi maintains that:

> Goodness is equal to greatness: If the one elevates, the other inspires, and
> if greatness advances material prosperity, goodness gives a powerful boost
> to moral progress, which is no less useful and necessary for the happiness
> of peoples and families.

These rather convoluted and forced remarks have, from what follows, a clear purpose: They are intended to demonstrate that whatever the circumstances—even the most dismal, like those of that poor woman of whom we speak—Jews were always distinguished in gifts and in blessings. And in fact the writer comes to speak of

> a Religion that gave Jewish History that succession of heroic martyrs, that
> array of philanthropists and benefactors who sustained one another, simul-
> taneously admired even though downtrodden, who are now esteemed and
> applauded by the peoples and the nations among whom we live.

Another blow struck to show that the hopes upon which Emancipation was based were well founded, and all the more so when one could appreciate instances like the one of which we are speaking.

And here Levi moves on to sketch the character of this exceptional angel, with the delicate attention of one who embroiders threads of silver on fine silk cloth. The embroiderer of the cloth has had the good fortune of knowing this poor flower, a modest violet hidden in the grass that reveals itself only "with the welcome emergence of its delicate, small leaves." A guileless old lady, all smiles, caresses, and sweetness. I can never forget that white face, plump and full of such goodness, that smiled at me from the highest window of the house across from mine, that smooth and pure forehead which the world's fury and rancor seemed to pass over without stopping, and on the sides of which were set two bunches of wrinkles, like knots, furrowed into her temples, the only trace of time and misfortune.

What furies and misfortunes could have left such deep furrows on that angelic face? The mystery thickens and stirs the natural curiosity of the reader, and all the more so since the merits and virtues of this modest violet don't stop here. In fact, she not only taught the Shema [an important Jewish prayer] and spoke about God but also kept a caring eye on those who, after the innocence of childhood, faced the turbulence of youth. Levi herself, the author of this moving commemoration, is forever grateful to this angel of goodness because

> with the beginning of youth, sweet dreams came to disturb me, and disheartening doubt to penetrate me. There was that tumult of passions, the hundred fevers of desire, the yearning of a knowledge which, like the fatal apple in which it was contained, understands and destroys, enlivens and suffocates. But there was still that spotless figure who kept me in my faith.

In short, the "fatal apple" aside, this utterly exceptional woman must also have carried out, with commitment and success, an activity that would seem to be reserved specifically for a rabbi who was conscientious and responsible for the faithful entrusted to him.

Notwithstanding all these merits—and others will be recalled later—the fate of this unfortunate was extremely sad. The truth about this great mystery comes out a little at a time. At a certain point Levi alludes to "that prejudice that renders the child responsible for the sins of the father." This concept appears briefly, without the slightest attempt to criticize its false and perverse routine morality. It serves only to emphasize that this angel of Casale Monferrato was a "poor soul, rejected and forsaken, whose presence, more tolerated than protected by distant relatives, was a stain on the family's honor" and who therefore "bore all the burdens of life without enjoying a single one of its small privileges" and was "constrained to perform the most humiliating services." Levi, the author of these comments—without even a hint of resistance to a mentality that was so retrograde and full of hypocritical puritanism and that condemned an innocent without appeal—accepts this ugly reality, limiting herself to saying that "those who knew her for her whole life call her a martyr." What matters, apparently, is that it would be best not to connect a name to these events, nor too precise a memory to such "mud," even though "from such mud the immortal soul arises, ever purer and more beautiful." How very kind of her! We should note that there isn't much that's Jewish in these comments, and to be a bit pedantic, one could add that some Christianizing concepts crop up here, according to which, the more one suffers, the better it is for the salvation of the soul, and the more one is persecuted and oppressed, the greater the merits that one acquires at the throne of the Lord. And human kindness and justice, which are important foundations of Judaism, where had they gone?

The dismaying details come out with difficulty, barely touched on: "She was the daughter of an unknown father and of a mother who went crazy from grief and shame." That's everything, but already it's a true Greek tragedy, a disastrous fate that not even the gods of the ancient world could ward off.

After this brief clarification, mentioned as though in parentheses, she returns to sing the praises and the virtues of this poor creature, with undertones of a Hasidic flavor. For one thing, it is declared that "the more she was rejected and isolated, the more angelic virtues developed within her." Can it be that real angels, who perform acts of such uplifting goodness, also have equally dubious and painful origins? The modest violet always managed to deprive herself of something "for someone with a greater misfortune," and she was "happy" when she was "at the bedside of someone who was suffering, at the side of someone who was unhappy—always simple, affectionate, smiling." Later, when "she became the owner" of a pension for life of 400 lire, her beneficence toward those who were more poverty-stricken than her grew. The author's comment, with coy sarcasm, and at any rate rather generic, is this:

> Four hundred lire is such a paltry thing! And it would certainly get smiles from the gracious ladies who, in the rosy haze of their carnivalesque reveries, see tidy sums vanish, sums for which that amount could hardly lay claim to being the legal interest.

But our poor and neglected heroine, with such a sum at her disposal, "came to regard herself as a little Rothschild," partly because "with that fabulous fortune, she constructed the most ingenious budget that mathematical skill and the mind of a speculator could construct." Enough is as good as a feast! And here is our heroic angel, carrying on her shoulders bundles of wood and "packages full of all you could desire, of which she regarded herself unworthy" (why on earth?), visiting the homes of the most wretched, to whom "she raced, to cheer and comfort with words of affection and faith." The story comes to mind of the rabbi who, during the Days of Repentance,[1] dressed as a woodcutter, brought wood to a poor sick woman, presenting himself as an ordinary *goy* [non-Jew] who was in too much of a hurry to collect his payment.[2] But that was a rabbi who knew how to fulfill what he taught his faithful through good deeds. Here, instead, in this festival of good and generous works, neither the rich nor even the rabbi appear. This does not mean that neither of them occupied themselves with the poor, may the Lord free us from such doubts. But there is one thing that can and should be said: Is it at all possible that the religious and secular bigwigs in a small Community were not aware of such a painful story? And how, then, at least based on this bit of reportage, can it be that those responsible for the moral and material welfare of their fellow Jews never considered it their explicit duty to try to combat such prejudice, to resolve such a sorrowful situation, and to give a hand to an unfortunate woman, excluded by everyone but from whom everyone was ready to accept assistance and gifts? Nor does the author of this sad account dare face this awkward problem, limiting herself to conclude, "May the righteous live by their faith!" Amen!

The fact remains that even from this story, which is subtitled "Society Sketches" (!), it is possible to draw a few useful features for judging at least some of the structures of that Jewish world, which, happily emancipated, went on fitting itself more and more into the world around it. It was a world sustained by a vague, abstract morality, by superstitions, and by those forms of prudishness that often served to hide real immorality and in which galloping assimilation was becoming ever more comfortable.

---

1   The annual period preceding Rosh Hashanah, the Jewish new year.

2   Segre is referring to a widespread Hasidic legend that was retold by I. L. Peretz in his short story "If Not Higher," in Irving Howe and Eliezer Greenberg, eds., *A Treasury of Yiddish Stories* (New York: Viking Press, 1954), 231–33. For an orally collected version, see "Mitsveh," in Jerome Mintz, *Legends of the Hasidim: An Introduction to Hasidic Culture and Oral Tradition in the New World* (Chicago: University of Chicago Press, 1968), 176–77.

JACHETU'S RING

Born and raised between the Della Palma alley and what was called the Clava Gate, Isacco belonged to a poor family. His playmates and schoolchildren and later others called him Jachetu. Who knows why? In the small Jewish world of what had once been the ghetto, many of the fine traditions that had been carefully preserved for years were already disappearing. But even after the Emancipation the custom of giving nicknames, which local gossips invented with great imagination, had not weakened and had maintained all its potency for humor and irony.

Maybe people in the Community used this dialectical diminutive, Jachetu, in place of Isacco to play up something about his physical stature and character. Closed within himself, introverted, and obviously shy, he sometimes exploded, in words and actions, almost as though he wanted to show that he wasn't afraid of anything. It could by no means be said that he had been furnished with an outstanding intellect—certainly not from looking over the grades he brought home during those few years in which he attended school, irregularly.

Shaking his head disconsolately and shrugging his shoulders, *sur murenu*, the rabbi himself, had often declared Jachetu to be an authentic *'am haárez* (ignoramus), a *chamòr* (donkey) the likes of which he had never seen in his entire life. He ignored Jachetu for years and even had him excluded from the weekly Jewish catechism classes. The good pastor, making this painful decision, justified it with the saying that you can't get blood from a turnip.

Notwithstanding these negative comments delivered from such a lofty post, which had made Jachetu's life within the Community even more difficult, he possessed that simple shrewdness that strives to make some kind of profit straightaway, even if in socially questionable ways. But Jachetu was never violent, in spite of what happened to him later, when he was swept away in a sea of woes. Nor was he dishonest. He had learned quite quickly how difficult it was merely to get a crust of bread, especially if you were poor. More than once he was obliged to take note of how bare the plate that his mother put in front of him was; nor did his parents' sighs escape his notice when his father, putting his hand in his pocket, turned it inside out to emphasize, visually as well as verbally, that he didn't have one cent.

Jachetu hadn't learned to read Hebrew, not even the common prayers and blessings, and he read Italian only with difficulty. Still, at a very young age he grasped the tough and scrimy game of procuring things of value, even in implausible circumstances. Thus, for example, during Purim he turned himself into a shrewd entrepreneur for his affluent friends. He quickly assessed the worth of the gifts they received for the holiday and then traded and sold them to the highest bidder, all the while anticipating a good slice of fresh sweet-smelling bread, which, seasoned with hunger, is the tastiest food there can possibly be and which no cook, no matter how talented, has ever been able to prepare without that one spice.

Jachetu spoke few words and made instinctive, abrupt decisions. Most of the time he was gruff and uncouth, as though to shield his poverty as well as he could. He learned quickly, on his own initiative, to go around to the piazzas on market days and rummage through the rubbish to find anything that he could fix and sell. Thus it was that sometimes, to the great surprise of his own family, Jachetu himself brought home a little of that chronically scarce bread, which he put in the cupboard without drawing attention to himself. Clearly, he was a generous young man, even if only toward his closest relatives. It could be said of him that he was a self-made man. Trying to pull himself away from the vortex of hunger that can drag one into the abyss without salvation, he stubbornly set aside penny after penny, with that tenacity that only desperation can engender. When he could allow himself something, he would sit at a table in a tavern, with the hauteur of a lord who can grant himself whatever he wants.

In time Jachetu succeeded in making contacts and agreements with traders and wholesalers for damaged and rejected goods—sheets, blankets, fabrics for men and women. He brought these goods to the city market on Tuesdays and Fridays on a small pushcart. On the other days, he rolled up his merchandise in a big bundle, put it on his back, and went from farmhouse to farmhouse, making some use of the train but usually covering several kilometers on foot.

The effort was enormous. From dawn until dusk, nonstop, he traveled on until he found a hospitable stable or an abandoned cottage where he would spend the night. Neither the suffocating heat nor the piercing cold ever stopped him. He sustained himself with a few frugal slices of plain bread and a few glasses of wine—although he wasn't so frugal with the wine. According to him, the wine gave him strength and confidence.

It can't be said that his character had altered in any way. He was what he always had been: an oyster, unsociable, but more receptive toward the *goìm* (non-Jews), who gave him a way to make a living and with whom he seemed to have found a thread of human relationships. He had never been able to find acceptance in his own Community, not with laymen (neither the more nor the less well-to-do), and not with the so-called religious authorities, who had long since abandoned him to his fate.

Besides his well-known personality, there were other grave defects that aggravated relations with his fellow Jews in an almost irreversible way. The language that he used was the typical dialect of the countryside, which had become familiar to him, and he dressed shabbily, more like the *goìm* than a Jew who respected himself. (One might have observed that as the simple Jewish traditions continued to disappear, the fashion of appearing entirely—in dress, language, and behavior—as "refined people" who would be respected and admired by the Gentiles, spread and was consolidated.) Among the other negatives the Community held against Jachetu, there was his rather limited attendance at prayers in the Holy Temple—as though in this he was a rare exception, worthy of excommunication, and was not outstripped in this grave failing and in so many others by numerous coreligionists. They, however, had the not insignificant advantage of being classified among the "respectable people" and they were, moreover, from a more substantial economic class.

Still, no one could claim Jachetu was without faith. Every morning, barely awake, he briefly washed his face and hands, even when he found himself in open country, and recited the Shema, the only prayer he knew by heart, in a low voice. True, he didn't go beyond the first passage, but those few words, recited with folded hands (sturdy, calloused hands that had the strength of a stone carver), had a great unconscious value for him. They gave him a resiliency that perhaps other persons who were more cultured and more religious had never experienced. In short, even his modest prayer was something concrete, almost visible. Is it really possible, then, to say with certainty that a person like him lacked faith and didn't believe in anything?

Unlucky in the military draft lottery, which was then in use, Jachetu also did his duty as a soldier for the homeland. He performed his military service in Sardinia, and he did not bring back any particular souvenir except a metal ring, worked in a basket-weave style with a bezel in the middle in which a hard stone was set. The ring was of little value, but from that time on Jachetu never took it off the little finger of his left hand, and he considered the ring a good luck charm. Was it only a matter of an obsessive personal superstition, or did the ring instead recall the memory of some gallant adventure, a gift received from a middle-aged woman who had often welcomed him in her home? Such were the rumors, vague but persistent, that made the rounds of the ghetto when it was noted that this ex-infantry soldier never missed an opportunity to show off that trinket.

As everyone knows, to marry and raise a family is an important religious norm. The ancient masters say that he who doesn't marry lives without joy, without blessing, and without well-being, and he who is celibate cannot be considered a man in the full sense of the word. These high moral teachings were certainly unknown to Jachetu. Nevertheless, one day, with his habitual decisiveness, of course, he convinced himself that getting married was a step he ought to take, without losing any more time.

This idea gradually took shape in his head on the train while he was going to a nearby town with his big bundle. Seated facing him was a coreligionist, a woman who lived in a house near his in the courtyard of the Clava Gate. He had known her since he was a boy. Orphaned for many years, she lived with relatives and worked as a maid for Jews and non-Jews. That day she was going to Vercelli, where she had offers of work. Her name was Bona, but she was known by the nickname Bunina. She was an enterprising girl, willing to do all the work that was requested of her.

Curious to know why she was traveling, Jachetu struck up a conversation with this young woman. Learning why she was on the train, he fell silent while his mind, to the rhythmic cadence of the slow-train's wheels, was immediately taken with the idea of matrimony.

Who knows why certain ideas come to mind when one least expects them. He didn't even ask himself why that woman, already in her 30s, wasn't yet married, although he knew quite well that generally, and all the more so in his world, it wasn't so easy for a poor girl to find a husband, not even by resorting to the match-makers, who were numerous in every Community. The line of reasoning that was coming to fruition in him was simple and straightforward: She was single, and a woman so full of energy like her would be a great help to him. Bunina wasn't the type of woman who would sit on her hands all day, and she wasn't bad-looking, either. By then he had convinced himself that she was his woman, and he who finds a woman, it is said, finds a blessing, and he had found her.

Having made the decision, he didn't want to lose time. He said to her, "Listen to me. How long are you going to keep going around like this, looking for work?"

"What are you saying? This is my life."

"That's not true. Everyone tries to create a life for himself, not just put up with it."

"That's all very well, but . . ."

"I never talk nonsense. I speak from personal experience. When you want something, you go after it with everything and you get something. If not, then you don't."

"Well then, according to you, what should I do?" Her voice was full of bitterness.

"Why don't you get married?"

Bunina's eyes opened wide and her jaw dropped, but she quickly recovered and in a weak voice said, "And with whom? Who would want to take a poor thing like me?"

"Me, for example." And he put his hand on his chest.

"Come on! Don't joke. It's not true."

Jachetu's tone of voice became hard. "You know me. You know that I never joke, that I'm of few words, but that I keep my word."

Bunina nodded in agreement while her face—he noticed it immediately—was becoming suffused with a soft red color.

"I promise you a modest but secure life, and, take note, an independent life. I'll be a good husband, a little grouchy, but you know that, too. Well then?"

"Well then what?"

"Well then, tell me yes, cancel your trip to Vercelli, and let everyone go to hell. I'll drop my business for today, and we'll go back to town and start the process right away—"

"What? Like this, all of a sudden, without thinking about it even a little?" Her blush was even more noticeable now, and she raised her hands to her face as if to hide it.

"Of course. There's really nothing else to think about—I've already thought of everything. If it suits you, fine, and you know that you can count on me one hundred percent"—here he raised his voice, which was heard by the other travelers as well—"and if not, let it go and—"

"Yes, yes," Bunina hurried to say, "but please speak softly—"

"Since that's the case, I'm very grateful to you." And for once Jachetu smiled. "I'm very grateful to you, here's my hand and—" And here he stopped himself in time because he was about to say, "that's settled."

The bridegroom did things in a big way, in his own style. He didn't want to lose this opportunity to show all his fellow Jews that for one thing he wasn't marrying a *goià*, a non-Jew (a fashion which by then was already quite widespread, even among families considered religious). And for another, getting married meant, particularly, that he was also in a position to maintain a family. The news of this wedding was like a bomb throughout the entire *chazèr* (courtyard, ghetto). There were many theories, partly because the thing happened so quickly that not even the most expert connoisseurs of other people's business had the slightest inkling of this matrimonial combination. That's not to say that there weren't those who took careful note of the date of the wedding, which allowed them to make simple calculations in expectation of the first prospective baby. But their calculations were mistaken, because no child came to cheer the life of the two newlyweds. Nevertheless, they did not lack for a vast, reciprocal fondness, shaped by mutual trust and similar harsh past experiences, seasoned with unceasing hopes, which are all the more numerous the poorer one is.

Jachetu went back to work, driven by a new motivation, which made him increase his effort and commitment. His business grew, his earnings multiplied, but unfortunately so did the number of bottles of wine. With the passing years he felt the hard work ever more strongly, and he had the illusion that a good glass of wine—in reality it was a matter of bottles—was the panacea for everything. Bunina, by hook or by crook as they say, tried her best to restrain her husband from this mad race toward the total degradation caused by alcohol. It's true that Jachetu had long since overcome hard times, that hunger was a distant memory, and so he was able to do work that was calmer and more circumscribed. In fact, however, it wasn't the labor that excused this vice; rather, by then the wine was a reliable pretext for maintaining that the more one drank, the better one worked.

When he came home drunk, arguments with his wife were inevitable, and unpleasant words and even the menace of Jachetu's strong hands flew through the air; but then, after the drunkenness passed, everything returned to normal, or almost. Jachetu didn't justify himself—maybe he didn't remember. At any rate he never acknowledged his faults. Bunina, affectionate toward her husband as always, did not lose courage but pondered a possible solution, night and day.

One day a good opportunity presented itself: Living quarters had become available close to where they lived. There were many rooms, which could be rented singly to travelers, merchants, and students. If they could obtain all the necessary permits, the business would be simple and lucrative. Bunina, with the experience and competence that came from the cleaning she had done for many families in the past, would attend to keeping the inn in order. Besides—and this was what mattered most—Jachetu would be able to confine his work to the market days, Tuesdays and Fridays, thus ending his traveling around the country-side definitively. The earnings from the inn would fully and more readily compensate for this limitation on his business. Not only that, this way he would be under the direct surveillance of his wife. Of course, convincing Jachetu to agree to this kind of revolution in his daily life was not easy. But one day when he had been in a deep sleep, dead to the world, in bed because he had been battered by a variety of illnesses, was weaker than usual, and was being nursed with maternal care by Bunina, he was finally convinced by her repeated appeals and gave his consent.

There were enormous difficulties arranging things everywhere they turned. The relevant authorities examined the request to open an inn with excessive zeal; Jews asked, "Right in the neighborhood of the ex-ghetto?" and other coreligionists wanted to know what this "new thing" could possibly be. Since when had anyone ever heard of such a thing? Could it be that hidden beneath was some other ulterior motive, shady and unacceptable?

Unfortunately, the world, as we know, is full of corruption. But our two protagonists continued confidently on their way: Jachetu's always hard-nosed replies along with Bunina's clear, lucid, and modest answers made many suppositions vanish, even though the gossip continued for a long time. What mattered was that in the end, after a few months, the Speranza Inn was open and began to function. Was it a triumph for the able, hard-working, and devoted Bunina? After some initial success, one would have to say that for her it was, to say the least, a grave error of judgment. The entire undertaking was conceived with the intention of being able to monitor her husband and his wine more closely, but things didn't go as it had been reasonable to expect. Jachetu, now freer from his usual business activities, began to frequent the Centrale Tavern, which was a short walk from their home, with greater diligence. Worse, he got himself drunk more than he had before, and not only that, he played long, interminable card games for money. Thus the quarrels resurfaced even more often, and they became more bitter, until it all came to a head in an unimaginable tragedy—certainly not intentional but no less appalling for that.

Jachetu had spent the late afternoon at the Centrale, as usual, getting together with his drinking and card-playing friends. Toward evening he had something to eat at the tavern with the others so as not to interrupt the game, which had been favorable to him and which had already earned him a considerable sum. They say that a card player isn't culpable until he becomes an expert. And Jachetu had long since become a skillful player.

That evening, luck, which was helping him, was more shameless than usual. The cards continued to go around, and wine continued to flow from bottles into glasses and down throats, which were drier than ever because of all the shouting and cigar smoke. At a certain moment the tension manifested itself clearly; the players who were losing began to grouse, and one word led to another. Was there someone who, hinting at first but then plainly, made an unpleasant allusion to Jachetu being a Jew? Was there someone else who felt it his duty to up the ante, hissing that Jews were always the same, that they were good at stealing money from Christians? Was there yet another who recalled the fine times of the ghetto when, at least in the evening, you didn't see so many Jewish faces around? Anything is possible in such an atmosphere, heated by the influence of wine, but precisely what happened was never known. Even when the judicial investigation got to the Centrale, no one, as often happens, had heard or seen anything. Nevertheless, it was a fact that when Jachetu's winnings had grown even greater and the words had become more inflamed, he suddenly jumped to his feet and threw cards and money in the faces of his fellow card players. If he hadn't been restrained, barely, by some coreligionists who were there, he would have hurled himself against them. He was led outside and, still shouting, set out, staggering, for home.

Bunina couldn't contain herself. She vented all her anger, all her pain, and all her bitterness at seeing that yet again her hopes had collapsed, this time definitively, and that the family's ruin was now at hand. Jachetu, slumped on a chair, his head bowed, muttered meandering nonsense between one belch and another and tried to convince his wife that what had happened had nothing to do with the wine at all (what gall!) but with his attempt to defend the honor of the Jews.

"I'm not worth anything . . . I'm less than a . . . everyone despises me . . . but still, I'll always be a Jew, that matters to me, and there's things I just won't swallow . . . those *sonè judìm* (anti-Semites), they're the same as ever . . . they'll never change . . . there's some things I just won't swallow . . ."

Bunina by then had completely lost control and cried harder and harder and trembled. She railed with growing vehemence against the disgrace that, as she stressed, was none other than her husband himself: "Of course those *sonè judìm*, you say, you won't swallow them, but the wine, damn it, you sure swallow it. You gulp it down like a lunatic and—"

At this point Jachetu had a violent outburst; he stood up and struck his wife with his left hand, shouting at the top of his voice, "That's enough, shut up, damn you!" As fate would have it, he hit her right in the temple with that bezel ring, a vestige of his distant military life and gallant adventures. With a piercing scream, she fell to the floor. A few minutes went by and Bunina was dead.

The trial took place a while later. It was an entirely merciless indictment of the guilty man. No testimony that could have reduced the charges in any way was given. The Jewish Community seemed to have vanished, as though it had never existed. Even *sur murenu*, questioned by someone, stated that he did not intend to get mixed up in such shameful things, above all for the sake of the honor of the Community and all its members, nor would he waste a single word for that man, who had behaved like the worst of the *goìm*.

And yet some effort could have been made on behalf of that unfortunate wretch. For example, there had certainly not been any intention to commit the crime, and the affection and respect that the accused had always held for his wife was well known to everyone. Besides that, it would have been possible to argue that given the state he was in, he was not, at that moment, of sound mind. Once again Jachetu was abandoned to himself, and the judges were extremely severe with him. In the *chazèr* there was even a rumor that the absence of any reference to extenuating circumstances was nothing other than a renewed act of anti-Semitism, which unfortunately gave one pause. Look at how life's strange events sometimes play out: Anti-Semitism has such deep and persisting roots that it can show up anywhere, even at the bottom of a glass of wine.

The sentence, without any extenuating circumstances, was thirty years in prison. Jachetu spent a long time in a confused mental state, from which he slowly recovered. When he realized exactly what had happened, he abandoned himself to despair without end, which must have stayed with him the rest of his life. Depressed to the breaking point, it was only his obstinacy, which had never left him, his stubborn character, that allowed him to survive by his own devices. By then he was already a broken man.

A model prisoner, he no longer drank, not even a drop of wine; he was always commendably diligent in all the jobs with which he was entrusted. During all those desperate years of expiation, he received no visitors, not even from those who, given their specialized spiritual functions, should have brought at least some words of comfort to a suffering soul. It is professed that it is a *mizvà* (precept, good deed, [mitzvah]) to visit not only the sick but also whoever is in prison. He received no packages, which usually would have been sent from the public charity to prisoners, and he received only one single visit, from the *shammàsh* (synagogue attendant), who brought him a prayer book, translated into Italian. The *shammàsh* told him that *sur murenu*, concerned in a fatherly way for his spiritual fate, had sent him this precious gift, counseling him to meditate upon those holy texts, to pray, and to ask forgiveness from the Lord, if at least he wanted to try to save his soul.

Jachetu was pardoned after twenty years for good behavior, and he returned to his old home, between the narrow Della Palma alley and the Clava Gate. At first he met with a great deal of suspicion and utter reserve, and then he was tolerated, in the way people are accustomed to act to some extent in all milieus. With the passing of time, which inexorably erodes and flattens everything and causes the good as well as the bad to be forgotten, the life of the ex-convict became, relatively speaking, a little more tolerable.

The tragic ring, the main incriminating evidence, had by then lain among the exhibits in some office of the criminal court for a long time. On Jachetu's hand there now remained a single ring, his wedding ring, the only thing to remind him of a great love and a torment without end. Prematurely aged, with white hair and an unkempt beard as pure white as snow, Jachetu had a slow, almost obsequious walk. He had lost all the haughtiness that once characterized him, and his words, which had always been few and measured, were, nevertheless, spoken slowly, with humility, as if to beg, always and from everyone, for understanding and forgiveness. He passed the time, often frequenting the synagogue for prayers and the reciting of the psalms that preceded or followed prayers on the occasion of memorial anniversaries in honor of persons who had left special funds for this purpose (almost as a guarantee of a more certain admittance into heaven).

He lived from public charity, circumspectly, never lavishly. That is how he was remembered, even among his youngest coreligionists, who had known him at the holy temple and who had heard him whisper about that bloody crime. Then we lose track of him. Many years later, when the conversation turned to this topic, which had disrupted the placid life of the Community for so long, the question that regularly came up was this: "So, by the way, what ever became of him?" No one remembered.

PURCHASE OF GOODS OF DUBIOUS ORIGIN

Concerning work, the holy texts and educated people have said quite beautiful, important, and edifying things, even if the hard reality of life doesn't always coincide with their wise aphorisms. Thus, for example, there are the well-known words "You shall eat your bread by the sweat of your brow." But it is not always so. Actually, as everyone knows quite well, there are those who drip sweat, and not only from the face, because of their hard, daily work—still they barely manage to earn a crust of bread. On the other hand, there are those who don't sweat because they make others sweat, and yet they always have a sumptuously laid table.

One must, however, be careful and not allow oneself to be misled by hasty, superficial interpretations like these. Certain gnomic statements are meant to be projected into a distant future, to messianic times, and thus we have to wait with faithful expectation and, in the meantime, do things of value to draw this wondrous era nearer. And this has to be done with unshakable faith, even if it has happened more than once that the ideals and hopes of those who labored diligently for their entire lives, whatever their work may have been, have collapsed disastrously, and with them, as in our case, all the expectations of an energetic family uprightly engaged in labor for generations.

In the large Courtyard of the Geese—which was called that because of the intense and remunerative work with these fowl that took place on the ground floor—to the right, just past the front gate, there was a big storeroom of scrap metal. It was a vast room where the most varied kinds of scrap metal were piled up: stoves, locks, keys, iron construction rods, beds, safes, all styles of trunks, plows, and other agricultural implements. Elia Levi had run the business, which he inherited from his parents, for longer than anyone could remember. It wasn't necessarily a simple job because there was not only the matter of selling but also of arranging for new acquisitions and thus maintaining a stock that could always meet the strangest requests. Elia was well known not just in the city but especially in the surrounding area, in the nearby countryside where he often went to track down something of interest to buy. This restocking would also take place right in the store itself when someone turned up who wanted to get rid of things that no longer served him or who had a pressing need to put together a few lire. Levi was well known in the Community too, particularly as the assistant to the *Coén* [Jewish priest (a Cohen)] when he would bless the faithful with the traditional blessing.

The life of the Levi family was modest, like that of so many other families, but secure and dignified because it was perfectly balanced between faith, plainness, and honesty in business. Besides, Elia had come to understand the new times quite well. He certainly would not have changed his accustomed work, which he was quite fond of—not for the world, not at his age. But his children, he was convinced, had to change ways in order to take advantage of the new, better opportunities that the great freedom of the Emancipation could offer them. Thus they could create a better life for themselves in the midst of that varied and attractive world in which they had been learning to live for several decades. Elia had three children, two girls and one boy. The two girls had married fellow Jews who were shopkeepers, and Elia thanked the Lord again and again for this gift, given the unhappy way things were these days with the ever more overwhelming wave of mixed marriages. The two sons-in-law had opened a splendid fabric shop, on Via Roma no less, and the joy of the old father was indescribable when he went to visit his daughters in the shop or in their homes, modern and pleasant, in a new quarter of the city. It was a significant step up, economically speaking, in quality and space, that consoled him fully for the many sacrifices he had made and continued to make, all for the benefit of his children. What's more, he had done it without ever asking anything from anybody, habituated as he always had been to standing on his own two feet.

Then there was his son, Giuseppe, who had been the special object of his dreams and plans. He was an intelligent, quick-witted boy. It had not been hard to get him to study, notwithstanding the onerous expenses that Elia had sustained, besides having to forgo the help of the one who, according to the informal tradition, should have been his closest aide and heir in business. But the progress that his son regularly achieved in his studies, always shining, had driven the father to support him, to encourage him to go forward at all costs, even when the father realized that Giuseppe wanted to break off his studies, so as not to continue to burden the family's expenses.

When the gates of the university opened before him, the economic problems reached substantial proportions. Elia did not lose courage; at that point a prestigious goal had appeared not only before the son but also before the father himself, who in a little while would be able to pride himself on having a son with a degree. He redoubled and tripled his efforts at work; he enlarged his activities a great deal and his business as much as possible, making new contacts in new milieus, always guided by his extreme prudence as a shrewd businessman. He felt confident in himself; he had the kind of experience—inherited for generations and consolidated by decades of work—that made him a true expert in dealing with ironmongery. This was demonstrated by the fact that he was often consulted by other shopkeepers to judge the quality of certain merchandise and the terms for selling or buying, which were no less important than the value of the merchandise itself.

When Giuseppe graduated in jurisprudence, there was a celebration in the family and in the entire Community. At the reception, organized in grand style by Elia, *sur murenu*, the rabbi, and even the already multidegreed president of the Community, spoke. The latter, to tell the truth, took part in the celebration mainly because he was driven by curiosity to see up close this strange type of graduate—the *homo novus*—who had sprouted miraculously amid the scrap metal of that store in the Courtyard of the Geese. *Sur murenu*, for his part, didn't miss the opportunity, after the formalities, to point out how even this splendid result was the fruit of the Emancipation, which had freely and generously given the most complete freedom to the Jews, and that it was their express duty to demonstrate—always, on every occasion—their gratitude toward the House of Savoy, increasing their commitment as upright citizens and as Italians devoted to their Sacred Homeland.

With his diploma in hand Giuseppe did not yet have a job, but there were plenty of possibilities; all he had to do was get on with it. Elia did not fail to contact all the authorities he knew. When his son, being free for the moment, dropped by the warehouse on his own, he wandered happily between those walls of his childhood and told his father that in the meantime he could lend him a hand. This elicited the sharpest protests from his father. Precisely now he wanted to ruin everything? Someone with a degree should not be in the middle of scrap metal but in an office. Everyone in his place, doing his own work.

And Giuseppe found his place, in an office, and it was nothing less than the local law court. He was presented with the possibility of a career in the judiciary. It was a prestigious position, of great responsibility, that would automatically rank him among the highest levels of local society. He would be able to become a judge, maybe even president of a law court, in one of those courtrooms that Elia Levi had sometimes visited out of curiosity when trials took place in which people he knew were involved.

A few years later, however, something happened that never should have happened, something that Elia Levi would never have been able to imagine could happen. One day, in fact, Elia Levi was to be found in one of those courtrooms not out of curiosity but as a defendant. Unimaginable!

In the warehouse in the Courtyard of the Geese, two individuals had appeared whom Levi knew vaguely, having occasionally run into them at some market and, now he remembered, in the café that he frequented on Tuesdays and Fridays, the market days. They proposed to him the acquisition of rolled-iron sections, a very good deal, for both the quality and the price. The deal concerned a consignment of goods taken over because of a bankruptcy, and it seemed genuine. The only condition, somewhat burdensome, was the payment in cash upon the delivery of the merchandise. As was usual in all his dealings, and in this case too, more than a few doubts presented themselves to the mind of the old shopkeeper, who began asking questions endlessly. The answers, however, were always detailed and thorough, and the official documents presented to him were exemplary. Still not completely convinced, however, Levi wanted to see the merchandise. He was accompanied by the two friends who led him to a warehouse at the edge of the city. What was there were rolled-iron sections of prime quality—of that there was no doubt—that had belonged to a firm that he did not know but whose name appeared clearly in the official papers that were produced and that had gone bankrupt a long time before. He reexamined these papers with the greatest care; they were authentic, according to him, in every detail. The deal was concluded, and the merchandise arrived at Levi's warehouse toward evening, when the first shadows had already spread over the old courtyard of the ex-ghetto. Payment for the delivered merchandise was made, according to the agreement, in cash. A few weeks went by, and then the bomb exploded. One morning when the store had just opened, a fellow—wearing dark colors, with a southern accent—presented himself and handed Elia a subpoena to appear before the examining magistrate.

"But what's this about?" asked Elia in a trembling voice.

"This, my task it is not. To deliver I must the document, and you, sir, to sign here, you sir must." And he handed Elia a notebook, after having written "delivered to the same" on the document. Raising two fingers to the brim of his hat signifying an official goodbye, the man left.

Levi felt faint. He seated himself in a chair and read and reread that strange document, which didn't seem at all clear to him. "Purchase of goods of dubious origin"—what did that mean, what did it refer to? And—this part he did understand—he was summoned to the examining magistrate "for information" in three days.

When Giuseppe returned home—in the meantime, after several competitive examinations (passed with flying colors), he had reached the position of clerk of the court—his father, who was still distraught, had him look at the summons. The son was also astonished, and he subjected his father to many questions about his recent business activities. Elia responded with his usual precision; he kept a register in which all the activity of the storeroom was scrupulously recorded. Giuseppe, with the technical eye of the profession, set himself to study all the documentation with a great deal of care. All of a sudden his attention was arrested by the acquisition of the rolled-iron sections, which still lay in the storeroom. He examined the merchandise and was surprised to see the disparity between the quantity of the goods and the price paid for them.

He turned to his father: "Whatever possessed you to make such a purchase? I get the feeling that deep underneath this there's something that's not so clean. How is it possible?"

"Listen, don't talk nonsense. I'm not a novice," responded his father, all but offended. "I certainly didn't buy with my eyes closed. For me too, at first, the deal wasn't convincing, but then I saw the papers and looked them over—several times—and they were in perfect order, without any doubt. It was a clearance sale due to bankruptcy."

"But are you really sure?"

"How can you have any doubt? It's not the first time I've dealt with business like this. I've always bought goods from bankruptcies—a lot."

"But given the importance of the transaction, why didn't you have me look over these papers?"

"What need was there? They were very clear and understandable even for me, who has no degree. Maybe you've forgotten that your father isn't a simpleton and that he has long-standing experience? I'm not exactly the type who can be fooled so readily."

But this time, unfortunately for him, Elia Levi had been fooled and in the most banal way. The documents were false, the merchandise was the fruit of receiving stolen goods, and so he was indicted for the purchase of goods of dubious origin and sentenced to several months, with a suspended sentence (being treated as a first offender) and the confiscation of the relevant merchandise. From which we learn, yet again, that among the accused seated in court there may also be honorable people.

This entire sad affair devastated not only the old shopkeeper, but especially, and it could be said, more directly, his son, the clerk of the court. How would he be able to continue his work in that building where his father, his own father, had been convicted? He opened his heart to several colleagues, who took pains to tell him that for one thing he was blameless, and in the end so was his old father, a shopkeeper of flawless honesty, a fact openly acknowledged by everyone in the city, including even the president of the tribunal, who at the conclusion of the trial said to the convicted man, "I am enormously displeased that you, sir, having reached your age after an irreproachable life would have fallen into this trap. What does it mean? That when you work, you never stop learning, whatever your age, even when you are old. On the other hand, the law is the law, equal for everyone."

All fine words, mulled over in Giuseppe's mind, even at night when he couldn't sleep and tossed and turned from one side to the other. His career, he thought, was ruined forever. There was no doubt, especially considering his completely unique situation: Giuseppe was not just any magistrate's clerk—he was a Jew, the first to occupy such an important position in that small city. It might seem strange that there could be anyone who would want to link what had happened with a magistrate's clerk who was Jewish, but it's not that hard to imagine, at least in certain circles. Something vague, barely whispered, had been reported about him, something said completely in confidence by someone who, in instances like this, was careful to declare himself a friend of the Jews ("and I always have been"): "It's well known"—it was supposedly said—"that the Jews, inside or outside the ghetto, always look after their own interests, just as they always have, and they're not too particular when it comes to making money. They haven't changed, and they never will . . . even if they get degrees."

One afternoon Giuseppe was at his worktable when an office boy came in and put some files on the table. He examined them one at a time, then stopped and stared at a folder opened before his eyes, thunderstruck. It dealt with the sentence pronounced against his father, which he would have to register. Was it simply a coincidence, or was it instead the special gift of some colleague, for some personal reason of his own? Giuseppe's head swirled and he felt faint. He closed the file slowly and left the office to wander aimlessly here and there throughout the city. He walked along the bank of the Po, staring persistently at the flowing water and the dizzying whirlpools of the current. The river was in spate. But he quickly turned away from that view and tried to push away certain thoughts that had suddenly appeared in his mind. He returned home.

It wasn't the first time since this family disaster that Giuseppe had tried to comfort his old father through the compassionate devotion he felt for him, even though it cost him great effort, because by then he considered himself a failure in life, facing the same dead end as his father. Entering the store, he saw his father seated behind his table. It was heartbreaking to see once again how much he had aged in such a short time. Deep wrinkles marked his face, and his eyes, staring sadly into space, signaled the measure of his despair. The father, who had finally become aware of Giuseppe's presence, made as if to get up. But the son, solicitous, was near him and affectionately put a hand on his shoulder and repeated words of comfort and resignation for the umpteenth time—as usual, without results.

"Listen, Papà," he said, looking at the gold watch his father had given him on the occasion of his graduation. "It's almost time for *'arvith* (evening prayers); why don't you go to the *scola* (synagogue)?"

"Yes, you're right," sighed Elia.

He got up with great effort, took off his *kippà* (cap, skullcap), picked up his black hat, gently waved goodbye to his son, and went out, walking slowly. His father, to whom he had always been lovingly close, had grown even more tender to him now.

As soon as he was left alone Giuseppe was overtaken by his tortured thoughts in a nearly obsessive way. Finding himself in that storeroom, which, one could say, had made a magistrate's clerk of him but had then also destroyed his career, gave him a sense of despair without end that sunk far down, down to his heart, to the deepest part of his soul. He walked slowly in the midst of all that merchandise, and he noticed that toward the right side there was a big empty space, occupied up until a few weeks earlier by those cursed rolled-iron sections. He stopped at length in that corner, so empty and so full of appalling memories, and he felt something like a knot in his throat suffocating him. All that iron, in the midst of which he had spent so many carefree hours in childhood and adolescence, now seemed to him as though it had been transformed into so many bars in a prison in which he found himself enclosed, without probation. He wandered around, here and there until, guided almost by instinct, he stopped in front of a display case filled with iron that was not for sale. It contained weapons that were precisely catalogued and duly registered and that had been used in the various wars of the Risorgimento, in which so many Jews had distinguished themselves with heroic deeds, even giving their lives for the beloved homeland. Rifles, pistols, swords, bayonets, and bullets of different calibers were lined up perfectly and scrupulously maintained without a grain of dust; polished and well oiled, they shined, as though they had to be ready for use. Authentic pieces, undoubtedly, awaiting lovers of antique weapons. Giuseppe studied those arms at length, flooded by a hundred uncertainties, by ever more oppressive thoughts.

Almost reflexively he stretched out his hand and took a pistol. His movements, at first uncertain, became sure. He looked for and found bullets of the right caliber. He loaded the pistol, closed the display case, and set off with uncertain steps toward the rear of the storeroom, which was slowly dissolving into the first shadows of the evening. Suddenly a shot was heard.

The glorious, alluring Emancipation had offered a new sacrifice on the altar of Liberty and of the Country of Laws.

CHRONICLE OF
A JOURNEY

During the summer of 1878, Chief Rabbi Flaminio Servi, editor of *The Israelite Banner*, made a trip "from Casale to Ancona," and he reported his impressions from his travels in several issues of the review. Things that were completely ordinary were recorded—descriptions of the rather everyday Community situations of the era, descriptions that would also be repeated in the following years, with some variations, depending on the different leaders of the Communities. Still, it might be worth summarizing the reports here because they provide a general portrait of Jewish life during those years.

Servi was a good journalist, classically Tuscan in style—in his sarcasm too, to which he abandoned himself willingly. He was a cultured man, a steadfast champion of all the patriotic values of the Jews, to the point of having always been resolutely anti-Zionist at every turn. It so happened that from a small Community—that of Pitigliano—there arose, as it were, two leaders of movements: Flaminio Servi, the leader of anti-Zionist Italian nationalism, and Dante Lattes, the leader of Zionist Judaism.

At the beginning of these impressions from his travels, Servi abandons himself to his reflections with the joyful exultation of a student on vacation.

> To live all year long—as rabbis or as journalists—amid the needs of the public, in the midst of the tediousness of the hard-to-please, under the weight of those who would like to command and those who don't know how or don't want to obey, of many who don't understand, and of more

who maliciously misunderstand—oh! say it, my readers, isn't life a bit too monotonous? So . . . off to the sea breeze, to the open air.

First stop, Alessandria [Italy]. Here, Servi asks if a new rabbi has been chosen in this Community "of about 600 individuals, completely wrapped up in itself. Seldom do they speak about the rabbi. Is he good? Is he bad? They don't want to say." Thus he comes to find out that "the one who was chosen wasn't an applicant. . . . In fact, he had stated that because of his rather advanced age, and for other reasons, he wouldn't be able to devote himself fully to that solemn undertaking."

To his question "How are things going in the Community?" we hear them responding

> with that listlessness, that glacial indifference which makes the glory of the past unrecognizable. The schools are deserted, the temple barely attended. . . . And yet, there are two great teachers, Foa and Vitale, who deserve titles . . . more than some who are given them . . . and are so inferior to them.

A brief stop in Bologna, to a Community that appears

> to the eye of the observer like a new bride. Everything about her is new . . . minus the habits of certain old men who come from different parts of Italy and who want to keep their customs . . . of shouting, of talking idly, of giving orders . . . even during the most devout passages. The new, gas-lit temple is a credit to Bologna; it is not, so to speak, lavish or opulent—it is not even, I would almost say, completed. It lacks those decorative ornaments, that flat blue color, that austere order that gives a building a certain sacredness. . . . But for Bologna, it must be admitted, it's a lot. . . . Bologna has done a lot better than other Communities.

This state of affairs, so it seems, is better than the preceding one—excepting the sacredness of the building, which has not yet been finished—and not in the least because Rabbi Momigliano, "a small man in his fifties," is "filled with religion and with such a lot of heart." It's a shame, Servi observes, that there are still "certain old men who come from different parts of Italy" to disturb this atmosphere so permeated with religion.

On his way from Cento, where, however much "it is engulfed by Bologna, the soul of religion hovers about and is still powerful," Servi meets briefly with Rabbi M. Sorani.

> He is a man who in terms of learning, ability, and orthodoxy, of course, would deserve to fill one of the major rabbinic posts of Italy. Modest—maybe too modest—he lives and vegetates in Cento. But merit will rise on its own, and if Israelite Italy, rather than opening misleading competitions for positions . . . were to seek out the best wherever they might be found, without waiting for them to come and beg, we would have the best rabbis in the best Communities. But what are we doing about such considerations?

Our journalist reaches Ancona, which, "as a city and as a Jewish Community, one does not forget so quickly. . . . The Jews number about 1,800, and they form one of the most respectable, orderly, and religious Communities that is known . . . we might even say the most religious. The current rabbi is His Excellency I. Tedeschi, past rabbi of Bologna and of Corfù—orthodox, modest, and extremely learned—and in his Community he preserves everything that is worthy of yielding him preeminence in devotion to the ancestral faith."

After having briefly described the Great Temple of 1505, critically observing that this "gracious, old-fashioned temple has the *ducan* (the raised platform where prayers are recited) at the back, while the *aron* (the ark) is at the opposite end and thus the distance is too great and the effect of the choir is lost," he notes that certain "anomalies ought to be removed." For example, the fact that the rabbi, not having a "distinguished position" does not wear "distinguished clothing," and how the custom of sounding a trumpet on Friday to announce the arrival of the Sabbath still continues. These and other things "are not suitable for the times in which we live." Beautiful, on the other hand, and appreciated, are some small placards placed at the sides of the *tevà* (the ark that contains the scrolls of the Torah, the Pentateuch). The placards, "which the *hazanim* (cantors) need," record, in hendecasyllabic verses, their duties and those of the public. After a brief visit to the new temple of the Levantine rite—"elegant without ostentation, modest without stinginess, one of the most beautiful, in its simplicity, that we have seen"—the most surprising and emotional visit is the one that Chief Rabbi Servi makes to the preschool.

"It's Jewish?" I asked my friend who accompanied me.

"It's for everyone, Catholics and Jews."

"How? How?"

"I understand your astonishment. But wait, and with me you'll say, 'Long live brotherhood.'"

"It's a brotherhood, it seems to me, that contradicts religious principles . . ."

"That's exactly what needs to be explained to you. Our preschool provides the first example of merging with the city's preschools while preserving— in the religious teaching, in the kitchen, etc.—the tenets and the special rituals of the Jewish faith."

I entered the room set aside for the Jewish children. A gentle teacher, with a grace and pleasantness all her own, had those dear children—about fifty between the boys and girls—recite some prayers in Hebrew. They performed several poems, and they did gymnastic exercises, always with a great deal of order and precision. A curious observation: The teacher gave orders to the children in a rather quiet voice, and she was understood right away. And to think that so many teachers shout themselves hoarse and yell all day long!

I tested several children on religious subjects, and they were truly good students.

Order and silence were not disturbed for a single moment in the course of an hour. Food is prepared by a Jewish woman in a separate kitchen, in accord with our customs.

And thus fusion takes place as religion and true liberty would wish it to happen. The institution is one for all, as is the principal, the distinguished religious teachers, and the distinguished grade school teachers.

Later, during their recess time, those dear children, some three hundred in all, were joined together, entering and leaving together, and thus brotherhood is instilled in those virgin hearts from infancy.

I confess that leaving I was so moved that I agreed with my friend, and with him I shouted, "Long live brotherhood!"

Notwithstanding these touching surprises and this unanimous salute to brotherhood, after having visited a Jewish girls' elementary school (twenty-seven students) and a Jewish boys' elementary school, or *Talmud Torà* (thirty students), this keen observer of Jewish life in Ancona feels the need, who knows why, to conclude, "In Ancona religious instruction is quite thorough, although certain fathers don't want to hear about it . . . with such damage to their children as they'll discover one day."

It makes one ask whether such a heavy liability ought to weigh only on "certain fathers."

A quick trip to Senigallia, which counts 300 individuals, plus about 80 spread out in the nearby towns, and which has a budget of 12,000 lire annually, "which pays the salaries, besides the rabbi's, of two *hazanim* (cantors), two *sciohatìm* (ritual slaughterers), two *schiammascìm* (attendants), and other minor employees. Very good if you want to take care of the common good."

The exceptional chronicler does not specify how much each of these associates or employees received monthly, bearing in mind that there were also other expenses that the Community obviously had to meet.

The Community of Senigallia had "arisen from the ashes" after some "brigands," had entered the temple with the "fury of lions" many years earlier, destroying everything. Then they had broken into the homes of the Jews, "stripping the helpless . . . and stripping is meant literally, for they left for Ancona completely naked."

The resurrected Community

> has, however, a double merit. Arisen from the ashes, young and beautiful, it has not surrendered to the facile love of fashionable reforms. (They say that not long ago in a Community in Piedmont the *Bircat Cohanìm*—the blessing of the priests—was abolished! Where are we going with this fad for unilateral reforms?) It is as if religion were a lady . . . coquettish, changing dresses with every change of season. And rising again, the Community understands that faith, charity, and patriotism can save it from new dangers. . . . The blessing of heaven and ardent faith have brought about a true miracle.

On the return trip, another stopover at Ancona, where Servi spends a Saturday. He is touched by the fact that there are still as many as four academies of sacred studies (*limmudìm* or *iescivòth*), where, with the help of "good holy books and good editions," the participants can still dedicate themselves to those Talmudic discussions "which were once the joy of our fathers and which today, unfortunately, are greatly neglected."

"Look!" a friend said to me, pointing out several conscientious scholars, all of whom were over fifty years of age. "Here is what's left of the old school. Who, in a little while, will take their place? Why don't the rabbis think about that?"

"Rabbis! The rabbis! It's up to the Jewish Communities, the wealthy, to encourage holy studies! That there still are rabbis is already a lot, given the lack of reward they receive and the prospects they are offered. Why would it ever occur to anyone to sweat for years and years (the best years of one's life) in order to gain nothing but disappointment, to see nothing but scandals, and not to earn enough for an honorable living for one's own family?"

"And the Rabbinic College? Isn't it still open?"

"I don't know what it will do given the current state of affairs—there are so many opinions and so many obstacles to overcome. But I believe that first of all steps must be taken such that the Italian Communities will give that importance to the rabbinate that it has in France, England, and America."

From what emerges, at least in this conversation, which is not without a certain historical and ideological interest, one would think that the difficulties of the Italian rabbinate are long-standing. Someone else, maybe without studying this very important problem in depth as one should, might, even on this occasion, repeat the famous words and ask himself, "Is there nothing new under the sun?"[1]

Before returning to Casale, Chief Rabbi Servi makes another brief stop, in Parma, where he meets with the librarian of the renowned Derossiana Library. He is Cavaliere[2]—better still, Officer of the Crown of Italy—Pietro Perreau, "our longtime good friend," who is pleased to have an expert on Jewish matters appreciate the precious De Rossi manuscripts.

In Perreau one recognizes the passion that rules him and that does him such great honor. He is an abbot, bound in friendship to many rabbis. He once said to me, joking, "When I don't have anything more to do, I, too, will become a rabbi. . . . Do you think that someone like me would be able to do it?"

"Why not!" I answered and clasped his hand.

---

1   Ecclesiastes 1:9.

2   Literally, "knight," an honorary title bestowed by the Italian state.

Passing through Alessandria again, Servi found out that "certain difficulties still hadn't been smoothed out" and that therefore the new rabbi still hadn't been named. And not even when Servi published the fourth and final installment of his travelogue either. Chief Rabbi Flaminio Servi, concluding his *reportage* a little bitterly with these final observations, invokes both Petrarch—"I go crying peace, peace, peace"[3]—and the sages of the Talmud, according to whom the wise increase the peace of the world.[4] Although Servi ended his journalistic labor somewhat disconsolate, might the famous editor of the *Israelite Banner* have also considered the friendly, joking declaration of the abbot Pietro Perreau, Officer of the Italian Crown, librarian of the Derossiana of Parma, as an extreme means of resolving the difficult rabbinic problem in Italy?

---

3   From the *Rime sparse*, poem 128, line 122.
4   Babylonian Talmud, *Berakot* 64a.

FIFTY YEARS OF ISRAELITE JOURNALISM

In 1903 a book titled *Album Containing Prose, Verse, Opinions, and Sayings by Various Writers, Compiled by Cav. F. Servi for the Fiftieth Anniversary of The Israelite Banner*[1] was published, on glossy paper, by Luigi Simondetti's Doyen House in Torino. Actually, this commemoration also included the run of *The Israelite Educator* [*l'Educatore Israelita*], a literary newspaper for Jewish families, the first issue of which came out in Vercelli in 1853, edited by Professors Giuseppe Levi and Esdra Pontremoli. From 1874 on, the *Israelite Educator*, based in Casale, assumed the title of *The Israelite Banner*.

In the preface, the editor, Flaminio Servi, emphasizes the importance of the *Album* as an acknowledgment of all those who had worked for the increasingly flourishing life of the periodical. He also touches on the different problems, which were not just economic, that had been encountered in bringing the idea of the publication to fruition. He finishes by thanking "all those who, looking over our *Album*, will bless the great persons of the past and the present, thanks to whom we were able to complete our modest work, which is a testimony of the heart and the mind of the Italian Israelites."

Servi himself then summarizes the history of the principal events of these two periodicals, *The Israelite Educator* and *The Israelite Banner*. In a note he recalls that the first attempt at a Jewish newspaper in Italy had been made in Parma in

---

1 The original Italian title is *Album, contenente prose-versi-pensieri-sentenze di vari scrittori, compilato dal Cav. F. Servi per il Cinquantesimo Anniversario del Vessillo Israelitico. Il Vessillo Israelitico* is the original Italian name of *The Israelite Banner*.

1846—*The Israelite Review* [*La Rivista Israelitica*], "under the steady editorship of Rovighi, who later died as colonel aide-de-camp of His Majesty the King Vittorio Emanuele II." The newspaper lasted until 1848, "the epoch in which the editor, abandoning the pen for the sword, enlisted as a soldier and covered himself with glory." At that time in Vercelli there was a thriving college where the teaching was done by scholarly professors "who understood that the range of their mission was too restricted in that small city and that as much as they taught in the classroom, it didn't go beyond the borders of little Piedmont." Thus emerged the idea of publishing a periodical for Jews, and in January 1853, the first issue of the *Israelite Educator* appeared. The newspaper was intended "to be dedicated to the education of young people," but quite quickly, seeing "that the best writers in Israelite Italy were with them" (S. D. Luzzatto, Della Torre, Benamozegh, and Angelo Paggi), the *Educator* extended its commitment to all readers. Not only that, the *Educator* also promoted proposals that were "manifestations of the Israelite spirit." Among these:

1. Gold medals, minted by public subscription in 1854, the first given to Albert Cohn, "for his magnificent work in the Holy Land. The others to the Rothschilds, who through their generous donations had founded charitable institutions there; to Sir Moses Montefiore, for the victory of innocence that he obtained in the Damascus affair[2] and for his repeated trips to Jerusalem and elsewhere for the relief of suffering coreligionists; and to Philippson, tireless advocate as a freelance journalist of the Jews of the Orient."

2. In 1855, when talk about the Law for the Israelite Communities in Piedmont began, "the *Educator* made itself the center of Assemblies and Committees in which the foundations were laid for the coordination that is still the linchpin and the lifeblood of many religious Communities in Italy."

3. Another proposal was advocated by this periodical in 1858: the creation of a central fund "to which Israelites around the world would send aid to benefit their brothers in the Holy Land, donating part of the funds to Training Schools for crafts, trades, and the advancement

---

2   In the Damascus affair (1840), a blood libel accusation was made against Jewish leaders in Damascus, Syria, who were accused of killing a Christian monk to make Passover matzo. The rumor resulted in anti-Jewish riots in Damascus and the Middle East. The accused, though imprisoned and tortured, were eventually exonerated completely, thanks to the efforts of Montefiore and others.

of agriculture. And it was proposed to begin with an appeal to the Italian Communities." After twenty-two Jewish Communities had already given their assent, "the matter was suspended because of the famous Mortara affair,[3] which greatly distressed the Israelites in the ex-Pontifical States, and they spared no effort to gain the support of foreign governments."

As one can see, from the gold medals of 1854 on, a certain interest in the Holy Land, even though philanthropic in tone, was being bolstered by the periodical in its readers. In the *Banner*'s comments regarding major events, however, the Holy Land, as will be seen, is completely ignored. Even though, in 1903, when Theodor Herzl was already near the end of his short life, the Sixth Zionist Congress was about to take place.

4. In 1859, when the war for Italian independence broke out, "the *Educator* roused Israelite souls to participate with all their strength in the unification of Italy, to flock to the fields of glory, and to contribute with their offering to all the appeals! And how gratifying it is to note in its pages the dead and the wounded and the honorable heroic deeds they carried out!" By then "the *Educator* was the organ of Judaism for our Peninsula."

After having recalled the unconditional support that the newspaper gave to the Alliance Israelite Universelle,[4] which originated in Paris in 1860, Servi underscores the paper's backing of the project for a congress of the Italian "Communions," which took place in Ferrara in 1863. One of the editors of the periodical, Cavaliere Professor Giuseppe Levi, was chosen to preside over the meeting. The second congress took place in Florence in 1867, supported again by the *Educator*, which, at every event and with all its strength, spared no effort to "reaffirm the principles of freedom of conscience, freedom of religion, and love for our Italy."

---

3   In the Mortara affair (1857), a Christian servant in Bologna secretly baptized Edgardo Mortara, a Jewish infant, when he was ill. At age 6 he was kidnapped and taken to Pope Pius IX, who ruled that the baptism was valid and could not be revoked. The case became an international scandal, but the boy was kept in Rome and never returned to his family. He became a priest.

4   A major international Jewish organization, which was founded to defend human rights of Jews around the world but which mainly followed an educational agenda among Jews in North Africa and the Middle East.

These comments regarding the *Israelite Educator* conclude by mentioning how, thanks to its editor, Esdra Pontremoli, it had succeeded, with "indisputable arguments," in obtaining a statement from D. Margotti, editor of *Catholic Unity* [*Unità Cattolica*] (May 12, 1872, n112). In the statement he said that "the slander of using Christians' blood for Passover is 'true slander for which the Jews were cleared by the Popes themselves, among whom Gregory IX and Innocence IV must be counted first and foremost.' He added that he had not been able to find any text in the Talmud that commanded or counseled Jews to murder Christian children to celebrate Passover." The comment about this statement is the following: "It was a fine victory for the *Educator*. The Catholics of the entire world cannot, ought not, believe any longer in a libel unmasked so absolutely by Margotti."

After 1874 the periodical continued with a new masthead, *Israelite Banner*, and with "new" intentions, dictated "by the momentum of the times and by the will of public opinion, which charges us with a vaster domain, a more pleasing diversity, and a more practical and attainable goal than that which was pursued up to now."

Thus Servi regards it his duty to point out straightaway, as a significant event, that in 1876 "the Government and the Honorable King gave a new commitment to freedom of religion, which should be a universal law, by elevating two eminent Israelites, Artom and Massarani, to the rank of senators." Artom wrote the newspaper's editor regarding the rightful prominence that it gave to this event, emphasizing that the road toward religious freedom was "one of the claims of glory of our Italy." Massarani recalled that "civil equality cannot be better defended than by displaying its noble results: hard work and the dignity of life." He added that if "the religious minorities are naturally called upon to be on the front line defending that glorious flag upon which is written 'freedom of conscience,' it is also natural that they be the first to remember that along with being the standard-bearer goes the duty of being the best of the soldiers."

Servi recalls the involvement of the *Banner* with the relevant authorities when a commercial treaty was concluded between Italy and Romania to support the principle of "complete equality between nations of different religions" and the backing of Italy, even though afterward the Romanian government failed to keep the accords.

Then he goes on to talk about two *Albums*. One can see that they were in fashion back then whenever there was a desire to immortalize particular events. There is the one sent in 1884 to Sir Moses Montefiore—"the glory of world philanthropy, who the *Banner* claimed for Italy"—on the completion of his hundredth year of life. This album, which contained texts in Italian, Hebrew, English, German, French, and Greek, was presented to him by his grandson, H. Guedalla, "in the name of Italy, his homeland." A second album, with signatures "of thousands and thousands of Italian Israelites, who many Catholics wanted to join," was presented to Alfred Dreyfus when, having just been freed, he arrived in Switzerland.

All the events of the House of Savoy, happy or sad, were "always carefully recorded by the *Banner*, and displays of the joy or the pain of the Israelite Communities were extremely welcome at Court because they knew that in the Israelites they had faithful subjects, devoted children, and grateful citizens."

Servi makes a brief mention of the fact that news of no event relative to his brothers in faith had ever been suppressed, nor had "any ritual, religious, literary, scientific, social, or civil question" that had any connection with Judaism. Then Servi's article, which was titled "A Half Century of Israelite Life," concludes with these words: "Always forward! That is our cry, our hope. May the sun of liberty that illuminates our homeland shine everywhere there are Israelites. That is the most ardent wish of our Israelite and Italian hearts."

Among the various items that follow are poems, opinions, and sayings in which, in most cases, faith and patriotism march together, proud and happy, arm-in-arm, in front of the large public of fellow Jews. They are moved and—save for a few exceptions—cheer any passages that add new, significant details to a portrait that is idyllic, thanks to the shining results achieved with the Emancipation and the certainty of a future still more dazzling in its affluence and glory.

A certain Arturo Foà of Torino in "For the *Banner* and for Us," writes, among other things:

> The *Israelite Banner* demonstrates almost every time that the sensible behavior of the Italian Jews is no small part of the reason for the peaceful conditions they enjoy in Italy. Thus it teaches how much practicality applied to matters of religion can do.
>
> Indeed, we see ourselves through your pages—tenacious but not blind; observant, yes, but without the excesses of ludicrous practices; memories of the past, yes, but intensely absorbed in the future. All of us intent, therefore, on making ourselves better: more lively, more youthful, and better prepared for the battles ahead. Therefore the *Banner* was and is

like a mutual friend and a mirror. Don't say, "Proclaim yourself superior to others by the right of race or of belief," but say, "Recognizing the pure beauty of others' faiths, acknowledge and respect their beliefs." Don't say, "Prepare to exile yourselves from your country for a new Semitic kingdom because the land in which you were born is not a homeland for you," but say, "This is your homeland; this is the domain of your labor; be manfully grateful to the dynasty and the people who have given you the dignity of free people and exert yourselves harmoniously to make yourselves ever more worthy of your new destiny as Italians and as Jews."

Even if that dangerous word, *Zionism*, doesn't get mentioned here, at least the issue, which Servi didn't feel obligated to at least refer to in his broad treatment, emerges, with even a certain evasive clarity, although it is condemned without appeal and without any second thoughts. But this stance is a foregone conclusion that comes as no surprise and that over the years had already been seasoned with every possible sauce, beginning with Servi himself. Thus the phrase with which we return to a favorite topic of the Jews of the era seems somewhat comic—the topic, that is, of gratitude toward the House of Savoy and the Italians for their freedom, obtained as a gracious gift and not as a right that is due every human being. The comic quality lies in that adverb: What can "manfully" mean? But patriotic enthusiasm didn't question rhetoric.

Leone Ravenna, from Ferrara, in "The Duty of Israelite Journalism," reflects on the critical problem of assimilation.

It is no longer necessary to concentrate our efforts on urging our youth to prepare themselves to win honorable positions among their compatriots; the desire not to lose the terrain that's been won and to prove themselves equal to new destinies is widespread in the rising generations, who therefore will not fall short of their glorious goals. The grave, pressing danger instead is indifference, the irreligiousness that is rampant, and in the ever growing tendency toward assimilation with fellow citizens, which amounts to a commitment to suicide. We need to exorcise this danger.

Ravenna concludes with this pointed observation: "I have hope and trust that the *Banner* will never lose sight of this objective, which is so suitable to the followers of the periodical that has the name of *Educator*."

To educate, certainly, was also one of the purposes of the *Banner*, but in what direction and for which authentically Jewish goals?

With a style that is very rich in bombast, a gracious woman, Emma Boghen Conigliani, in "Religion and Homeland," observes, among other things, that

> the Italian Israelite woman is, by necessity, an outsider to the conflict between the State and the Catholic Church, due to which, even high-minded female souls believe themselves constrained to choose between faith and homeland. But the more our religion itself remains distant from every reactionary, ostentatious piety, from every unwholesome mysticism, and from every chain that restricts the circle of ideas and affections, the more it intrinsically has free and open principles in which the love of country, humanitarian sentiment, enthusiasm for science and art, and devotion to civilization are welcomed in their full intensity. The religious principles of the Israelite woman do not constrain anything, do not encumber anything, and do not give offense to anything in intellectual and civil life. Rather, like an intimate, benevolent hearth, they radiate heat and light on the family, on the homeland, and on humanity. . . . Our contemplative faith, upon which an unextinguished, ancient glory shines across the ages, lives securely under the sun of Italy, and the Israelite spirit gives this ancient mother, to which it is bound by the tenderness and gratitude of a child, the magnificent flowers and fruits of art, science, and industrious works. Womanly kindness thus gives Italy illustrious examples of gentle, domestic virtues and powerful, civic virtues.

In "The Israelite Spirit and Social Progress," Felice Momigliano, a well-known historian, philosopher, and sociologist, deals, as one would expect, with the vast problem of justice.

> Humanity, now more than ever, is troubled by this *nisus*, by this struggle to destroy the most glaring injustices. Precisely because vacillating belief in justice beyond the grave is not sufficient comfort for those who suffer, we want at least approximate justice here below. The best and noblest portion of humanity aims for this with all its strength. God, says Isaiah, hasn't created the world for desolation; he has formed it for human habitation. All humans have the right to justice and happiness; thus the prophets are democratic and, to a certain extent—the word is intended with

discretion—socialist. Like the modern revolutionaries, Marx and Bakunin, for instance, they concern themselves with the masses, with the destiny of nations, to whom, here below, they have to explain their stances in a harmonious way, preordained by God, so that the cause of the Lord will triumph in the world. Reread the radiant visions of Isaiah and Micah: no more borders, no more oppressed, no more oppressors. All peoples are brothers, Jahweh is the God of all people, his house is a house of prayer for all humanity. The ideal of universal peace ignites the enthusiasm of the son of Amos; he exalts peace with dazzling hymns of praise that anticipate the political vow of Sully, the idyll of Saint-Pierre, the philosophical hope of Bentham and of Kant, and the vigorous dialectics of the *Communist Manifesto*. Who can deny that the precepts for interpreting economic and social laws—trembling with revolutionary daring and called the "doctrine of added value," "the class struggle," and "economic determinism"—with which Karl Marx tries to demolish modern society, are conceptual structures based on the humanitarian sensibility that is older than reasoning? A messianic ideal smiled on Marx, who was of Semitic origin too; according to him, although the current ruinous course of humanity is determined by the tragic class struggle, a day will come in which this struggle will cease, and in which this society, born of injustice, will end. A smaller and smaller minority will rule despotically until the exploited majority rises again, throwing off the disgraceful capitalist shroud.

While being open to all the currents of thought and action of his era, Momigliano here gives, so to speak, a secular interpretation of the prophetic biblical teaching, with all those suggestions of utopian socialism that were then in fashion. But at least for once, in this piece of his writing, we hear a new voice—more natural, more humane, more dignified, and more Jewish—which distances itself clearly from the nearly blanket chorus praising the House of Savoy and arousing a facile patriotism, sustained by fanatic zeal.

Thus the *Album* contains a series of "thoughts, sayings, and miscellanea, published and unpublished, gathered from Israelite writers," some well known, like Elia Benamozegh and S. D. Luzzatto, and others less well known. It concludes with a type of appendix, an "Album of Portraits," which is subdivided into four parts: (1) "Writers and Rabbis," in which one can see sixty-five photographs of rabbis, whose titles go from Chief Rabbi to Rabbi to Deputy Rabbi to Honorary Rabbi, among whom, besides Servi, who has a full-page photo, are those whose photos are smaller (a quarter of a page), like S. D. Luzzatto, Elia Benamozegh, Lelio Della Torre, Lelio Cantoni, G. Sonino, and others—no less than four of Servi's sons appear as rabbis and contributors; (2) "Contributors and Correspondents," among whom are Samuele Alatri, Cesare Lombroso, Abraham Berliner, Leone Ravenna, Alessandro D'Ancona, Luigi Luzzatti, Felice Momigliano, and Giacomo Dina; (3) "Women Contributors," eleven photographs in which one can also see women's fashion of the era; and (4) "Patrons," among whom are Moses Montefiore, Alberto Cohn, and Isacco Artom.

To sum up, at least partly, we can repeat the words of Servi himself, where he says that this "*Album* is a testimony of the heart and the mind of the Italian Israelites." The editor of the *Banner* speaks the truth, namely, how at least a large part, though certainly not all, of his coreligionists thought. There is no doubt that this volume offers a faithful picture of community life from 1853 to 1903, even in its diversity of ideas and forceful styles that praise the patriotism of the new Italians. We can, especially today, make all the critiques we want to make and should make regarding those distant years, especially from a historical point of view, taking into account all the different experiences, which were usually bitter, that the ensuing decades held for the Jews in Italy. But we have to judge very carefully, not simply trusting to hindsight. Even from these pages, in fact, the situation seems rather clear: Emancipation, with all its freedoms—even though sometimes they were merely formal—had truly been a kind of gift that was unexpected until then. Certainly, around 1848, there had been a great deal of ferment that had advanced this possibility more than once. But the equality of rights that arrived after so many centuries of harsh suffering and futile waiting was almost, one can readily say, a bolt of lightning from a blue sky—at least for the majority of the common people, unprepared as they were culturally and ideologically for such an event. Thus most were dazzled and swept away by events that were bigger than themselves and very hard. What happened, happened, and one certainly can't deny a large measure of spontaneous good faith and honest enthusiasm in the face of an event that could not help but appear to be anything other than a gift from heaven transmitted through official channels to King Carlo Alberto and offered by him to his new, completely Italian subjects. Later, having gotten past the emotions of the first years, which must have been very great—namely, when community life was normalizing itself according to the new royal policies—Jews increasingly wanted to consolidate the status that they had achieved. And more than before they were ready to renounce a good deal of the authenticity that the Jewish ideal offered, now that the joys of liberty were many and varied. This renunciation was part of what could be defined as a second phase of the Emancipation, the most dangerous and polluting phase with respect to traditional life centered on the Torah and its teachings. Assimilation had kept pace with the declaration of all these freedoms; it consolidated itself firmly and thus continued to grow more and more with improper ideas and pride.

The first signs of the Zionist movement, toward the end of the nineteenth century, made themselves felt in Italy too, thanks to a small group of individuals who took it upon themselves to see to it that Herzl's idea would be a return to Judaism even before it was a return to Eretz Yisrael. But the opposition of the majority was immediate, strong, and definite. In the picture of Jewish life of the era that Servi's *Album* presents us, these new stirrings of spiritual and national rebirth do not find any space except for the indirect and vague reference from Arturo Foà to a strange "new Semitic kingdom." One should not confuse the sacred with the profane, the celestial Jerusalem with the terrestrial. History, then, turned out as it did, at the expense of Zionists and non-Zionists alike. Afterward—after everything that happened and unfortunately is still happening, and in many parts of the world—one still gets the impression that even though times and ideas have changed, we fall back into patterns that have already been harshly tested by past events. One might at least add that it is not true that the past is always a great teacher.

Regarding the small Jewish nucleus in Italy and especially in Piedmont, the following observation might also be made. Reviewing the pages of this entire story of yesterday and today, one notices that the complex events of this local Piedmontese history seem to unfold following a thread that connects them symbolically it seems as though everything has proceeded and goes forward under the symbolism of flags. The *Educator* had already chosen for its motto the passage from Psalms (60:6) "Thou hast given a banner to them that fear Thee." But this banner, according to the poet, was to be for the Jewish people a symbol of faith in God and defense of the truth. It would bring help during the most serious moments on the battlefields and in the struggles of life. But to which battlefields did the *Educator* want to commit itself? Servi, later on, gave the new publication the straightforward name of *Banner*, which did not distance it very much from the previous name. In an era closer to us there was a new Piedmontese banner, *Our*

Flag,[5] which was not only of patriotic inspiration but above all fascist and decidedly anti-Zionist. Today, then, there are many other flags, of different colors, that are waved with a great deal of zeal—no less than that of their newly emancipated coreligionists of long ago—but at the same time, without any Jewish commitment and without any Jewish hope.

---

5   Ettore Ovazza edited the newspaper *Our Flag* (*Nostra Bandiera*) beginning in 1934. For an excellent account of the story of this Jewish anti-Zionist, fascist publication and the tragedy of the Ovazza family, see Alexander Stille, *Benevolence and Betrayal: Five Italian Jewish Families Under Fascism* (New York: Penguin, 1991), 17–89.

GIUSEPIN'S SHARP TONGUE

Under the long arcades that flank Via Roma, Giusepin had a stall where he sold used books and a hundred other odds and ends jumbled together in a colorful disorder that intrigued and attracted the attention of anyone who walked by that strange display. He had pursued this line of business for many years. His was an unpretentious labor, but it gave him the means of sustaining his family in a reasonably tolerable way, mainly because Giusepin's mind was a veritable volcano of ideas and initiatives. He knew and cultivated many acquaintances, which enabled him to be aware at all times of what was happening in the Community as well as outside the *chazèr*, the ex-ghetto. And that was why, when he went from house to house in the afternoon, he always found a way to sell or buy something at a good price.

However, his tongue, just like his mind, was always ready and sharp. You had to be very careful when you got into a conversation with him. He spared no one—not the poor nor the rich and not even those who had one or more university degrees—and he enjoyed a certain prestige in the Jewish Community. He answered with the same self-confidence and usual biting irony whether it was to *sur murenu*, the president of the Community, or Baron Vitta. He observed the Sabbath scrupulously, and the food on his modest table was always kosher. If he was appreciated for his crystal-clear honesty and his active Jewish faith, he was also greatly feared for his opinions, which, it was said, skinned you alive and left you dumbstruck and breathless. He was proud of never having held back anything in his throat (*an tal gavaz*). Maybe his behavior was due not only to his self-assured, clever quickness in giving sharp retorts whenever necessary, but also to his poverty-stricken life, which he had to face every day and which perhaps compelled him not to fear anything, because it couldn't get any worse. Of course it shouldn't be ruled out that he also may have found a certain entertainment value in saying things without holding anything back when he felt he was in the right. Furthermore, precisely because he was a man of faith, honest and uncompromising, he was ready to help his neighbor, to the extent his means allowed, or to procure help for others, turning, with his usual directness, to anyone who had the means to do so. All this was because he never forgot the teaching that even the poor person who lives by charity is not exempt from the obligation to help those who are poorer in some way or another. Thus, when he was unable to give immediate, practical assistance, he didn't fail to comfort and give counsel to those he found in difficult straits. He would often begin these conversations with a few words that were dear to him: "Poverty is nothing to be ashamed of, but there's also no need to be excessively pleased with being poor, and so you have to get busy." His good counsel was always judiciously calibrated and distilled with great good sense. What is said in the holy texts—that the wisdom of the poor man is held in contempt and that his words are disregarded—could certainly not be said of him, for Giusepin was listened to and feared by everyone.

Many stories were told about him—and they will continue to fuel wittiness for generations, even after his passing—but no one knows if they were all true or if they just naturally got attributed to the kind of person, like him, who knew how to create a truly extraordinary reputation around a sharp tongue. It is told, for instance, that one weekday, not tied to any Jewish holiday, a well-off fellow Jew offered him a chicken as a gift. Giusepin, however, refused it resolutely with these words, "Thank you, but I won't take it. You know, when a poor person eats a chicken, either he's sick or the chicken is sick, and I, thank God, am well!"[1]

It is well known that to perform Havdalah, the brief ceremony that signals the end of the Sabbath, three small stars must have appeared. Now it happened once that at the end of the Sabbath, *sur murenu*, suspecting that the Sabbath had already ended, turned to Giusepin, who was near him, and said to him, "Please, Giusepin, go outside to see if the three stars have appeared." It was winter and

---

1   Compare with "When a poor man eats a chicken, one of them is sick," a Yiddish proverb popularized by Sholem Aleichem and later the Broadway musical and movie, *Fiddler on the Roof*. Another variant is "When a Jew eats a chicken, one of them is sick."

very cold. The voice of Giusepin was heard to say, "*Sur murenu*, stretch out your own foot, and I'll make you see all the stars you want!" And Giusepin didn't move.

Another time Giusepin was busy concluding a very good business deal, buying and selling flour. It was an exceptional transaction that would not only give him a good profit but would also set aside a few kilos of the excellent product for his family's use. Thus, in a few days his wife would be able to prepare a wonderful plate of tagliatelle, or *tajarìn*, as they were called in dialect. But on that very day Giusepin was forced to go to bed with a high fever of 102 degrees. It's easy to imagine his despair, especially when he was brought a cup of broth, which meant forgoing the dish he had dreamed about so much during all the negotiations over the business deal and that would have been a great delicacy for him, because he could not always allow himself such luxury. Outraged that he might have to abandon that delicacy, he raised himself up in bed, exclaiming, in dialect, "Cal crepa Giusepin, ma 'l mangia i tajarìn" ("Giusepin may die, but he'll eat the tagliatelle").

These and other of *sur* Giusepin's witty remarks circulated throughout the *chazèr*, but one of them became well known and famous in other Communities as well. Once, a leader of the temple, well-off and quite parsimonious in everything, imprudently let himself get pulled into an argument with the old merchant, who maintained that in business there was no reason to be afraid of dealing with anyone, regardless of religion or nationality. The council member, however, a teacher and *commendatore*[2] who was extremely circumspect in every one of his actions, would have nothing to do with this opinion and, pontificating from on high, had said, "To discuss, yes, of course that's normal, but you always have to be very careful, especially a Jew, because he who trusts a *goi* (non-Jew), ends up eating *chazìr* (pig)." To which, to the shared and genuine shock of those who were present, Giusepin, ready as always, answered, "And he who trusts Jews like you, doesn't even eat that!"[3]

In the new cemetery, on his headstone—which was one of the first to occupy a place there—a long inscription written by someone who knew Greek and Latin is

---

2   A title awarded by the Italian state.

3   I heard two versions of this proverb in Venice in 1978: "Chi di goy si fida, hazir ahlá. Chi si fida di un judio, non mangia neanche hazir" ("He who trusts a goy, will eat pig. He who trusts a Jew, won't even eat pig") (Signor Giuseppe Salvadori and Signor Marco Salvadori, June 22, 1978); and "Chi di ngarel si fida, hazir manya" ("He who trusts a non-Jew, eats pig") (Signor Bruno Calimani, September 23, 1978). Umberto Fortis, in *La parlata degli ebrei di Venezia e le parlate giudeo-italiane* (Florence: Giuntina, 2006), 271–72, cites other variants of this proverb, from Torino, Trieste, Modena, Ferrara, Livorno, Ancona, and Pitigliano, attesting to its widespread popularity.

still legible today. After having described (not without pompousness, but also successfully) the gifts of the deceased Giusepin—his extraordinary capacity for work and his great faith—the inscription concluded: "Rest, rest in peace." The verb, repeated twice, was sometimes interpreted in a way that was not very respectful to the deceased. It was said that it meant, in essence, "Now you're fine where you are. We won't hear your tongue badmouthing everything and everyone anymore!" Regarding this unsympathetic interpretation, many doubts could be raised, but it is undeniable that the author of this funeral eulogy, when he found himself in the cemetery for the yearly visit, enjoyed reading aloud the words that he had suggested to the occasional visitors who accompanied him. Coming to those final words, he would read them slowly, winking, as though to say, "Get it?" Then he would go on to read other inscriptions—always those he had written—which he recited as though the people who were assembled there had gathered to hear those passages of high funereal literature rather than prayers.

One morning, Giusepin, hands in his pockets and cigar in his mouth as though he were sucking on a piece of candy, was behind his stall, wearing the sly look of someone waiting for good customers—that is, for those ready to make a good deal. He studied whoever stopped in front of him, and his expert eye rarely erred. When he thought the person being considered wasn't from his city, he would murmur some words in Hebrew. If the unfamiliar person didn't respond, he would mutter to himself, "He's an *arèl* (uncircumcised)." He always had the book of Psalms open, in the middle of the counter, and he read from it frequently, between one sale and another.

Giusepin saw one of his fellow Jews go by, one of the familiar *minianisti*—those who, being paid to do so, would be present at the synagogue to ensure the minimum number of ten men required to recite certain prayers. He, too, was in search of a daily bowl of soup, which could be procured not only with work, but with gossip, by spreading news he had elaborated, thus gaining a few coins from people interested in certain events. An informer sui generis. He was called, who knows why, Muciapàn. He had made himself a reputation in this respect, to such an extent that in the Community, "He's a *muciapàn*" meant, indisputably, someone who habitually told lies. He was walking, briskly as usual, with his hat shifted slightly forward, as though he didn't want to be delayed from collecting the news of the day, which he would resell later for a good price to the highest bidder.

Giusepin called to him and asked, "Beh! What's new today?"

"Mah, nothing new or special," Muciapàn replied cautiously and with a sad tone of resignation.

"How can that be?" Giusepin pressed on with a slight smile. "Haven't you heard the big, unheard-of news of the day? It should interest you personally."

"What? What?" His eyes were wide open, and his gaping mouth appeared to be waiting to drink up the big news, which he would later fashion for his own use and consumption.

"Since yesterday, over and over, the rumor has been spreading that finally you said something that was true! Is that really the case?"

After removing a *mezzo Toscano* [a type of cigar], soaking with saliva, from his mouth, Giusepin broke into a loud laugh. Tears nearly came to his eyes from laughing so hard. Muciapàn just gestured with his hand and went on without taking leave, offended by the outrageous things Giusepin had said about him.

Now "Bona del Moru," the wife of one of the most adept *minianisti* in the Community, was approaching. Her hair was drawn back hard and tight and held in place with small combs on the nape of her neck. She had an oversized aquiline nose, which always pointed upward as though smelling who knows what. She usually walked with a hand on her hip, swaying slightly, like a model on the catwalk displaying fashionable clothes. Exaggerating a little, you could make a bit of an analogy to models, considering that she had quite a few clothes at her disposal, which she had carefully collected by going door to door, begging for "something to throw on." Wearing fine clothes from high society, even if they weren't exactly new, was a reliable, lovely novelty for getting the whole *chazèr* to admire her. La Bona also had a role, not to be overlooked, in collecting and circulating news, carefully served up according to the circumstances and the person. If one can speak of specialization within this genre of curious activities, one could say that Bona del Moru was an expert at knowing thoroughly who was who among almost all the families of her fellow Jews. Frequently you would see her standing at some strategic point, usually a corner, on the small streets of the old ghetto, so she could monitor a larger area. Hand on her hip, she often seemed to be chewing something, but she was actually talking to herself. The gossips said she chewed tobacco and at home even smoked cigars. Sometimes it was enough for her to take a glance at the coming and going of people, observing their behavior, in order to make conjectures and draw conclusions, rarely mistaken, even if such conclusions were flavored with a bit of the fantasy that is indispensable to the life of every ghetto in this world. She approached Giusepin, stepped around the counter to be closer, and whispered, "Have you heard anything about Juchanàn's daughter?"

"No, what?" Giusepin was waiting to find out where the secret would lead and what price might be requested.

"L'hai sentì che l'an gnusàla."[4] ("I heard that she's had intimate relations.")

"But no, how can that be, with whom?" The merchant's surprise was great; he knew the family, which was always perfectly respectable in everything.

"Yes, yes, I understood it from many things." Saying this, she raised a hand and brushed it against her stomach. "How? The way it happens in all these cases." She smiled maliciously. "And with whom?" She stopped herself for an instant; she wanted to keep Giusepin's curiosity, which kept growing and growing, in suspense. "With whom? I think I know who it is, but I'm still not sure. At any rate, it seems that it's nothing less than a *goy*, a real *cherpà* (shame) for that poor family!"

Giusepin realized that things were getting awkward, and not intending to go any further, he cut it short with one of his wisecracks. Getting serious and speaking softly, he said, "Tell the truth, you're sorry, right? I understand—it's something that can't happen to you anymore! You're jealous, right?" And he broke into a big laugh. Bona pulled back, as though she were horrified by what she had heard, and she left, offended, swaying her hips more than usual, her face completely red, not saying a word.

Having rearranged the objects on display so they took up the least amount of space possible and covering everything with a tarpaulin that was then secured with rope, Giusepin pushed his stall toward the courtyard of the house where he lived. It was Friday, and he had closed his ambulatory shop early so he could get himself ready in time to welcome the Sabbath. This weekly festive day was, both for him and his entire family, a symbol of deliverance from all the daily worries. He dressed during the week in the most unassuming way, in clothes that were more than used and not always tidy—in army boots, with a black, threadbare woolen scarf around his neck, and a cap that by then had lost any semblance of color on his head. But on the day of the Sabbath, Giusepin was transformed into a true *signore*. In the holy temple, beginning with *'arvith* (the evening prayer service) on Friday evening, he would appear in a dignified suit, a white shirt and well-matched tie, perfectly tidy shoes carefully shined, and an impeccable homburg on his head. At the temple he held a place of respect, as befitting one who knew

---

4   In Jewish Piedmontese dialect.

Torah and all the numerous liturgical chants in the most thorough manner. Woe to that *chazàn* (cantor) who erred with one word or one note. Only on such occasions did Giusepin's tongue resume its regular, harsh weekday tone, and his voice, almost angry, made itself heard even though it was the Sabbath. Later, at home, by the light of the Sabbath lamp, he conducted the traditional chants as only he knew how, and family members followed him with respectful attention and interest, not in the least because, after supper, Giusepin would comment on several passages from the Sabbath Torah reading, in his own style, of course, and usually in dialect, but with sure knowledge.

On the Sabbath everything about Giusepin was transformed, and he seemed to be another man. One could practically see that in him, truly, the second soul—the Sabbath soul, as a mystical tradition has it—had descended. Our sages say that on the Sabbath even weekday language should abate, and we should speak in another way. Whoever was his guest on this day—and there was always some guest because Giusepin never forgot those who were hungrier than him—would have gotten the impression of finding himself in front of another person, entirely different. Clearly he was completely different from the person one could observe during the week, behind his stall along the arcades of the Via Roma. Then, the Sabbath over, he would return to the man he always had been, and he could even seem to be a cantankerous old captain, on the bridge of his ship, ready to attack the crew, without hesitation and mercilessly, with that tongue of his that could bite and didn't spare anyone, ever, on any occasion. But on the Sabbath, no. With his clothes, he changed his manner, his behavior, and his usual, hazardous speech.

THEY'RE NOT ALL CRAZY

It is said that on the facade of a well-known psychiatric hospital, it was written, "They're not all here, and they're not all crazy." Great truths are concentrated in these few words. They lead us to think seriously about the eternal perplexities that accompany the great human adventure in all its most complex and peculiar repercussions. They also persuade us to keep on investigating the effects of the historical and social vicissitudes of individuals, groups, and the community on a given historical period and on customs and traditions. These vicissitudes may leave profound and painful marks on the unconscious mind, and are transmitted, just like life, from generation to generation. There is also a special aspect of so-called craziness in which it can be a very useful instrument for resolving situations that are particular and tricky from a social and political point of view, like the case of David, who pretended to be crazy in front of Akhish, the king of Gad, or times when craziness can be used effectively to protect a given regime. In cases like these, whoever doesn't think exactly like whoever is firmly in power can't be anything other than a crazy person who, for his own good and the good of the general public, must be interned. Hence it is worth considering whether the most dangerous madmen might not be those who, given their position, enjoy the broadest liberties and hold the levers of government in their hands. Therefore, when one faces this type of problem, one must proceed with maximum caution before attempting a definitive judgment.

Nonna [Grandmother] Celeste had asked her grandson Moshè to accompany her to this type of hospital, where they would visit a little old lady in her 90s, originally from Rome. Still sprightly and, as they say, self-sufficient, nevertheless she sometimes seemed senile, not realizing what era she was living in. They hoped they would find her having one of her better days and so could take her for a short walk in the city. The spring weather was perfect, inviting for going out, and the presence of the grandson would be a type of assurance and a help in case the old lady, on the way, might have second thoughts, so to speak. Angela—that was the name of the patient—was firing on all cylinders, and permission was immediately and gladly granted.

They went out and headed toward the center of the city. They were about to turn into the long row of arcades when Angela stopped and moved closer to the first column, almost as though she wanted to hide herself, and said, "It's not at all wise to go under the arcades."

"And why not?" asked Nonna.

"What, don't you know? Quite often the Pope's guards are lying in ambush behind the columns."

"The Pope's guards?"

"Of course, and it's not the first time. They hide themselves, and if someone goes by who they think is a Jew, they kidnap him, and then who can save him?"

Moshè intervened: "So then it would be wiser to avoid passing under the arcades, even though I found out a little while ago that the Pope's guards aren't here today. They're all at the palace."

"You're a smart boy, and you understand things right away," Angela remarked, smiling and in better spirits.

After having walked around for about an hour, Nonna Celeste invited her friend to have coffee at home, and that way they would also be able to rest a little. The little old lady accepted with pleasure. They were comfortably seated on the sofa, sipping excellent coffee after having enjoyed traditional homemade sweets, when Angela suddenly put the small cup of coffee that she was drinking on the table, stood up, and ran to the window. She raised the curtain while she signaled them to be silent with the other hand. Then, almost running, she went to the door and checked to see whether it was really locked.

"What's happening?" Nonna asked, smiling.

"Here we go again! I think I heard the distinctive footsteps of the Pope's guards."

"And what if that's what it is?" Celeste ventured imprudently.

Angela opened her eyes wide, terrified, and exclaimed, "What? Are you from *charànna?*"—that is, from far away, referring to *Charàn*, where Abraham came from—"Haven't you understood yet that if they take a Jew, there's nothing more to be done, they baptize him by force?"

Nonna Celeste took Angela lovingly by the hand, brought her to the window, opened it and showed her that there was no one in the street below. Then she opened the door and had her look to see that the landing was empty. The little old lady brightened up, but by then it was better to take the lady back to her home and not run any more risks.

The grandmother gave her grandson the explanation for all of Angela's worries while they were returning home: "You need to realize that this lady lived in the Papal States[1] for many years, and forced baptisms, more or less like what Angela fears, actually happened, and not rarely. Exactly how those kidnappings were carried out, I don't know. I'm a woman without an education, and so I don't even know if it happened through the initiative of the guards themselves or through the selfish suggestion of some Christian citizen. But I've heard stories about many such episodes, especially concerning the kidnapping of babies still in diapers. It's not impossible that something like this happened in Angela's own family or in the family of some relative or friend of our dear old lady. If this is what happened, some distant memory of these shameful things must have remained in her mind, and now that she's reached a venerable age and she sometimes loses control of herself, these recollections return to her distraught mind as if they were current . . . a very distressing matter," the grandmother concluded as a caution to her grandson. "One of many that we Jews should never forget."

Next, the chronicles of the small, ancient Monferrato Community record a case that wasn't connected to the persecutions (in whatever manner they manifested themselves, even "to save a soul," as in the preceding example) but rather was a consequence of the Emancipation and regained freedom. In the private history of Jewish individuals and groups, paradoxes that are difficult to explain occur, and they are not unusual.

In the same hospital, there was a man, a patient for many years, who was classified by the experts as completely incurable. He had been admitted the same day on which he had received, with flying colors, his degree in engineering from the University of Torino. Whoever would visit him would notice that most of the

---

1   The Papal States were a large area of central Italy ruled directly by the pope, including major parts of the regions of Lazio, Umbria, Marche, Romagna, and Emilia. They were integrated into the Kingdom of Italy during the Risorgimento. Rome with its ghetto, the largest in Italy, still intact, was added last, in 1870.

time, except for brief interludes of relative lucidity, he was in a constant state of agitation, consumed with repeating mathematical formulas to the point of exasperation, from ordinary algebra to the most complex calculations. He was a son of the generation emancipated by King Carlo Alberto. His parents, realizing that they had a son endowed with special intelligence, had decided to push him toward engineering, convinced—who knows why—that being an engineer would mean having a splendid profession, a high social position, and, something not to be discounted, adding new honors to the entire Community. The young man had accepted this advice, so to speak, after a great deal of uncertainty and not a few doubts. But, once having chosen this path, he had had to follow it to the end. That was because at the slightest wavering—and more than once during the long years of university studies, misgivings arose in him—the family threatened him not only with an uncertain future if he stopped his studies, but also one full of shame for him and for everyone. Thus the studies came to an end—brilliantly but no less laboriously in the midst of difficulties and spiritual grief that one can only try to imagine. And so insanity awaited him at the gates of the university itself. A well-known doctor once said that if one becomes mad, it is because in reality he has always been mad. Maybe so, but in this case one has to ask oneself whether that young man would have been reduced to such a state if he had been able to follow his natural inclination instead and had not had to bend to his family's commands.

Even given the extreme fragility of such cases, there are some others, no less serious to all intents and purposes, which can still give rise to a bit of humor. In the same Community, people remember the case of a coreligionist who, in order to receive the appropriate care, had to be transferred to the provincial psychiatric hospital. The problem lay in convincing the poor fellow to get into the car. Attempts made by the doctor and the family failed. Then someone thought to turn to the rabbi, whom the ill fellow knew well. *Sur murenu* went to the fellow's home, started up a general conversation, and then, as though just at that moment he'd gotten a good idea, said to him, "Listen, the weather today is really quite beautiful. Why don't we go together for a ride in the car? I've got a friend who could go with us."

The invitation, to general surprise, was accepted immediately and happily, and so they set out on the trip. During the short ride, the conversation continued in a most logical and normal manner on various subjects, including those regarding the countryside through which they were passing and of which that odd individual demonstrated his considerable knowledge, at practically a scientific level. The rabbi himself, afterward, on the way back, said that all during that long conversation, he had asked himself more than once what was actually wrong about the mental condition of the person he was accompanying, so logical and lucid was his reasoning. And yet, he added, there shouldn't have been any doubt given the certainty of the thorough medical statement. Having arrived in front of the hospital, a wide gate opened, and the car entered and stopped near a small staircase that led to the office. A doctor and some nurses were already there, but in normal clothes, without white coats. At this point, having just gotten out of the car, the patient, preceding the rabbi with incredible speed, approached the doctor and pointing with a finger at *sur murenu*, said, "I've brought you this madman!"

With all the respect due distinguished people like a rabbi, one might still repeat the already-quoted words in this case, too: "They're not all here, and they're not all crazy."

Nonna Celeste herself, when she was almost 90 years old, began to suffer from arteriosclerosis, a serious hardship for her and a great sorrow and worry for her family. Everything possible was done to ease those moments when the poor woman was seized by outbursts of the illness that afflicted her. She would even spend hours in peaceful serenity, which sometimes created the illusion that the situation could somehow be more normal; but then she would lapse into outbursts of rage, which alarmed even the next-door neighbors. However, it never crossed the minds of her family to institutionalize her, because they were convinced that affection and loving care could often be more effective than generic medical care.

When she was well, she also attended the synagogue, following the recitation of the *tefillòth* (prayers), which she knew by heart, perfectly. One day during vacation her grandson Moshè, by then a university student at the faculty of jurisprudence and at the rabbinic college, came to visit her. His grandmother received him with a great deal of love, and she inquired in detail about his studies, in which she took particular pleasure: "It's a great joy for me and an extraordinary honor to have a grandson like you," she had said, almost overwhelmed emotionally. Not only that, she also wanted to know whether he had enough to eat at the boarding house where he stayed and whether he "took a great deal of care with his personal appearance." Suddenly, however, her face turning dark, she changed her tone and addressed him curtly: "What are all these tales? Why did you go so far away from home? To study? And do you really study? They tell me that you want to become a lawyer and a rabbi. Will it happen? What do you think? That I'm afraid of you? You make me laugh. Tell me instead: How are we at practicing our Jewish laws?

A FORBIDDEN MARRIAGE

Laws concerning sexual morality and the sanctity of the family are numerous in the Torah. It is clearly stated in the text that Jews should do neither what was done in the land of Egypt, where they had lived for many years in slavery, nor in the land of Canaan, where the Lord was leading them. These provisions, extensive and detailed, are so important and unchanging in the life of the Jewish generations, that even on Yom Kippur, a solemn day of fasting and prayer, they are read from the sacred scroll of the Torah and meditated upon, this being the most appropriate day for realizing that sexual purity is purity of the spirit as well and that so-called loose morals are a sure path to all the other transgressions against morality in general and against the good of common decency. The Egyptians and the Canaanites had actually raised many sexual aberrations to a religious level, so that there needed to be a clear break, without compromises of any kind, between pagan polytheism and the idea of pure monotheism.

While taking into account human weakness, which can overwhelm a person whatever faith he belongs to, it can be said in general that even in the small Communities, with their modest educational standards, these laws were well known and applied scrupulously. Still, incidents could happen—God forbid—even in one of these small Communities, incidents that were connected to what is written in Leviticus 18. In this passage of the Torah, and specifically in verses 12–13, it is stated, "Thou shalt not uncover the nakedness of thy father's sister; she is thy father's near kinswoman. Thou shalt not uncover the nakedness of thy mother's sister, for she is thy mother's near kinswoman." It was precisely in connection with this law, so clear and exact, that things happened that can readily be classified

You know, there are some things I know quite well—young men far from home can often get into a sea of troubles. So, for example, how are we at *tefillòth*? Do you still recite them? Did you say the Shema (a daily prayer) this morning, yes or no? Tell me the truth!"

She didn't give her grandson time to respond but took him by the hand and led him into the kitchen. There was a prayer book on the table. She took it, opened it, and handing it to him, said, "Kiss it here, Mr. Rabbi-and-Lawyer! This is what counts, not the rest!"

It was obvious that there was no need for the grandson to try to respond to that cascade of questions. He obeyed the peremptory order of his grandmother, who with her finger also indicated the precise spot where he should place the kiss, which was the passage of the Shema!

"Good," the grandmother commented. "This is what you should do, and not follow such *chalomòth* (dreams), which, besides, you don't know where they'll lead. The daily prayer is what counts, not the rest. Today young people have so many new things in their heads, and they're no longer like they used to be."

Well then, were certain ancient peoples right when they reserved special honors for those who were victims of mental derangement, convinced as they were that precious sparks of wisdom and truth might arise from these people too?

with ignorance, slander, and popular superstition. They devastated the religious life of one of these Communities for a long time and also fed a great deal of idle chatter.

It happened that a fellow became infatuated with his aunt, and she didn't remain indifferent to the attentions of her nephew. It was unheard of, but it kept on, just like that, provoking incredulous surprise from the start, and then, when more became known, disgrace without end. The rabbi regarded it as his explicit duty to call the young man *ad audiendum* ["for a hearing"]. In his office, in private, a rather difficult conversation took place, difficult not so much for what was said by the rabbi, who explained in a fatherly but clear way the exact rules that absolutely prohibited such relationships, but for the words and the ideas of the young man who had been summoned: "But Signor Rabbi, I have serious intentions; I want to marry, and my aunt wants the same thing. Neither I nor she wants to provoke a scandal in the Community."

"But the scandal, my boy, already exists, and either you haven't understood me or don't want to. I've shown you the laws of the Torah concerning this clearly, and so it's just as clear that this is an absolutely forbidden marriage and no rabbi in this world could ever officiate for it."

"I very much dislike being forced into having only a civil marriage," the young man insisted stubbornly, "but if there's no other solution, I'll choose this way, though certainly with great regret."

"Whatever way you choose," the rabbi patiently persisted, "it's my duty to remind you that any eventual children would all be *mamzerìm* (born of incest) and in that way you would start a disastrous chain of events that would never end but would continue over the generations to come, except for one exception, which need not be examined here. Desist, my son, from this insane plan; it's against the Law, against morality, against common sense."

Unfortunately, the attempt by the spiritual leader did not succeed and neither did other conversations he tried to set up with the two young people and with family members. They all failed miserably. In the *chazèr*, the area of the ex-ghetto, the chatter kept heating up more and more. The young man and his aunt, in the eye of this storm, were having a difficult time, but they ignored all the appeals they heard in the meantime from individuals, relatives, and friends. The prospective groom in this impossible marriage, unconvinced by the words of *sur murenu*, even went to consult with rabbis from the nearby Communities, some of which, it was known, were quite "liberal." Nevertheless the response, in this case, had been unanimous: Nothing could be done. Thus, if they wanted to get married, the only way was through city hall. They were talking about this one evening at the groom's home, with several relatives present. The atmosphere was a little strained, partly because, in spite of the clear and well-grounded words of the rabbis, the bitterness of being obliged to have only a civil wedding persisted for everyone. At this stage, the religious prohibition stirred up many doubts; actually no one, in their ignorance of the Law, was convinced that it really had to be this way. Happily, times had changed; we were living in a new era of complete freedom, so why, then, should we continue to observe laws that were ancient and no longer in harmony with the progress of modern civilization? Long silences frequently punctuated these sorts of remarks until, to the renewed question, "Is it really impossible to find another solution?" suddenly, a relative, a first cousin, slapping his forehead, exclaimed, "Of course, my dear friends, there is a solution, a good one, and we didn't think of it!"

Attention quickened as though an electric shock had struck everyone. The cousin looked around himself with an air of triumph. There was complete silence and then pleas from everyone: "Come on, out with it, don't keep us on tenterhooks."

"Pay attention and listen to me. There's a solution, and it's simple, very simple. Who ever said that a religious wedding can only be performed with the participation of a rabbi?"

"No?" was the unanimous question.

"Definitely no. The rabbi, in this case, doesn't matter at all. What matters is the ring, the words of the ritual, and the presence of witnesses. And then there's also the reading of the *ketubbà* (the document of the obligations of the husband toward his wife), but that's not indispensable in my opinion. So the indispensable things are three: the giving of the ring from the groom to the bride, the words of the ritual spoken by the groom, and the presence of witnesses. That's everything, and the marriage is sealed, and it's completely valid, even without the authoritative presence of a rabbi!"

Completely valid when the marriage is permitted, certainly not when it is forbidden. But neither the cousin nor the other relatives worried about such trifles. They only asked, "But you, how do you know this? And then, if it's true, who's going to see to it all?"

"First of all, I know because I've studied a little, in due course," the person addressed said, with false modesty. "And then, I myself am available, and I'll organize everything as it should be done. Remember, too, that the *beth kenéseth* (synagogue) isn't necessary. The wedding can be performed at home, even outside in the courtyard, like they used to do in the good old days. Don't worry, I myself am ready to be in charge and to conduct the entire ceremony as it should be done."

Having found this unexpected solution, thanks to that genius of the Jewish laws, the cousin, the go-ahead was given for preparations, and the date of the "religious wedding" was set. The cousin became the center of this exceptional ceremony, and, to tell the truth, he went through a lot of trouble with the greatest dedication imaginable so that everything would succeed in the best way possible. *Sur murenu*, having gotten news of the disaster about to befall his Community, tried again many times. He also spoke with the cousin, explaining to him the gravity of his initiative and the illegality he was about to commit, but everything was futile. The preparations continued according to the plan. Not only was the room where the ceremony would take place transformed from top to bottom—furniture removed, new and elegant wallpaper, etc.—but the invitations to the ceremony were also printed on special cards and sent to the greatest number of people possible, not leaving out those who had opened their mouths more than necessary. It was certain they wouldn't come, but it was enough that the wedding announcement had arrived at their homes, so they would know. The menu for the reception was taken care of in all its details. It was more faithful, so to speak, to the importance of the ceremony and the guests—among whom were more than a few Catholics—than to the traditional Jewish laws regarding food (*kashrut*). How was it possible, even with the best good intentions, to follow all the Jewish laws in all circumstances, since there were so many, and they never end? Was it for this that freedom, the chance to leave the ghetto, had been given? Why should we continue to be closed off in a new kind of ghetto, one that actually distanced the observant Jew from the entire vast, surrounding world?

The big day arrived. The servants, coming to the house quite early, had taken the situation in hand, and silently, as is fitting, they were getting every detail ready. Numerous bottles of champagne were ready for the toasts to the happy newlyweds and thus to conclude the sacred ceremony as one should. The room was dominated by the canopy, symbol of the new family that was arising and an auspicious omen for the new home being built with the indispensable support of the religion.

The bride appeared all in white, with ornate lace and with the inevitable orange blossoms; the groom was in formal dress with a flower in his buttonhole.

The guests began to stream in, and they were numerous. No one remembers whether there were more or less Jews than Catholics, but there were many people. Small groups formed—chatting, recalling similar occasions, and not failing to tell the usual jokes that are customary at such events. The laughter and the good humor spread throughout the room, and a chorus of greetings and good wishes, together with endless embraces, encircled the bride and groom. Everyone was already there; only the cousin-officiant was missing.

Continuing to chat, they waited a while, while the groom—a little nervous, as befits such occasions—turned over the wedding ring in the pocket of his vest, trying to make sense of the delay. But the time passed inexorably, and there was no sign of the cousin. The bride and groom and their respective parents held a kind of family council in a room apart. It made no sense; maybe it would be a good idea to send someone to find out what had happened. They had decided to do just that when the doorbell rang, long and insistently.

"Finally," everyone said. The door opened, and the cousin's son rushed in, his face distraught. He approached the bride and groom and their respective parents, and between the tears, because he was crying without restraint, he communicated that his father had died suddenly, a short time before.

This wedding, upon which a gloomy shadow of mystery and fear weighed heavily for a long time in the Community, opening the door to the most impertinent and strange interpretations, was concluded sometime later before the mayor of the city.

THE SMALL
WINTER TEMPLE

At the *tefillàth shachrìth*, the morning prayer, there was barely a *miniàn* (the minimum number of ten men prescribed for certain liturgical activities), and the requests to move the *beth kenèseth* to the small winter temple, which was only a large room in the old preschool, were more numerous and urgent every day. Winter was already at the gates, and in the Great Synagogue the cold was becoming bitter and unbearable. This move usually took place at the end of November, and the congregants prayed there until the eve of Purim.[1] An ordinary cabinet, with a *paròkheth* (curtain) that was too long and too wide, was transformed into the *Aron ha-Kòdesh* (Holy Ark). Five or six benches were dragged, with difficulty, from the Great Temple and then arranged on the right side of the room. This job, directed by the *shammàsh* (synagogue attendant) with unusual authority, was to all intents and purposes done by the *minianisti*. Dealing, for once, with "real work," the impromptu "workers," both before and after, started up long, interminable debates about the compensation they should receive. Only Babandu—who, along with Zajòth, the janitor of the temple, worked harder than anyone else and never complained—accepted whatever was offered right away, arousing protests from the others for his gullibility. He limited himself only to shaking his head disconsolately when he wasn't really satisfied with the pay. Not so the others; their demands were concerted and robust, and even supported with passages from the Torah, cited more or less appropriately and more or less accurately. The shouting of the impromptu laborers and the scraping of the long, heavy benches on

---

1   The holiday of Purim falls between late February and late March, depending on the year.

the cement pavement as they crossed through the short colonnade that led to the room of the former preschool, jeopardizing the rather stable structures, created an atmosphere that was similar, almost, to that of a work site in full swing. Thus, having arranged the benches—here, too, with interminable debates—the tradition of the *minianisti* contemplated a proper rest, relatively long, to take a sip, or more, of wine, to catch one's breath, and to return doggedly to the wage claims again. It was surely curious to observe how people who for the most part had never worked in their lives, except occasionally and for a very short time, and who were disinclined to commit themselves to any activity that was at all physical, were so expert at defending, right or wrong, the rights of workers.

After moving the benches, which constituted the heaviest work, the women's chairs were arranged on the left side of the same large room, near the two great windows that opened onto the small courtyard. Thus the division between men and women, traditional in synagogue worship, was relatively clear, although the most observant—who for years had continued to maintain that the separation couldn't be based solely on the difference between benches and chairs—were not completely convinced. Different rooms were also needed. If not, what kind of *beth kenéseth* was it? It was above all the old men who grumbled, dissatisfied on this occasion too. For them, everything was, unfortunately, going to the dogs. From the Emancipation on, the plunge toward assimilation was taking ever greater strides. Where would it end? In church? In the case at hand, nothing was normal, and so it was against the Law. Modern crazes on the part of the Council, someone added. It was always getting farther away from everything that was Jewish—what do you expect? Even *sur murenu*. He was a *learned* person, of course, but even he is already indulgent, bitten by the bug of new ideas. For decades this had been the way that the small winter temple was put in order to try to resolve the problem of the great coldness. Still, the protestations arrived punctually like the first coldness and the first fog.

"In my times," the oldest among them observed disconsolately, "We certainly didn't abandon our *scola* (temple) because of a little cold. Today there's a generation of softies, without faith. The cold made itself felt then, too, of course. What do you think, that winter was warm? Each of us brought his own brazier with him, and everything was fine."

"But what about Shabbat?" one of the youths pressed, in a provocative tone of voice.

The little old man—who in the meantime had drawn closer to the small temple's big majolica stove and, having placed his hands on its gleaming tiles, was enjoying the pleasant heat—knitted his eyebrows, perhaps offended. Angrily raising his tone of voice, he said, "We"—and he brought his hand to his chest—"we," he repeated to emphasize the enormous difference between the old and new generations even more, "had much more, *much* more, respect for the observance of the laws than you." He pointed an accusatory finger at the imprudent youth. "So we, on Shabbat, suffered a little more from the cold, without braziers, obviously, with an extra sweater wrapped more tightly under our *talleth* (prayer shawl). That was it, and nothing bad ever happened to anyone."

Arguments like these were often repeated ad nauseam while waiting for the start of daily prayers. On one side, the youths, already few by then, who amused themselves by needling the old men, and on the other side, the old men who, acting offended, took pleasure, without saying so, in responding, to these verbal challenges, because such exchanges gave them a way to underscore the richness and the soundness of their faith even more.

When *sur murenu* entered, the arguments ceased, as though by magic, and everyone rose to their feet respectfully. The rabbi responded with a smile and with a brief wave of his hand. The spiritual leader was never interested in knowing what the subject was that his faithful argued about in the temple. Certainly not the Torah, he thought regretfully, but about the same old things, which he already knew and knew well, and for a long time past.

THE JEWISH NATIONAL ANTHEM

In 1897 the Tonietto Printers in Modena published *The Jewish National Anthem, Sung at the Congress in Basel, Translated in Verse by Canon Professor Antonino Castiglione.*

When he wrote the following lines, Castiglione (1845–1915) was an admirer of the Jewish people, a sincere friend of several Jews, and clearly an enthusiast for the Zionist movement, which was then taking its first, still uncertain steps:

> There where the cedar soars, yearning
> to kiss the sky with a chaste kiss;
> where the Jordan flows and spreads,
> leaping happily, with abundance and waves;
> where the tomb of my fathers lies,
> and the blood of the Maccabees runs—
> that is the shore my heart desires,
> the sweet land that is my homeland!
>
> Even though I was torn from there by force,
> and I was exiled among strangers,
> my heart, Zion, was not removed,
> and it leaps to the sound of your beautiful name with emotion!
> My eyes—oh, how many times,
> wet with tears, have I turned to You!
> And every day my gaze sought
> to see you again, oh my homeland!

If it must be—oh, too harsh a thought—
that I am to die in this land of exile,
then, within the grave, may my gaze
be fixed ever eastward
toward that beautiful country, where the sun,
which quickens this earthly mass, is born.
My eyes imploring, my heart desiring,
May they be turned toward my homeland!

I will go down to the grave with hope alive,
my ear alert, trusting that the hour will come
when all my ancestors' sins
will be forgiven by God.
And the ordeals, overflowing—
the Savior will relieve the suffering!
As a single family, one day
we will all return to the homeland!

There where the cedar soars, yearning
to kiss the sky with a chaste kiss;
where the Jordan flows and spreads,
leaping happily, the waters fecund;
where the tomb of my fathers lies,
and the blood of the Maccabees runs—
on that shore, which is blessed,
the sweet land: we all await!

These lines are simple, affected, if you like. They reflect the style and taste of the era, and they have a rhythm that seems to have been made especially for singing by preschool children on the occasion of some particular festival. Regarding the construction of this poem, which interprets the classic national anthem "Hatikvah" (The Hope) by Imber in its own way, all these comments and more can be made, but certainly not regarding the content, which is limpid, clear, and enthusiastic about the return of the Jewish people to the ancient land of their ancestors. To emphasize even more strongly the unquestionable historical value of these verses written by the Canon Professor Castiglione in sharp contrast to what many Jews of the era thought of Herzl and Zionism, it is enough to print what, in the same year, 1897, the president of the Community of Casale Monferrato, Cavaliere Giuseppe Pavia, was thinking when he wrote a letter to all the presidents of the Israelite Communities immediately after the conclusion of the first Zionist Congress in Basel. One reads, among other things:

> You will no doubt have had news of the deliberations of the Zionist Congress in Basel last August, the intention of which, as it appears from the very title that it assumed, was that of promoting the establishment of a new "Kingdom of Israel" in the ancient abode of our fathers. Although this ideal is generous and humanitarian regarding the offer of a secure and peaceful asylum to the wretched who suffer blind, ignorant persecution, even in the midst of the glorious civilization of our century, it cannot be said, however, to be either practical or advisable. Because not without the grave danger of reawakening lamentable arguments about race, which have been put to rest forever among some peoples, and of exacerbating the persecution that already rages so severely among others, could the reestablishment of a state that the laws of history demonstrate to be irretrievably ended, be attempted.

Between Canon Professor Castiglione's joyous, exultant poem with a genuinely biblical tone and the pedantic, overly prudent considerations of an Israelite, president of an Israelite Community, the contrast and the distance are too clear and obvious. They don't require any further comments, which would be superfluous.

UNEXPECTED DEATH NOTICE

That day, the *tefillà* (prayers) finished and breakfast done, the rabbi had retired to his study. It was simply a room separated from the apartment and situated in the rear, to the right of one of the doorways that led to the women's gallery. The door, which was small and made of dark wood, had an old lock that was opened, creaking, with a heavy key, some twenty centimeters in length. Inside the room, to the right, two wide, deep, built-in cabinets held hundreds of volumes in several rows, enclosed by doors with ornamental designs of classical inspiration. On the opposite wall were bookshelves filled with books. Near the two small windows that opened on an internal courtyard sat a long table that was used for the weekly Hebrew lessons. Facing it was *sur murenu*'s desk, covered with paperwork "in loose order," as he himself would say. Several pen holders filled with goose quills (which the rabbi used, with rare skill, to write in Hebrew), caught one's eye. On the left, on a small table, there was a cast-iron press for copying letters, after first moistening the thin sheets from the "letter copies" register with a brush. An old Remington typewriter, virtually a museum piece—maintained, however, with great care—gave the rabbi's office a touch of modernity, so to speak.

Seated at his table, *sur murenu* took care of the most urgent portion of the correspondence. But his thoughts already ran to the lessons he had to prepare: Hebrew language, with exercises, and history. Then he had to finish his commentary on the weekly *parashà* (Torah passage), which he would explain in the *beth kenéseth* Saturday afternoon, between *minchà* and *'arvìth* (two prayer services).

Having left his study, the rabbi was crossing the women's gallery to reach his apartment when someone rang at the door. He went to open it. Wearing a black leather cap and jacket and dripping rain, a man the rabbi didn't know addressed him. After having asked for His Eminence, "the bishop of the Jews," and receiving confirmation that he was in fact the person facing him, the man gave the rabbi a letter, adding, "Excellency, at your convenience. Don't worry. I will wait below, in the car."

In the letter it was communicated that a fellow Jew had died at a nearby country place, and the funeral had already been set for early afternoon that very day. It was asked, with words of great deference, if the Israelite pastor would be willing to attend to the funeral rites. He vaguely recognized the family, and he knew they were Jews, even though they were never seen at any religious event and were notoriously distant from every form of Jewish life. Nevertheless, it was useless to remain there thinking about what he should do. He had been asked to fulfill a mitzvah (precept; good deed), and it is known that every mitzvah fulfilled is like lighting a flame before the Lord, blessed be he. Therefore the rabbi decided to go, heedless of the criticism, of which there would be no lack and from many quarters. The notables, it was only to be expected, would once again point out that the rabbi was paid to discharge his community tasks and was not allowed to absent himself without the approval of the Council. Then there were the old people, survivors of a religious world that had already disappeared. They wouldn't fail to criticize him, with the usual comments: "What kind of Jews are they? They remember they're Jews when they're born and when they die, and not even when they marry, since mixed marriage is all the rage. So, then, why should *sur murenu* waste his time on people like them?"

Shortly afterward, seated next to the driver (who, to no avail and with a great deal of awkwardness had respectfully insisted that His Eminence the bishop take a place in the backseat of the car), the rabbi traveled toward the hills that surrounded the city. They were ascending a road that was all curves, bumpy, and full of puddles; the fog was thinning out and turning decidedly to rain. The countryside had already put on the humble, melancholy clothing of late autumn. The trees were almost bare, and the grapevines clung to a few pale red leaves and many of an intense yellow. The fields were deserted, and under the sheds in the empty barnyards were the dogs, fastened to long wires, dripping wet, howling and barking at every sound. The farmhouses, seen below from the upper part of the road that rose higher and higher, presented old tiles glistening in the rain, while blasts of dirty gray smoke escaped from the blackened chimneys and, pushed by the wind, danced around the buildings, spreading the odor of burning wood mingled with that of manure, which was less intense for having been softened by the rain.

At the entrance to the built-up area at the top of a hill, there was a road paved with large stones that made the driver's hands shake. Bordering the left side of the main road was a long, low colonnade with shops, a bar, and a bank. In the middle of the road were two ruts, paved with worn slabs of stone and full of bumps. Toward the end of Via Roma, the car turned right, sped up a dirt road, and shortly afterward stopped in front of a villa with a garden and an iron gate handsomely worked in the style of grape leaves. A low wall with small columns of fretted bricks bordered the property. The furious barking of two dogs greeted the two travelers.

Some of the members of the family came to meet them, solicitous and deferential as is befitting the priests of any religion. Everyone, men and women, were already clothed in strict mourning. One person even tried, in vain, to kiss the hand of the pastor, after having made a slight genuflection. It became clear right away how difficult an undertaking it would be to try to give the ceremony something of a Jewish atmosphere. But, faithful as always to his mission as a teacher, the rabbi didn't give up, and taking the closest relatives aside, he explained in the simplest but clearest way the laws to be followed, both for the dead and for the living. The general silence that accompanied his words could not, of course, be interpreted as agreement with all he said. More than anything else there was a pervasive sense of curiosity and surprise in hearing all these novelties, but there was no sign of serious interest. The rabbi had the distinct impression that his words fell on deaf ears. The glances those present occasionally exchanged with one another left no room for doubt. But *sur murenu* did not lose heart and calmly, in a friendly tone, brought out all his best skills. He concluded by saying that he himself would personally take care of everything, without inconveniencing anyone, including the *rechizà* (ritual washing of the deceased), which absolutely could not be circumvented. When he had finished saying everything that needed to be said, one of the sons, after exchanging a quick, knowing look with the other relatives, began to speak. He said, always in the most completely deferential tone, that everyone understood perfectly well that those were the ancient religious laws of Mosaism, even if they had been superseded a long time ago, but that one's social obligations toward the entire local population and the traditions of the place also could not be forgotten. Shortly, he took care to point out, the authorities of the town (several priests and a monsignor, the mayor, who was a dear friend of the family, and even the provincial party secretary from the nearby city, with whom the dear departed had founded the local branch of the Fascist Party) would be coming to pay respects to the departed. Now, the worried son concluded, how would it be possible, after the traditional washing, for the dear departed to be wrapped in a simple sheet and placed on the floor? The social position of the family could not be ignored, particularly on a solemn occasion like this. Thus, they arrived at a kind of compromise—there was no choice. After the *rechizà*, performed by the rabbi alone because no one, it was said, felt up to helping him, the deceased, dressed in his best clothes, in a black shirt, was placed in a lavish coffin, in order to be displayed to the homage of the citizenry.

Sitting around a table, sumptuously prepared as if for a wedding, the rabbi continued to surprise more than a few of those present when it was realized that the eminent pastor of the Israelite religion satisfied himself with just raw vegetables, fruit, and plain water. The appetizing food did, however, get the conversation going more readily, and it was therefore a good and rare opportunity to put an unending string of questions to the very special guest. He was asked whether he ate that way for reasons of health or because of special dietary rules. When it was then learned that a Jew was supposed to follow fixed rules even in dining, the surprise was great, and someone who knew a bit more than the others reproved his friends, telling them that what the rabbi had referred to were ancient precepts known for thousands of years. But, he added with an ironic little smile to himself, he failed to understand how, in an era of such great civil progress, one could continue to live—may it be said without giving offense to anyone—like cavemen. *Sur murenu* tried to explain as well as possible exactly how things were, but to go into this topic in depth would not be worth the trouble, not at all. Then the discussion broadened, and he was asked how the Israelite religion understood heaven and hell, not to mention purgatory. Because there were few foods the rabbi could eat, he responded to these and to many other questions, always calmly, smiling, plainly, and with the tone of a teacher who is giving the very first religious lessons to children. The conversation would have continued for who knows how long, but in the meantime the people and the civil and military authorities began to pour in. Respects were paid to His Eminence, the bishop of the Jews, by everyone in an entirely peculiar way.

Having left the old cemetery, in which there was a separate area for the non-Catholics, including the family tomb of the deceased, the rabbi was accompanied by several members of the family to Via Roma, to get coffee before returning home. The car stopped in front of the bar. At the entrance, affixed to a column, were death notices. When he got closer and was able to read what was printed, *sur murenu*'s eyebrows were raised in great surprise. Still incredulous, he stared with greater attention, hoping to be wrong, but his eyes remained fixed, glued to that notice. There was no doubt, he couldn't be wrong: the name was that of the co-religionist just now buried, and above it there was a big black cross! The members of the family were going into the bar, as though they hadn't seen anything.

Can it be assumed that it was just a matter of a simple, inadvertent oversight by the printer?

OCCUPATIONAL HAZARDS

The rabbi had come to the end of a commentary by Abrabanel. It was a folio volume from the 1700s, unusually precious both for its content, which always renewed the rabbi's personal interest in the intriguing mystical aura that Abrabanel was able to create about every passage of the Torah, and for the edition itself, which was valuable and perhaps rare. He carefully turned a page, soft as blotting paper, and glanced at the following two pages. It was a commentary that, as usual, seemed never to end. From the small pocket of his vest he took out his steel Longines watch, a gift from his children on his twenty-fifth wedding anniversary. It was already late, almost midnight. He put a bookmark in the book, closed it, and left the study. In the great silence of the night, the large key, turning in the lock, reverberated with a sharp click. To reach his apartment, he had to cross the women's gallery of the temple, a gloomy corridor that ran the whole length of the *beth kenéseth*, immersed in darkness and illuminated here and there by the weak light of the *ner tamìd* (eternal light) that filtered through the openings in the wooden, basket-weave style screens. Near the exit he approached the last screen, which faced the *tevà* (ark), and sat down on a bench. By then it was midnight, the proper time for reciting the *Tiqqùn Chazòth*, several prayers in memory of the destruction of the Temple in Jerusalem. He took a small book out of his pocket and immersed himself in the reading; the lack of light was not an impediment because he knew the text by heart. Having finished the nocturnal prayers, he stopped again for a few moments to look at the *ner tamìd*, which always made him think about many things. For him that perpetual, flickering light was not only a symbol of faith, which burns without ceasing, but also a call to Jewish history, which continues across time. Surrounded by total darkness, a small, modest flame stood as a symbol of age-old hopes in the midst of the absence of conscience, black as the night, and other evils that always lay in ambush. He left the women's gallery, turned to the right, went up a few stairs, turned to the left, and entered his home. A small lightbulb that shed a faint reddish light hung from the high ceiling, attached by a long wire.

He undressed in the bathroom and, having put on his slippers, was on his way to the bedroom when he thought he heard a voice calling from the alley. He retraced his steps, and from the balcony he tried to figure out who it could be. More clearly now, he heard a female voice: "*Sur murenu, sur murenu—*"

"Who is it?"

"It's me, Rusìn—"

"What's happened?"

"It's Duardo, Duardo—"

"I'm coming right away. Meanwhile, go back home."

He returned to the bathroom, put his clothes back on, took the small, hand-written notebook that the circumstances called for, and hurried off to the house of the sick person, who, given the urgency of the nighttime summons, might by then have already come to the end of his long suffering.

When he happened to get called out at night, in circumstances such as these, he would often recall a similar episode that happened to his grandfather many years earlier. Grandfather Gherson was the person everyone turned to for mitzvahs like this, even though he was well known for being unsociable, for his habitually gruff behavior. He was renowned for his faith and for his ready willingness to help anyone, without any purpose other than that of fulfilling a duty. Once, in the middle of a winter of deep snow and bitter cold, the old grandfather had been awakened by just such a summons. In his nightshirt, which came down to his feet and was white as snow, he had opened the window and, knowing that the person for whom he had been summoned was already dead, he had said, "By now the Lord is already busy with him. I can just as well come tomorrow morning. There's no hurry." And he shut the window and went back to bed.

The rabbi climbed a couple of flights of stairs, which were dark and had slippery steps. With a sick feeling, he entered an atmosphere heavy with kitchen odors, but even more with the smells of the *tampa*, which was put at the entrance to collect everyone's garbage.

He went into Duardo's lodgings, a bare, wretched room that was used for everything, even dying. Partly wrapped in a sheet of indeterminate color, Duardo lay gasping for breath, stretched out on a type of mattress filled with corn husks, barely supported by a small military cot. Gathered around him were his three sisters, with their habitually untidy hair. They were in tears, each one supporting the other. The reading of the traditional prayer didn't take long because the *murenu*, who had experience as a medic, soon realized that the old man had breathed his last. He looked at the sisters, who had not yet noticed anything, and drew near them.

One of them, Polda, murmured, "With the *murenu melda* (praying), Duardo will be saved—"

"The Lord has given, and the Lord has taken away, blessed be the name of the Lord,"[1] whispered the rabbi.

The tears, barely held back, could no longer be contained, and the sobs almost turned into shrieks. *Sur murenu* did his utmost to speak words of comfort, in dialect naturally. He had them sit down on the wobbly chairs and gave them a little water to drink, trying gradually to draw their attention to what they had to do next. The three women became a little calmer when they realized that the rabbi was actively fulfilling the precepts connected to the circumstances. He had removed his jacket, rolled up his shirt sleeves, and, by himself, had begun to attend to the dead person, with the traditional meticulousness and care, when—at first vaguely and then in an increasingly pronounced way—he noticed an itch, which spread over his body, increasingly intense and extensive. Before long this annoying sensation became nonstop, insistent, unceasing. It didn't take much to realize that yet again, just as had happened before, he was a complete and utter victim of bugs, maybe even lice; but right then he couldn't look into it more deeply. He went on with his work, except to scratch himself here and there, in accordance with the most urgent and unbearable needs.

Dawn had already broken by the time he headed home. He had fulfilled his duties, in keeping with the tradition, and what's more, it was for an old friend, a faithful *minianista*. The rabbi had stayed to talk with the sisters at length, going over the practical problems of assistance. In his mouth he still had the bitter, dubious taste of the coffee that the oldest of the sisters had insisted on making for him, hanging a small, very dark pan in the fireplace, which was as black as soot.

---

1   Job 1:21.

Between one scratch and another and between one sip and another of that disgusting concoction, he had still found a way to compliment them on the excellent coffee that he was forcing himself to drink. Sometimes, in certain circumstances, a compliment from an authority figure comforts more than theological reasoning and even makes the person to whom it is given smile.

Walking home, he continued to scratch himself, but more circumspectly now because there were already people on the street, and it certainly would not have been very edifying to observe the chief rabbi in certain positions that were unworthy of the office that he held.

He called to his wife from the courtyard: "Please, get a bath ready right away. And a change of clothes—underwear, suit, everything." He said it under his breath, making his situation understood more with gestures than with words.

"Yes, yes, I understand," mumbled his wife, who, drowsy, appeared at the window. "You're bringing home a present, like when—"

"Please, do what I told you—"

"It's OK to be poor, very poor, but a little cleanliness doesn't hurt anyone, not even the poor—"

"Don't judge—"

"No, no, I'm not judging, but meanwhile you're scratching . . ."

A BAR MITZVAH

It cannot be said that Moshè frequented the classrooms of the Balbo Royal Gymnasium-Lyceum with particular enthusiasm. It was not just because, having skipped fifth grade, he suddenly found himself among classmates he barely knew, who came from different backgrounds, even including a *marchese*. Nor was it because of Latin, which he had heartily detested for eight years. The reason might have seemed strange on the face of it, but it was of the greatest importance to him: his clothes. The third male in the family, he was usually destined to wear his older brothers' clothing, adjusted and mended, as was the rule in families of modest means. If his fellow students had been in the same situation as him, Moshè wouldn't have given this fate of his such great importance. At home he made mild protests, which, however, no one listened to except his mother, who, beseeched annoyingly on the subject, would cut him short, decreeing, "When your clothes are clean and tidy, they are perfect, in every way!"

Every day Moshè found himself side by side with companions who showed off new, elegant, fabulous clothes—at least that's how it seemed to him. One of them already wore long pants—to Moshè a truly glorious dream. We won't talk about the sailor suit with white piping and a real boatswain's whistle that hung in front. That one, too, was an outfit that Moshè dreamed about for a long time but that he never owned. In the same way, a Bianchi or a Legnano were part of his forbidden dreams. How would he actually have been able to ask his father for one of these bicycles, which cost as much as 120 lire? Still, it should be mentioned that although he was aware of this great and weighty difference between himself and his schoolmates regarding clothing, there were other things that to some degree balanced out the social state of affairs, as it were. And that happened precisely when the bimonthly grades arrived. If not always brilliant, his results were respectable and praiseworthy. What's more, the first in the class was even poorer and more ragged than him. The calculations, in a certain sense, evened out, or almost.

And now, besides his studies in classics, Moshè was also busy preparing himself for a religious ceremony of primary importance that would formally consecrate him as a bar mitzvah, a Jew of religious majority who takes upon himself the responsibility of observing all the mitzvahs. Engaged in this not-so-easy preparation, the boy's chief thoughts were concentrated on the dream, which now he would finally be able to realize: a new suit, completely and only for him. It was actually a widespread tradition that on that solemn day the young bar mitzvah would be presented before the Lord in a suit worthy of the ceremony and that therefore could not be one of the usual secondhand suits, even if it were "refurbished just like new." Moshè had never spoken a word on this subject to his family but was awaiting the big announcement in hopeful trepidation. While the boy was dreaming in anticipation, the parents, more practically, paper and pen in hand, had been busy for a long time making calculation upon calculation to find the means necessary not only for the suit but also for the Friday evening reception and the Saturday luncheon at noon. If at the end of so many calculations the accounts didn't balance, as often happened in such families, it would then be decided to take out a loan, studied and cautious, the minimum possible amount that was indispensable so as "not to cut a bad figure."

The long-awaited day finally arrived. It happened when his father, smiling and all but formal, told Moshè to get ready because in a short while they would be going out with Mother to buy cloth. He said it just like that, without specifying for whom the purchase would be made. But the announcement that he had been given rendered more precise information unnecessary. The boy's joy and excitement knew no limit. He quickly went over the foremost fabric shops along the so-called Long Colonnade of the main street and asked himself to which of these stores he would be taken. Already, during the preceding days, he had stopped many times in front of those shop windows to look, to do calculations, and to *choose*. His joy was great, partly because, since his parents had decided to bring him along with them, it could mean that they would leave all final decisions to him. Regarding this last matter, he had never really thought about it concretely, but now the big moment, the first in his life concerning clothes, had arrived. So then, what color to choose? It came to mind that his desk-mate frequently sported a magnificent light blue suit, a real beauty. Another, he now remembered, wore a pearl-gray one, exceptional. These and other no less beautiful and intriguing colors were intertwining and mingling together in his mind when, having gone out the main entrance, he realized that his parents, instead of turning right, toward Via Roma, had turned left, toward Via d'Azeglio.

"Where are we going?" he asked his father, surprised.

"To *sur* Riccardo's—"

"But—"

"Don't worry. I know what you want to say to me," his father continued, confident and calm. "On the Via Roma there are certainly very good shops, but their prices are impossible for us. *Sur* Deangelis, on the other hand, has a well-stocked store with a lot of choices, and besides, he has truly good merchandise that wears well, very good prices, and what's more, he's an old friend. He'll treat us well, you'll see . . ."

Somewhat disappointed, Moshè kept silent. Certainly he was unhappy with having to give up going inside one of those shops under the Long Colonnade—and it would have been the first time. Besides everything else, he might also have been seen by his classmates, and that was no small matter. But he didn't want to take any risks. The truth was that what mattered was to have a new piece of cloth, just for him. So he went on in silence with his parents. They came to Via Massimo d'Azeglio, and they stopped in front of a building with classical lines, the property of *sur* Riccardo. There was a front gate and a wide entrance leading under an arcade that encircled a small garden with the customary drinking fountain in the center and some greenery and modest plants around it. The father, followed by his wife and son, entered confidently; he knew where to go. He walked along the edge of the arcade to a place where some steps led to a basement. It was a huge room with endless shelves full of bolts of cloth of every imaginable color. Moshè's ideas regarding choice of color actually became even more confused; he never would have guessed that there could be so many different shades.

Behind a counter, smiling and welcoming, with open arms, was the good *sur* Riccardo. "Here I am," he said, still holding his arms open, as if he wanted to embrace everyone. "Here I am, at the complete disposal of *sur murenu* and our bar mitzvah."

Moshè, bewildered by that vast warehouse, was silent, waiting for his parents to start the conversation. His mother began: "Listen, *sur* Riccardo, we want a bolt of cloth—good material that will wear well, and naturally, at a good price."

"If that's what you want," he exclaimed, placing his hand on his chest, almost as if taking an oath, "If that's what you want, my dear lady, rest at ease; here we have only top quality cloth, as your husband knows, and knows quite well."

"I'm sure of that," his father intervened. "But we also want something that has a good price."

"Is this the kind of conversation to have with me?" the shopkeeper exclaimed, acting surprised. "Has there ever been a single time when you weren't pleased? Look, I don't yet know what material you'll choose, but for you, whatever material it might be, I'm guaranteeing you, in advance, a discount of 10 percent. And, mind you, such discounts cannot be given on all the fabrics. Then, as far as payment goes, if you want to do like you've done in the past, you can pay by installments too." And turning to Moshè, he asked, "What color would the boy prefer?"

"That isn't an issue," his mother immediately made clear.

However, the moment when Moshè would have to speak if he wanted to be the one to make the choice had arrived.

"Truthfully . . . ," he began, a little timidly.

"Truthfully what?" asked his father, smiling.

"Well," Moshè resumed, perhaps encouraged by his father's words, but still looking at the floor. "Well, I would like something in light blue—"

It was out. His parents looked at each other, genuinely surprised by the novelty they were hearing. But even before they were able to open their mouths, *sur* Riccardo had stepped in, turning himself to the boy and saying, "Yes, the color that you would like is undoubtedly very well chosen, because it's beautiful and makes you stand out. But I have to tell you that it's also a very delicate color that fades quickly in the sun and deteriorates before long. *Goyish* (non-Jewish) stuff,"[1] he said softly, so as not to be heard by the salesclerks.

"No, no, for heaven's sake," his mother interrupted. "That's all we need with all the expenses we've got. We want a reliable color, one that will last. Am I clear?"

There were a few moments of silence. Moshè had forgone speaking; he was afraid of putting his cloth at risk. His parents looked at him, shaking their heads, still incredulous over their son's original idea. Even *sur* Riccardo seemed lost in thought. He had also turned toward the shelves and was examining them

---

1   The Italian is *roba da goìm.*

attentively, or at least acting like he was, almost as though seeking an inspiration. Here and there he also picked up and examined several bolts of cloth. Then, suddenly, as if a good idea had come to his mind at just that moment, he turned toward his clients and put his hands on the counter.

"Here, this is a good solution," he said, completely satisfied. "There is a solution, and I don't mean good, but optimum. It offers all the advantages you've asked for, like the type of material and the price. Somewhere in here there's a remnant of one hundred percent reliable material. It's brown, a bit dark, but very good for a bar mitzvah—a serious suit, in short, for our Moshè to go to the *tevà*, no?"

His parents followed this speech with interest—Moshè did too, but with less enthusiasm. *Sur* Riccardo continued his speech, and, being an expert at his profession, it was clear that the transaction was about to come to a successful conclusion, according to preestablished plans.

He continued. "Since it's a remnant, you're the ones who are getting a deal, definitely not me. And obviously I'm going to give you a special discount, which for you—but only for you—will be 15 percent. With you, dear friends—and you know it's true—I really don't want to make money. I'm just asking you to keep it to yourselves, don't tell anyone else. I'm doing this favor only for you, a kind of present for the boy, but I can't do it for everyone. We just have to see if the yardage is OK."

He lowered his hands under the counter, bent down, and looked carefully, as if he were searching for something without knowing exactly where it was. Suddenly he said, "Oh, here it is," and pulled out the bolt of cloth as though he'd been quite lucky to track it down, as though it hadn't been put there early that morning when he'd learned of the visit of his customer/friends. He measured it as if for the first time. Pleased, he announced that it was fine, the yardage was right, and there would even be some left over, which was always useful. The father and mother began to feel the material, as if they were experts, and as, in any case, one must do in front of the seller. To tell the truth, that color would have been more appropriate for a person of a certain age and not for a 13-year-old boy. That was Moshè's remark—made, however, to himself. He didn't dare speak anymore, mainly because his parents seemed more and more pleased with the great bargain. Actually, that remnant of quite good cloth had lain in the warehouse for a long time and now had finally found a buyer. Regarding the price, there was a bit of dickering, another small discount, as an extra special favor, and the deal was concluded. The happiest of all, naturally, was *sur* Riccardo, pleased that his skill as a shopkeeper once again had resulted in complete success. And he was so glad that he even felt the need to congratulate the parents heartily—people, he said, who really knew how and what to buy, true connoisseurs. This was the finishing touch of *sur* Riccardo's commercial skill. Realizing, however, that the boy hadn't really shown great enthusiasm and desiring a complete victory for his professional dignity as well, he continued to perform masterfully, and said, "Just a moment, we haven't finished yet. If you will allow me, I would also like to give our Moshè a small gift."

He turned toward a nearby shelf, pulled out a bunch of ties that he placed next to the cloth, chose one, and handed it almost deferentially to Moshè, saying, "Here, for you. My little gift which, as you see, goes splendidly with the cloth. A bar mitzvah should also have a tie, right?"

Thus the parents were happy, *sur* Riccardo was very happy, and this time even Moshè, who had never thought about a tie and who only recognized the stylishness of the gift at that moment, was happy.

That evening, at supper, the conversation about the extraordinary event of the day continued. The conversation was coming to an end when the boy, as though he had been seized by a new thought, said, with some indecision, "Well then, I'd still like to ask about something, but I don't know where to begin."

"Why such a tone?" the mother asked, surprised. "Why such hesitation in talking with your parents? Since when? Speak already, freely."

"Yes, yes, I know," he said, his eyes glued to his plate. "Look, I would be very happy if, like some of my classmates, I could have a pair of long pants, too." It was out, and he heaved a great sigh as though he had removed a huge weight from his chest. Now what?

For a few moments there was a general silence. The request, it was seen, had arrived like a bolt of lightning from a clear sky. The father and the mother looked at each other with eyebrows raised in great surprise, and the brothers smiled indulgently. Then the mother raised her arms, almost as if to ask for help from the heavens, and exclaimed, "Good heavens! I've never heard of such a thing! What's gotten into your head? What's the world coming to? Have you ever seen a bar mitzvah in long pants?—"

"Yes, actually, Michele Levi . . ."

"A fine example, thank you," his father observed at this point. "But what kind of examples are these? Do you or do you not realize that that family lives as if they all were *goìm* and that for them a bar mitzvah is like a confirmation? And then—"

"And then," his mother immediately pressed on, "and then there are other more serious and consequently more practical reasons too. First of all, you should have expressed this desire of yours before the material was bought because now the yardage that we've got obviously won't allow for long pants, and then, even if it were possible, the most important thing is simply this: Do you or do you not realize that your brothers, both of them, mind you, entered the *miniàn*[2] in short pants?" And she looked at her son with an interrogatory expression, awaiting his response.

But Moshè wasn't able to organize his thoughts at all before his father continued: "That's exactly what I was about to say. This is one of our family traditions, and all of our traditions should be maintained and should not be altered with ill-considered ideas like these, just to keep up with the latest—" Here he stopped himself for a moment, almost as though to confirm that all members of the family were following his words carefully, and then he resumed, in a good-natured but frank tone: "Of course, what you asked for was a very small thing, but I particularly want to remind you, who are about to assume such important responsibilities as a Jew, that even from this small detail you need to know how to draw a useful lesson: From now on you should be very careful about the choices you'll make in the future. Look, sometimes you begin to change things that on the face of it have no significance, and later you don't know where it's going to end and you find yourself completely assimilated when you least expect it. May the Lord help you, my son!"

That was enough for everyone. Moshè now felt a knot in his throat, and he was on the verge of tears. But he didn't know exactly whether all he felt was due only to the negative response he had received or also due to a vague sense of guilt for this, his unintended assault on the family tradition—and who knows?— maybe against the Torah itself and the entire Jewish people . . .

Many years later, Moshè, who by then was also the father of a family, had occasion to recall that small episode, such an inconsequential part of his early

---

2   From the Hebrew *minyan*, "quorum," "number." A minyan is the minimum number of participants (ten) prescribed for particular prayers. Boys who have been bar mitzvahed "enter the minyan," that is, they can be counted in a prayer quorum because they have achieved religious majority and are bound by the observance of the precepts. Like "va in tevà," "entrare da miniàn" is another way of saying "become bar mitzvah."

adolescence, and he remarked on it with a smile and in a humorous tone because that minor event, long pants apart, had been part of a period of his life which was, as a whole, untroubled and tranquil.

He thought, "Just look at how things play out in this world. Even a simple pair of pants, long or short, can be the subject of a profound lesson. Essentially, it can be maintained that the tradition, the authentic one, is always present in everything we do and so it should be, even when dealing with minor things, like a simple, plain pair of pants."

Moshè was a person who loved to elaborate on everything, nearly entertaining himself, even at his own expense, and so he continued in this mode: "The poor knew how to find prompt and successful solutions between economy and religion, between the scarcity of resources and the tradition. These results, usually good, valid, and instructive, were what the rich Jewish middle class wouldn't allow itself." And so he also admired his parents who, through the strand of a tradition they followed with faithful integrity and common sense, were able to discover the fitting solutions to what poverty imposed.

It must be added in conclusion that those were not wandering thoughts arising just by chance but rather during a very happy event, similar to Moshè's, from so many years before. He thought back tranquilly to those years during the reception for his son Dani's bar mitzvah. Moshè saw Dani roaming about, happy, among the numerous guests who showered him with compliments, in a fine, light gray suit, with long pants, the cloth chosen and the length of the pants determined by the boy himself.

A COMMUNITY PRESIDENT FROM OTHER TIMES

From the council meeting minutes that a diligent secretary kept accurately down to the smallest detail, as well as from gathered evidence, one can try to reconstruct the activities of a Jewish Community council, including the president. More generally, even the communal atmosphere that always surrounded these coreligionists called to such a high responsibility might be pieced together. But an assumption that might seem obvious, yet isn't, must be ruled out from the start—that is, that because we are dealing with a small Jewish center, the duties of these leading figures must have been few and limited. Instead, the reality was quite different, beginning with the moment in which it was necessary to proceed to the naming of a new council. At that time a truly striking fact became noticeable: The sleepy indifference toward everything that smacked of Jewishness and that weighed heavily on small Communities such as this one suddenly gave way when the names of prospective candidates first began to circulate. The initial private negotiations, one might say, had begun, covertly. If afterward these secrets, whispered only to friendly ears, became known to everyone, it all served to set in motion other, broader conversations and to revive, almost magically, an unimaginable interest among everyone. Meanwhile, the old council members—who more than once had declared that they had had enough and no longer wanted to deal with so many pointless Community matters—were the first to try to persuade everyone, in private, confidential conversations, that no other prospective council member could be better than them at performing such delicate tasks with dignity and distinction.

The new candidates—discovered at the last moment by some activist and forced out of their habitual noninvolvement in Jewish matters—for their part, expressed many doubts but took pains nevertheless to declare that they would accept only in the eventuality that the previous council members were let go. Given the preceding council's obvious inability to manage the Community, new men and new ideas were needed. Thus one can conclude that even a humble seat on the council, in spite of everything, did not fail to exercise a great fascination upon even the more assimilated Jews, as though it were a matter of a true position at the ministerial level.

The naming of the new council members having taken place—leaving almost everyone unhappy, as usual—the real work, which in its totality was not inconsiderable, began. It is true that the council did not actually meet on official matters very often, but a council member, having taken office, found himself automatically involved in the public and private life of the entire Community. Besides, even those who had not made it their habit—and they were the majority—were obliged to attend the Holy Temple more regularly: on Saturdays and holidays and all the better if on weekdays too. One's absence would be noticed immediately and bitterly criticized. One's presence was enough—with a *tallith* (a prayer shawl for certain prayers) not of wool, in keeping with the custom, but of silk, and placed on one's shoulders like the priest's stole. Fulfilling these important public functions, which required time and, for the less proficient, patience as well, the new council member always had to be up-to-date on all the particulars that were part of the collective and private life, beginning with the rabbi himself. All this news was useful and valuable for keeping a finger on the pulse of the general state of affairs generally, serving not merely to satisfy, so to speak, a curiosity that kept growing with the passage of time. These bits of news facilitated solutions to urgent problems more than once, without having to raise the problems before an official meeting. It sufficed that in the president's home council members could discuss, without leaving a trace in any record, how to help a family in a precarious budget situation economically, or how to encourage deserving youths to continue their studies, or how to find them a good job. These solutions were good and praiseworthy, and they increased the general trust of fellow Jews. Of course, problems that were no less important but more complex were examined in council meetings, just as valuable time was dedicated to small matters as well. Thus, for example, in one set of minutes, it is recorded that the preschool teacher had returned the Italian-Hebrew dictionary borrowed a good two years earlier. This announcement must have cheered everyone up and produced renewed faith in the integrity of the employees.

Other "important" topics that were placed on the council's agenda:

—For the Festival of Tabernacles (Succòth [Sukkot]), it was necessary to procure *lulavìm* (palm leaves)[1] and *etroghìm* (citrons). Signor Rath of Trieste, however, requested payment in advance, and the price was rather high. Nevertheless, it was decided to buy a good four *lulavìm* and the respective *etroghìm*.

—A letter from the Israelite Community of Livorno announced the coming inauguration of an Israelite hospital in that city. The council, at its regular session, resolved to send a letter of congratulations, with the assurance of availing themselves of the hospital in case of necessity.

—And more: The schedule of synagogue services from now on—this was a resolution of the council—would be set not by the rabbi alone but agreed on with the *Signori* Supervisors of the Holy Temple.

As can be seen, there was no lack of issues, like promptly informing the subprefect of the adherence of the Community to the request to edge its official papers in black for 180 days because of the death of Her Majesty, the Queen Mother.

★ ★ ★

For the third consecutive time, Raffaele had been unanimously reelected president of the Community. He was a skilled businessman who, thanks to his intelligence and exceptional ability, had become wealthy. He was the ideal kind of president, and not only for a small Community. He observed the traditional precepts as well as he could, was a faithful keeper of the ancient synagogue chants, and was attached to reciting certain prayers, especially on the solemn holidays. Having come from humble origins, he had never forgotten what poverty is, and he was always ready to help his neighbor, generously and with the utmost discretion.

He took his gold watch out of the breast pocket of his vest, popped open the cover, and murmured, "It's time, I have to go."

Even in the midst of his numerous daily business engagements, he not only never forgot to be an old-school Jew, as he often declared with pride, but also

---

1   Besides the palm branch, a *lulav* also includes myrtle and willow branches.

always remembered all his Community obligations. He had scheduled a session of the council for that afternoon to examine several urgent issues and to make a special announcement. From the house where he lived, through an internal passageway that opened at the rear of the courtyard, he reached the entrance to the Community in a few minutes. At the doorway stood a young boy, about 15 years old.

"Greetings, Moshè." The president was first to greet him, with his customary smile, friendly and slightly ironic, as was his habit. "What are you doing here?"

"I'm waiting for a friend, to go for a walk in the park."

"Well, well." The president continued to look at him and to smile. "Come here, stand next to me, shoulder to shoulder. I think you're as tall as me." He laughed openly, taking his ever-present cigar from his mouth.

"Ok, but why?"

"Look, you are as big as me, which means we're still a bit small, but . . . we'll grow." Raffaele was enjoying himself. "And looking at you, I was reminded that I have a pair of suits, still quite good, that I don't wear anymore. You know, at home it's always the women who are in charge, and even if I still like the suits, and quite a bit, all the same my wife has the opposite opinion. So, if you come to my house tomorrow, I'll give them to you, and they'll fit you well, you'll see. I won't have to think about them anymore, and you'll make my wife happy too."

Actually, Raffaele had realized right away that the young boy's clothing was in rather pitiful condition, and knowing that he attended the first-year class of the classical lyceum, Raffaele had immediately thought, "A Jewish boy ought to attend such an important school dressed properly, not like this." And right then and there he had invented the story of the two suits no longer being worn due to his terrible wife!

At the opening of the meeting, the vice-president informed his colleagues that a family of immigrant coreligionists, which was also quite large, had arrived in town that morning. For years Jews in transit had constituted a huge problem that weighed on the budget of the Community, and to a considerable degree. People on the road, devoid of means, turned to the Community for counsel and lodging and train tickets to continue their journey. They were forced to leave their native lands, to prepare themselves to immigrate to some other country, sometimes even to Palestine, having had to abandon countries that had been centers of anti-Semitism and serious persecution for centuries. But among them it was not unusual for so-called local elements to have wormed their way in. They were Italians of the Mosaic faith, drifters who lived from day to day without any intention of finding a job and who went like this from Community to Community, without pause, certain of finding room and counsel at least for a day and, beyond that, a train ticket for getting to the next Community. This time, however, it was a family of *foreign* Jews, of Polish origin, who had arrived in Milano and was diverted from there to Vercelli and then to Casale. They were headed for Genova, where they would embark for America. Some doubts still remained regarding even this foreign family, because it seemed strange that, having been provided with ship tickets, these unfortunates would not have also received the means for the train trip. Still, as a rule, one didn't probe too deeply into such cases; the sooner they left the city, the better it would be for everyone. Besides, to whom could they turn? To the police, causing endless shame? What's more, sometimes rather strange types arrived, dressed bizarrely, with long, loose coats, side curls, black broad-brimmed hats, and white tassels sticking out from their shirts. People, naturally, turned to them, curious to look at them, to smile, sometimes to sneer. In cases like these, they were made to leave on the first train, regardless of the expense, and even fellow Jews who spontaneously offered money were to be found. An old coreligionist—liberal, as one would say, and therefore assimilated—having seen some of these strange types praying in the synagogue, writhing as though they had been bitten by the tarantula,[2] had exclaimed, "And then we complain that there's anti-Semitism! But really, when you see types like these, how can there not be? Even I would become an anti-Semite, even though it's true that I'm an Israelite. But I'm civilized!"

The treasurer hastened to point out that the relevant items—living expenses and travel—were such as to impose maximum frugality. If they were to leave by the end of the day, with a certain amount of sacrifice they could be sent on to Alessandria. From there the local Community would provide.

The president, who by shaking his head had already signaled that he didn't agree at all, spoke up. "No, we can't behave like this with people who have already made such a long journey, and just pack them off to another Community. And all the more so since they have children who are still babies."

---

2   Southern Italian folk tradition produced a folk cure for the bite of the tarantula (or wolf spider) in the form of a possession-like dance called the tarantella. For the great pioneering study of the whole complex, see Ernesto De Martino, *The Land of Remorse: A Study of Southern Italian Tarantism*, trans. Dorothy Louise Zinn (London: Free Association Books, 2005).

"What then?" asked the stern guardian of the local finances, stretching out his arms.

"Very simple," the president concluded. He put his hand on his wallet, took out 100 lire, and handing the money to the treasurer, told him exactly what to do. "Give it all to the *shammàsh*, who will have the job of buying the tickets to Genova. He'll give the difference to the family, which may need something. So, the only thing that remains for the Community to pay is their living expenses until tomorrow."

The old mathematics professor, a philosopher and follower of Mazzini, tried to launch into a small speech, as only he knew how, embellishing it with classical expressions, exalting the French Revolution and traditional, generous Jewish charity, but he was immediately stopped by the president, with these few words: "Excuse me if I allow myself to interrupt you, but there are still other important matters to examine."

And the next topic on the agenda was certainly of primary importance: The rabbi had resigned, having won a competition for the pulpit of a more important Community. It meant arranging the appointment of a new spiritual leader and, at the same time, considering what material possibilities the budget figures afforded.

The treasurer immediately felt himself obligated to remind his colleagues: "All right, obviously we have to deal with the problem of the replacement, but we also have to understand quite well what concrete terms we can offer the new prospective rabbi. And for how long?"

"And why?" asked a council member.

"The answer is simple," another council member, a lawyer, answered. "Let's suppose that these financial difficulties can be overcome, at least for the time being—so what? For how long, we have to ask ourselves, will we be in a position to honor this commitment? Let's not forget that the law of 1857, which is still in effect, establishes that rabbis are appointed for life. Regarding the rabbi who has resigned, everything's fine since it's him who is leaving. But if the future rabbi never has such intentions, what guarantees do we have of being able to bear the expenses, substantial expenses, for an indefinite period? Keep in mind that revenues keep diminishing."

The president followed the discussion attentively, in silence. The philosophy and mathematics professor, after having, almost coyly, straightened his gold-rimmed spectacles, shot a stealthy glance at his colleagues, and with a slightly ironic smile, began:

Dear colleagues, you are talking about budgets, and that's fair, and you do well to do so. I, however, ask myself if this is truly the most important facet of our problem. In all the Israelite Communities of this world, not only in our homeland, Italy, the rabbi has always represented a light, a beacon that focuses and at the same time spreads that light of civilization that came from Sinai when the world was still immersed in the night of paganism. This immortal light, which a spiritual leader transmits with his teaching and by his example, has illuminated and continues to illuminate the hope for true civil progress, for true freedom for all peoples, and for true justice in the entire civilized world. The most excellent *signori* rabbis therefore are also, at the same time, the most authoritative advocates of that universal religious ideal that will gather all the peoples of this world under its wings in peace and freedom. And you, dear friends, stop yourselves in the face of budget figures?

The president smiled, listening to that golden speech, but he continued to remain silent. Another council member spoke up: "Our dear professor colleague uses a tone, as he usually does, which for its loftiness deserves that he be granted the title of rabbi *honoris causa*."[3] Everyone smiled at this quip, even though it wasn't the first time the speaker had said it. "But meanwhile, who can we call upon to fill this position of ours? Should we announce a competition, or even before that—and it would be very advisable—convene a special assembly of dues-paying members to hear their opinion, too?"

At this point, the president asked leave to speak:

Listen to me. The problem is important, and it should be resolved as quickly as possible, without losing time. But meanwhile I'm ruling out the idea that we should turn to a general assembly. If once, having to face a big problem, we intend to dump the responsibility on others, then it would be better for all of us to resign immediately and go away. This is the first point. Second: the financial question. The necessary funds need not be lacking, and they will not be lacking. We will find a way to overcome these difficulties, which, frankly, do exist. We'll economize, we'll readjust the dues, we'll make bigger donations to the temple on various occasions, and, more specifically, each of us will put his hand in his pocket

---

3   That is, an honorary degree. The Latin phrase means "for the sake of honor."

and bring out as much he is really able to give. One way or another, I don't foresee that these difficulties will be insurmountable, not today or tomorrow; a Community like ours should not and will not be without a rabbi. Who might the candidate be?

At this point Raffaele paused, took a drink of water, and after having looked at his colleagues one by one, continued:

How is it that we think of competitions when we know how they always turn out? Either we don't receive any proposals, or whoever turns up is ill-suited, and then it ends up coming down to some kind of compromise, more or less good. Now, instead, we already have our candidate right here—in the business, let's say—and we know him very well because he's dedicated himself to our Community for decades, as only he knows how. Why don't we ask him if he's willing to assume this position?

The person alluded to by the president was well known to everyone, and there was no doubt that they were discussing a teacher who met all the necessary qualifications to occupy that pulpit. But, some council members—those with university degrees—felt the need to turn up their noses, and this attitude did not escape the president, who, undeterred, proceeded:

Yes, I know, and I thought as much. Not all of you agree, because there's still some among you who aren't convinced that his titles are authentic, which is not true. But let's suppose, as a hypothesis, that it is true; I would like to know if there is anyone among you who can in good conscience maintain that he does not have a good Jewish education, that he is not an excellent teacher, that he is not a magnificent *hazàn* (cantor), that he is not an honest person, and that he's not a man of sincere and certain faith. If there is someone who thinks that for these reasons and not for others he is not a person worthy of our attention, say so, but say it here, now, and immediately.

A chorus of voices drowned out his last words. Regarding the person in question, there was not any doubt, not even the shadow of a doubt; he was a person who was perfectly in order, from every point of view.

The lawyer, nevertheless, allowed himself to add something:

I declare and I confirm that I have no objections, personally speaking. Only there's the question of the rabbinic title, which does not seem clear to me. I would propose that he be entrusted with the position, with another title. I don't know . . . vice-rabbi, for instance, or else maybe even better, chief of worship. This way, it seems to me, everything would be all right.

Raffaele, who at this point realized that he had gotten his way, was happy about it, especially because the Community would not be left without leadership for an extended time, and he declared:

I'm happy that you agree with me. As far as the title goes, organize a commission, discuss it, and decide. I leave this task to you, mainly because I'm sure that our old friend, the candidate, would never raise this kind of question. Thank you for your valuable cooperation. Let's go on to the next topic.

You will recall that no later than two days ago, on the seventeenth of the current month, on my initiative and with your nearly unanimous consent, I thought it appropriate to send to Geneva, to the League of Nations, the following telegram, which I re-read: "Casalese Jewish Community affirms just Jewish Arab agreement. Palestine source prosperity in the Orient. Hopes for ratification Palestinian mandate. Help scattered martyred Jews through revival Jewish national center Holy Land."

Well then, I have the pleasure of communicating to you that, just two days afterward I received the following response from the director of the Mandates Section of the League of Nations: "Sir, I have the honor, in the name of the Secretary General, to acknowledge your telegram from Casale dated 2/17/1922. Please accept, sir, the assurance of my thorough consideration. Wm. E. Rappard, Director of the Mandates Section."[4]

There were some ironic little smiles from our professor and others who were well-known to be disinclined to share in these strange, new ideas, but on the whole everyone felt flattered by the official response.

An old friend of Raffaele who sat nearby, whispered to him, "Beh! Once again you did what you wanted and—"

---

4   The telegram is in French.

"No, no," the president immediately interrupted him. "I did what I should have done, what was my duty to do at such an important historical moment for our Jewish people."

The meeting ended like this, which was truly a little peculiar, given the classic anti-Zionist past that had dominated the Community with Chief Rabbi Flaminio Servi's well-known Jewish newspaper, the *Vessillo Israelitico*. With a little pedantry, one could observe that the expression "scattered and martyred Jews" excluded a priori those who, as in Italy, lived freely and enjoyed all civil rights. The allusion, then, to the "national center" echoed the vague "national home" of the 1917 Balfour Declaration, and finally, the expression "Holy Land" was the one that is still used today when someone doesn't want to say "Land of Israel." Along the same lines, one could also say something about the response, which, although prompt, nevertheless confirmed the sterile bureaucracy of the League of Nations. In spite of all that, this telegram is worth reporting, to the credit of the small Monferrato Jewish Community and its president, who was a good Jew.

PROMPT CHARITY

The ancient social teachings, among which those that concern taking care of the poor surpass all others, are one of the foundations of the Torah and of the age-old experiences of the Jewish people, who were often weighed down by great poverty in every time and place. It is not true that all Jews are rich, unless to material wealth one also means to add the spiritual richness that has sensitized the Jewish spirit to make provision for the needs of one's neighbor and has taught that one should intercede to try to rescue him from his daily worries. In the Hebrew language, one translates the word *charity* as *tzedakah*, which more literally means "justice," as if to say that what one gives to the poor is not an act of sheer generosity but an act of justice one is obligated to render to whoever has been struck by bad luck or by the wickedness of men.

There exist individuals who never forget these sound principles of deep morality and, even while carrying out their regular jobs, are always there when it comes to giving prompt and generous help. Then there are others who transform these acts of justice toward their neighbor into a true mission, to which they dedicate all their time and their intelligence. Among these there are also world-class, one even could say, scientific experts, considering how they present themselves and what they say to those to whom they turn for funds. And because, as is well known, the less public the charity one gives, the greater the merits acquired in heaven, it may well happen that from such people you never know exactly the reasons why certain donations are requested.

One afternoon, a little before 2 o'clock, Moshè was reading the newspaper after having eaten lunch, as was his habit. His father, the rabbi of the Community, was absent from the city because of professional commitments. The bell rang insistently. Who could it be at that hour? He went to open the front door, and he had barely moved it a few centimeters when a push from the outside suddenly flung the door wide open and in walked a stranger. He was small of stature, middle-aged, with a full beard, *peòth* (side curls), and a broad-brimmed hat; under his arm was a briefcase. Full of nervous energy, he seemed worried not to waste time, which in fact he did not do during that extremely brief visit to all or almost all of the Community.

He assailed Moshè immediately: "Do you speak Hebrew?"

"A little."

"And English?"

"Also a little—"

"Bad, very bad, you have to know how to speak many languages"—he was speaking in Hebrew—"so you have to understand that I'm traveling around and have been for a while." He stopped himself for a moment, sighing deeply, frowning, like someone weighed down with big problems. "But first of all the mission. I'm desperately making the rounds to collect funds that are indispensable for maintaining a center for study. Do you realize the importance of this mitzvah?"

"Of course," Moshè said, barely succeeding in making his own voice heard. "But look, the rabbi, my father, is gone and besides, the Community is small and the funds that could be collected—"

"All nonsense! If your father isn't here, you are, and as far as the funds go, I'll take care of that. When something important is needed, you're always helped by Heaven, by the Holy One, Blessed be he. Don't worry, with good will . . . Get moving, and don't waste time."

"But . . ."

"What? No 'buts.' Is that your hat?" He pointed at a hat hanging on the coat rack with his finger.

"Yes, it's mine. So?"

"So then, take it and come with me. Take me to families who you know can give, and give generously, and to whom I want to give the joy of being able to contribute to this fund for those who study the Torah. Don't waste any more precious time—we've wasted too much already."

And even before Moshè could take his hat, the man himself took it, stuck it on Moshè's head, and taking him by the hand, dragged him outside. Moshè had neither the time to get a clearer idea about this fund, nor to know where it was located, nor who the students were. No one ever knew, except the missionary concerned with the collection, who would have responded to requests for greater details with an inspired look: "Do you know, or do you not know, that whoever gives without asking a lot of questions, gives twice and therefore his merit is greater? Do you want to forgo this kind of mitzvah?"

Having gone a few steps, the little fellow suddenly stopped. "Where are we going for the first visit?"

"Really, I don't know. I don't have any idea, and then at this hour—"

"What does 'at this hour' mean?" His tone of voice was that of someone who was already losing his patience. "Maybe there's a fixed time for collecting funds for the study of Torah? The mitzvahs don't have a set time, and besides, going now, we'll find people at home and not wrong them by not finding them, in which case the sin would be ours, and serious—"

"Just a minute." Even before figuring out who to call on, Moshè was still asking himself whether it was really right to follow this stranger. Regarding this matter, of prime importance, he thought it over again, but it was at the last moment, and thus a bit late. He was unable to oppose the stranger right then and there because he was assaulted with angry words: "A minute, what? Are you, who are ready to refuse to come with me, against the Torah too? Are you an *apicòires* (heretic)? In Italy, unfortunately, there are many."

There was nothing to be done, and Moshè followed the fellow almost automatically, fascinated and overwhelmed by his ardor. Then he even received a quick compliment: "Good, bravo, I see that you are the right fellow for me. Let's go, let's run . . ."

Moshè thus found himself drawn into that strange fund-raising effort, swept away by the violence of a tornado that relentlessly hurls leaves in every direction. More than guiding the unexpected guest to the houses of fellow Jews, he had the sensation that it was he who was led, ceaselessly, from place to place, from one doorbell to another.

The rounds completed, there was finally a break, at a bar near the train station, where the boy was invited to drink a plain glass of mineral water since, as was pointed out to him, a good Jew shouldn't trust other drinks. The man drank quickly, while he looked, smiling, at his companion. It wasn't easy to classify that strange little smile—whether, for example, it was one of satisfaction for the results obtained, which weren't extraordinary but nothing to sneeze at either, or whether it was ironic, directed at someone who could be deceived with such ease.

Moshè was still sipping his water when the fellow, who had swallowed his drink in almost a single gulp, took his leave with a brief salutation, leaving the youth with the glass still pressed against his lips.

It was only toward evening, after having rested, stretched out on his bed, that Moshè began to review those few feverish hours spent with that unknown benefactor. The sayings that he had reeled off as they walked came back to mind, and he realized that, at any rate, he had dealt with a person who, as they say, was learned and profoundly knowledgeable in the Bible, the Talmud, and many other things. Was it this flood of wisdom that had immobilized him, preventing him from reasoning more calmly about the actual goodness of the undertaking? But when you listen to such beautiful sayings, how can you have any doubts about the piousness of such acts? For example, the man had said to him that he who gives charity receives a reward—without specifying exactly in what way and who the direct beneficiary of that reward might be. These words had their importance and attraction. Or else: "Charity is equal to all the mitzvahs and is the only one that remains after death." And another, which certainly isn't a small thing: "Charity opens the door of *kedushà* (holiness) and therefore hastens the coming of the Messiah." Moshè tried to remember all those wise words—not only because of the natural interest the man of faith and learning has for these things, but maybe also to find a justification for the cooperation, which, it must be said, had been given without thinking about it for even a minute. Maybe if he had considered it calmly for a moment, he would also have realized that good, true good, can be accomplished even without such wisdom, without so many words. Next his thoughts turned to the people they had encountered, when he had sought in some way or another to act as the interpreter between his unknown guest and his coreligionists. The reactions of the people they had approached had been varied and not without a certain interest.

An old lawyer, who had lived alone for years, took him aside and whispered, "Why this frightful sight? When I saw him, I was really afraid. I've never seen such a specter. Luckily you were there, but try to spare me such visits. It's not because of the money; it's because of my age. I'm old!"

Another professional, well known and learned, had muttered, "You see? And then you're always complaining about anti-Semitism! Come on! Do you really think people won't complain about someone who goes around dressed like that? We're Israelites too, but we're Italians and civilized people. But these people, who are they and what do they have to do with us?"

A third coreligionist, with several university degrees and a great deal of wealth, was not charmed by all the learned quotations but limited himself to saying, and to repeating several times, that times were hard and that if you had to give charity, first of all you should seek to help yourself and, that is to say, try to avoid financial collapse.

Yet another, an officer during World War I and a *commendatore*,[1] had refused categorically, declaring harshly, "How did you allow yourself to bring me someone who comes to collect funds for a country that I don't know and for a people who aren't Italians? We have a lot of people right here who need help, Jews and non-Jews, but they're all Italians."

When Moshè's father returned home, he immediately got angry with his son, who had acted with such irresponsibility, without finding out exactly with whom he was dealing. *Tzedakah*, of course, should always be given, and without paying attention to nationality or even religion—but after due consideration. He was a learned man? So what? Learning can be used in many ways. Moshè's father concluded the fatherly talking-to, telling his son that not all wrongs result in harm and that therefore this episode should serve him as a lesson, to open his eyes better so that he wouldn't be so gullible again.

The following Friday evening in the temple, Moshè found himself at the center of endless comments. Everyone had his say—bitterly, ironically, harshly—glancing unkindly at the imprudent youth at the center of that small tempest in the synagogue.

Even many years later there was always someone who, now and then, would remind Moshè of that episode that had caused such tension in the Community. Moshè would limit himself to making a vague gesture with his hand, without adding a word, still convinced, in spite of the brief fatherly talk, that maybe it was always worth the trouble of being "so gullible" when one hoped to be able, in some way, to help one's neighbor.

---

1   An honorary chivalric title bestowed by the Italian state.

THE PHILOSOPHER OF THE PO

If you were to cross the bridge over the Po, then turn left, you would enter a vast, grassy area that sweeps from the side of the river toward Casale Popolo. About a hundred meters from the bank, there are two knolls (the goal of the "ascents" of all the boys), behind which, in 1849, the Austrians encamped in the vain hope of conquering the city. Their siege failed. Even the artillery placed on the two small hills didn't do much; only a few cannonballs reached the center of the city. On a small building at the end of a street that opens on the right of Via Cavour and that leads to the station, a modest projectile framed by white paint crops out from the wall, even today, recording those glorious deeds. While King Carlo Alberto was losing the war and the throne in Novara, the Casalesi were repulsing the enemy. For two days, March 24 and 25, "they were able to defend themselves heroically," as a historian of our era scrupulously observes. From the fortifications—or from what remained of them, having been built by the Gonzagas toward the end of the 1500s—they replied to enemy fire with indomitable courage. Our historian, fulfilling his duty, does not neglect to record that "among the combatants who distinguished themselves, there were also Jews, specifically Benedetto Dina, a volunteer, and, among the National Guard soldiers, Edoardo Fiz and Raffaele Luria."

It should be emphasized, however, to the credit of the historical documentation, that this kind of action was not new to the Israelite Community of Casale. Since the distant days of Young Italy,[1] Jews were distinguished for their ardent

---

1   Young Italy (*Giovane Italia*) was an early part of the Risorgimento (resurgence, 1815-1871), the Italian national movement for unification and independence. Young Italy represented the radical wing of that

patriotism. In Vercelli the bookstore of Salvador Levi and his son Giuseppe, on Via San Michele, was the repository for Young Italy's literature, and incendiary publications from the Ticino Canton[2] as well as the conspirators' correspondence traveled to Casale, Asti, and Alessandria in baskets of Abram Lazzaro Levi's famous goose salami. The Monferrato Community was present in the Risorgimento, and in a worthy way, not only with the arms of its fighting sons but also with the pens of its poets and scholars of Jewish subjects. In memory of this historic battle, it was actually resolved—to continue the citation—to recall the happy event every year with a celebration called, appropriately, the Purim of the Germans [*Purim dei Tedeschi*].[3] Rabbi Gattinara wrote an extremely valuable account of the defense in Hebrew.

Near the Gonzaga fortress a bronze monument named *The Defense of Casale* later arose. It portrayed a young girl, glowing with health and wrapped in transparent veils, as though she were flying toward certain victory. During the regular evening stroll along Via Roma, students, without any reference to the exploits of the Risorgimento, would use the expression "the defense of Casale" for any girl who passed by and was notable for her graceful figure.

Between those two historic knolls and the bank of the Po arose a type of small hut made of wood, stones, cardboard, and pieces of sheet metal put there in the hope that the metal would serve as a roof. Inside there was one room, a couple of meters in length and width, with a few cheap things, the most important and precious of which was a bunch of rags and straw that served as a bed. Here one would encounter a strange fellow, pleasant and always reflective. His clothing, typical of a ragged beggar, made a lively contrast with his speech. His tone of voice, deliberately measured, revealed a person who was wise and of uncommon learning. He had a bushy beard, a mixture of black and white, and two bright eyes, often half-closed and ironic. He lived by collecting refuse and accepting, with dignity, offers

---

movement, having as its goal the establishment of a republic (rather than the monarchy, which ultimately triumphed). The movement was founded and headed by Giuseppe Mazzini in 1831 in Marseille, France.

2   In Switzerland, specifically the Italian-speaking canton bordering north Italy.

3   Purim is a Jewish holiday that celebrates the rescue of the Jews of Persia from annihilation. The biblical scroll of Esther, telling this story, is read on the holiday. When a particular Jewish community was similarly rescued from a tragedy (manmade or natural), a "local Purim" might be declared and celebrated annually. Local purims were particularly widespread and popular in Italy, and some communities had several. Casale's Purim of the Germans is a good example and shows that such local holidays were being established as late as the mid-nineteenth century.

of food and money, like someone who garners something that is due him by right; but he never asked for anything from anyone. He was called the philosopher of the Po. It has been said that the fool says what he knows and that the wise person knows what he says. The philosopher knew many things. Boys wandered around that area, and they often lingered in front of the hut to snoop around. The old man would put up with it for a while, but then he would brandish his cane and set them in flight. But there was also no lack of students from the high school who spent time with the philosopher, who could talk authoritatively about Socrates and Kant. With great wisdom, he drew the attention of the youths to existential problems and put forth original ideas.

One day Moshè and some friends had gone to visit him and chat, bringing as gifts a bottle of wine and some pipe tobacco, which the old fellow smoked in a small white clay pipe of his own making. He was asked, in particular, how it could be that a man of his education could have been reduced to such conditions. The philosopher, as though to gain time, filled his pipe in silence, lit it, took some puffs, looked at his friends one by one, and then, smiling, slowly began: "Look, in order to pose the question correctly, you would have to ask yourself, for one thing, if the choices that one makes are a 'reduction' in given conditions, as you claim. Yes and no, I would say. When one is young, like you, the horizon of your expectations and hopes is as vast as can be. You even think that you can take in everything. But that's not the way it is. From what you've said to me, this year you'll achieve what's called, I don't know why, 'maturity' [graduation: *maturità*]. In reality, you're never mature, not even at my age, and I've got a few years. And you, how do you feel?"

"Mature, extremely mature!" they exclaimed all together, enjoying themselves.

"Exactly so, super mature! But then, and you yourselves will realize it, go poke your nose into a department office at the university and right away you'll see that your horizon gets scaled down, that it necessarily becomes smaller. When you choose one thing, even a major, you give up many others. Little can be done about it, and you'll notice it many times after your university studies, too; all one's life is a continual choosing and at the same time a continual renunciation. Is this a 'reduction,' as you say? Of course—but, it's a fact. You have to be very careful when you decide to choose something, and that means you have to act with common sense and not by process of elimination, searching for the lesser evil and the most endurable compromise, accepting whatever comes along." And with his forefinger he pointed at the buttonhole of his jacket, to the left, where the fascist badge had been fastened, mischievously adding, "Like those who wear the 'bug,'[4] understand?"

He paused briefly, opened the bottle of barbera, brought it to his lips, and drank a long draught. He wiped his mouth with the back of his hand and continued: "At the point when, for example, you put on the black shirt, where does the horizon end? You don't see anything anymore, you can't even reason, you accept everything—for the sake of discipline, of course. You agree to lies and violence, you have to give yourself to everything you are ordered to do, and the only thing that you can still do is to applaud. Well, yes, in this case you have been 'reduced.'"

He stopped talking, and, screwing up his eyes, looked at his interlocutors to try to understand whether it was worth it to continue this delicate discourse. It seemed he was convinced, because he pointed to some fishing boats and then went on: "See those fishermen? They fulfill one of their dreams: they catch fish and eat them. And the fish, so it seems, are born to fall into the net. But I didn't let myself fall into the net; I saved myself in time. Of course, I, too, ran the risk of ending up in jail and disappearing, but as soon as I realized that in those conditions the suffering of anyone who loves liberty and their own spiritual independence were enormous, I made a hole in the net, I got out, and here I am, a free man, and forever. So, I'm not 'reduced' at all, on the contrary . . . Things weren't as simple and easy as the images I related to you, like the hole in the net. I was expelled from teaching, investigated in various ways, more or less civilized. I visited several convict prisons; then someone must have decided that I was a poor madman, and they let me live in peace in this villa of mine, on the bank of the Po. This is my short history, which really has nothing exceptional about it. It was my own choice when I realized that liberty wasn't there"—he pointed to the bell tower that could be seen in the distance—"but here, on this side of the river . . ."

He stopped himself for a few seconds and then, as though at that moment he had been reminded of something of great importance, he raised his voice along with his hand, a voice of fatherly authority, to say, "To me—at least I hope so—nothing worse than what happened to me during all these years can happen anymore. I learned that liberty is worth defending with courage and perseverance and that to maintain it, one must be able to give up many things. So because of this, I haven't been 'reduced,' but rather I've acquired space—absolutely! Judge these words of mine as you wish; it doesn't really matter to me at all.

---

4   A sarcastic nickname for the fascist emblem.

"I want to add just one more thing: be careful not to let yourselves be seen here often; it's not safe, not for me but for you. At your age, and I would say to your good fortune, you're already starting to become dangerous to certain regimes. And I say 'to your good fortune' because this way, if you want, before it's too late, you can rid yourself of many twisted ideas dictatorship imposes and learn to live as one should: responsibly free! My friends, learn to live this way, as soon as possible . . ."

Moshè never forgot that encounter and those words. He always considered them, together with the words of his father—which in parallel fashion, through the study of Torah, followed similar principles—to be a precious teaching. It guided him in many of his choices to *enlarge*, not to *reduce*, the area of his ethical research. And he also had many opportunities to mention to friends and to students, always with real gratitude, those words of great, honorable wisdom, even if they were bitter, as all truths to some extent, are.

TWO SCHOOLMATES

If in a small city you know everyone to some extent, and even if your knowledge isn't always direct, you know more or less everything about everyone, what can be said about someone in a small city who is part of a small Jewish Community? The same, but with something more: You know each other better and more deeply, and you also know more precisely how to maintain and strengthen certain friendships or keep them at a distance.

These considerations were important and carried weight for adults, but certainly not for children of the same generation, who met each other in preschool during the early years of their childhood. Even here certain nuances appeared in the children's clothes and in the meals they ate together that were delivered at lunchtime by family members or "persons of service," as they were called back then. But these were tiny details that small children were not yet able to judge. At the preschool, among themselves, the children weren't so subtle; friendship was spontaneous, they played together, they had a good time. They quarreled with each other too, but always as friends. And certain memories from early childhood are never forgotten.

So, just to mention a brief example, one of these children, many years later, received a visit from a fine lady at his office in Rome. After the usual pleasantries, both of them realized that they had been in preschool together in the same city. The man, who was head of the office, also remembered one of the games in vogue back then among the children, which was for a boy and a girl to introduce themselves to the others as "husband and wife," arm in arm, bowing, and proclaiming happily who they were. The man was certain that the woman facing him had been "his wife" in those far off times. But he didn't say anything, waiting to see whether she, too, would remember the game. The lady, now the real wife of a wealthy professional, made no allusion to the game. She talked, of course, about the pre-school and the two teachers, Signora Sofia and her daughter Sansonina, and of the by-then-vanished Community, but nothing more. That that memory had not also passed through the mind of the gentle visitor cannot be ruled out a priori; but the distance between the two—the economic distance, first and foremost—was such as not to allow them to mention certain things, even if it was a matter of a simple, innocent children's game.

Two children in those days had become good friends on the small benches of the Jewish preschool: Giuseppe and Moshè. The first, Giuseppe, belonged to a wealthy family, the father of which was a well-known and established professional. Moshè, the second, was born to a modest family, economically speaking, because his father occupied the rabbinic post in a tiny Community. In preschool they formed a great friendship, which was consolidated in middle school and high school. To be a bit picky, you could say that some differences surfaced here and there occasionally, like when both of them reached their bar mitzvah, or religious majority. For Giuseppe's family, religion had been relegated to the margins of a ceremony that was essentially social. And that was not only because many of those attending the ceremony were not Jews but especially because this varnish of religion allowed the family to cut a fine figure before the Christian world, making it understood that even though they were of the Mosaic faith, they were people who feared God, which gave a seal of reliability to their social and professional contacts. For Moshè's family, on the other hand, the chief concern was the intrinsic value of the ceremony itself: to be "bar mitzvah"—that is, "son of the mitzvah"—meant to take on all the responsibilities of a young Jew toward himself, his Community, and the entire Jewish people.

During the middle and high school years the friendship continued, in spite of the social positions of the two families. Seeing each other every day at school in the same class, doing at least part of their homework together, going on bike rides (there were some differences between the two bicycles, but it didn't matter), seeing a film or a soccer game together—all that couldn't help but maintain and strengthen this friendship. Here, too, there were gaps at times, but only an excessive scrupulousness could call attention to them, as, for example, when Moshè went to his friend's home. If his sister opened the door, Moshè would be left outside, hearing her say, "Giuseppe, *your* friend is here," with the pronoun strongly emphasized. It could also be added that once, when Giuseppe's mother was talking with Moshè's father about social and community topics, the discussion being somewhat heated, this comment slipped out: "But, then, don't forget that your son Moshè, after all, is welcomed in our home without any objections." A minor thing, even though it's understandable that Moshè, already sensitive to many things, avoided frequenting the home of his companion for a while afterward.

When they finished high school, they lost sight of each other, each one enrolling in universities in different cities, one in Torino, the other in Rome, although they had chosen to study the same subject.

Their encounters now happened more by chance when they were back in their small, native city. One time they ran into each other in the temple on the occasion of Giuseppe's sister's wedding. Moshè had not received an invitation. Giuseppe attended the ceremony in the uniform of an Alpine troops officer; from a distance he merely waved his hand toward his old high school companion in a vague gesture of greeting. When he finished university, Giuseppe began to travel around the world. He went to Paris, and he stayed longer in London, where he learned English well. Moshè, on the other hand, had been studying Hebrew for a while, and he had already begun to speak it. One might suppose that each of the two ex-schoolmates had chosen the language he preferred—there's no accounting for taste, it's moot. But in reality the issue wasn't so simple. The choice of English could open commercial and industrial business possibilities for Giuseppe internationally, as in fact it did. Not for nothing did Giuseppe settle in Milan upon returning from this period of living abroad.

Moshè's choice, instead, had been dictated by the desire to know Jewish culture and history more deeply, and given the times, with the Nazi persecution that had already broken out in Germany, to acquire a deeper experience of the current problems that were assailing the entire Jewish people. It was not by chance that ever since he was a student, he had been in contact with refugees, been a member of a committee to assist Jews in transit, and had begun to hold meetings for children and young people, to whom he spoke about Judaism in general and Zionism in particular. In Rome he had found an incomparable guide, having been a student and then friend of Dante Lattes, the most authoritative expert on the Jewish irredentist movement, which Zionism then was. Thus the choice of these two different languages was nothing other than the logical result of different family upbringings. The path of assimilation of the Jewish upper middle class had led a young man to the international language, the most widely diffused in the world, and that represented, in a sense, notable progress with respect to the preceding generation.

In the Jewish homes of the province, this Jewish upper middle class—well-off, energetic, and scrupulously honest—already spoke French as an old tradition, as an expression of high European culture. But speaking French was also a symbol of dutiful gratitude for the unforgettable ideals of the French Revolution, which had delivered the first crucial blow of the battering ram to the ghettos, giving everyone the equality of civil rights. It is true that opening the doors to the singing of the *Marseillaise* allowed free entry to the first flurries of assimilation, but wasn't it worth renouncing those many old religious traditions in order to enjoy fully all the light of this new and marvelous freedom?

It seemed almost an oddity, on the other hand, to think that among other families there might still be someone who dedicated his time to an ancient language, *dead* for centuries, which only now and then enlivened things through the synagogue chants that almost no one understood but which once in a while, for a variety of reasons, brought together both the religious faithful and the so-called liberals, who were the assimilated. It was not so much for the language in itself or as a sign of loyalty to an idea as it was for the melodies, which, learned in childhood, were always remembered with feeling by everyone.

And the racial laws came to Italy too, a wave of barbarism that, less than a century after Emancipation, intended once again to drive the Jews, observant and nonobservant, within the dark walls of a new ghetto, more modern and even more dangerous. These laws surprised the majority of the Jews. Their general conviction was this: The laws should be treated as a temporary measure that couldn't last long because, after all, Jews were Italians too, and many were also good fascists, and finally, they hadn't done anything at all wrong to deserve such treatment. Meanwhile the laws went into effect, and, save some attempts at evasion, which quickly failed, no one looked anyone else in the face, whether they spoke English or Hebrew.

Moshè and Giuseppe once again found themselves in the city of their childhood. Their affairs had taken a sharp, sudden turn, and their ideas were changing. Or at least for Giuseppe, more than for Moshè. Giuseppe's plans were collapsing; for Moshè, what was happening—which in any case did worry him, and not a little—when all was said and done, didn't represent a big novelty. For him, history, which he knew quite well by then, was repeating itself, even if on a different level. In other words, Moshè was ready to face the new times, but Giuseppe felt lost, and with a great deal of hesitation he sought to orient himself. This was almost certainly the fundamental reason that compelled Giuseppe to look up his old high school companion. Giuseppe was definitely a decent young man, morally sound, who still remained firmly Italian and to such an extent that when war broke out in 1940, he wrote his district recruiting office that, although he was a Jew, he wanted to defend the homeland under arms. But he also wanted to resist this inhuman situation with increasing resolve, thus becoming much more frankly antifascist than he had been before. It was a matter of a good Italian Jew, duty-bound to oppose this grave situation; his was a moral reaction, but gaps still remained in his awareness. To try to find some inner equilibrium, he recognized, virtually of his own accord, the indefinable need to reclaim his Jewish religiosity. From that he engaged in long discussions late into the night with Moshè, who this time was welcomed with the greatest warmth in the home of his old companion. There was a common denominator by then that firmly unified them: antifascism, even if the goals each of them held were, in essence, quite different. Moshè aimed, and not just beginning in 1938, at a complete solution to the Jewish problem, through Zionism. Giuseppe set forth a political change that would save Italy from the fascist dictatorship, thereby saving all Italians, among whom were Jews, without any doubt. Giuseppe and Moshè's interminable discussions concentrated on these points, and their respective positions were, and always remained, very far apart from each other. Those differences did not impede them from finding themselves in full accord regarding activities that were minor but at that time had a certain importance. Giuseppe had never forgotten the *niggunìm*, the traditional chants of the temple, and he had become even more passionate about these ancient melodies. He knew a little about music, and with the help of Moshè (even though he was quite tone deaf), Giuseppe zealously set out to put the notes of these ancient chants into writing. Close by the wheezy old organ, unused for decades, they spent many long hours attempting to reconstruct those musical notes. From a Jewish point of view, that was all Giuseppe could do; to go beyond that wasn't possible for him because he lacked a suitable education in history and ideas, which can't be improvised. Nevertheless, his stance was an honest one, because the synagogue songs were the most important point in his return to Judaism, even if for him it was provisional, awaiting better times.

Intermittently, each of the young men was busy with what was most at the center of his own interests: Moshè traveled around Italy, from Community to

Community, speaking to young people to prepare them for aliyah (immigration) to then-Palestine—which was still possible, the British permitting—and to give a hand to refugees in transit, victims of the shocking, bestial violence of the Nazis. Giuseppe tried to continue with some professional activities, seeking to protect his own economic position, the capital his family had honestly achieved.

During the German invasion they lost sight of one another, but each of the two took an active part in the Resistance. When the war ended, Moshè and Giuseppe returned to their old locations in Milan and Rome and no longer had frequent contact with each other. Moshè took up the same path as before, enriched by new experiences and new ideas that pushed him to dedicate himself exclusively to the Jewish community, to Zionism as the only historical solution to the age-old problem of his people. Giuseppe, who had fought hard during the Resistance, coming in contact with social problems that his previous upper-middle-class life hadn't given him any way of knowing more directly, had himself undergone a great shake-up (economically, too) from all the vicissitudes of persecution and war. He had taken a new path—that of communism, in which he became an active, authoritative participant. Judaism, as such, passed again into oblivion, and assimilation, for all intents and purposes, was even broader and by then irreversible.

Still, there was no shortage of visits between Moshè and Giuseppe, in the north and in the south, according to the professional engagements they had, and these encounters were always warm, lively, rich in ideas and feelings, and helpful to both of them. Moshè, even though he was not a communist—his Judaism sufficed to guide his actions toward everyone—was still invited to speak about Jewish history and Zionism in communist centers by his old study companion. Nor did he ever refuse, because wherever there was an interest in understanding the Jewish problem more deeply, Moshè would go readily, not taking notice of parties or religious or cultural attitudes. In 1947 Gromyko gave a famous speech in defense of the rights of the Jewish people at the United Nations, maintaining that "it was time to help the Jews, not in words but in deeds." He also said that "the fact that not a single Western European country had been capable of ensuring the protection of the basic rights of the Jewish people, nor of compensating them for the violence they suffered, explains the aspirations of the Jews for the creation of their own state. It would be unjust not to take this into account and to deny the Jewish people the realization of this aspiration." Between the two old schoolmates, it was a brief moment of reciprocal comprehension and the convergence of certain ideas.

But the idyll didn't last long. The problem of the so-called Palestinians rendered more difficult not only the situation in the Middle East but also the relationship between Moshè and Giuseppe.

One day, Moshè happened to read, in an Arab propaganda magazine, a letter from his friend in which he stated that, although he remained a Jew, he joined with the Arabs in defending their cause. The question, simple and immediate, that Moshè asked himself, was this: If Giuseppe had learned that his party had taken positions toward others that he personally did not share, would he have written a letter to the opposing party in analogous terms, that is, "I remain a communist, but I join you in defending your rights?" And he wrote Giuseppe in those terms. Maybe Moshè made a significant error of historical and ideological judgment—that of putting Judaism and communism on the same moral level, giving them both, at least formally, the same value. But evidently that wasn't so, because he never received any response from Giuseppe.

They lost sight of each other, and they never met again.

JUNE 22, 1941

After Italy's entry into the war in 1940, the activities that Moshè carried out in the various Communities were further reduced from what they had been before, for a variety of reasons. Transportation had become more difficult, visits by Zionists in the different Jewish centers were increasingly unwelcome, at least officially, and finally, police surveillance of Moshè had become even more thorough after war censorship had instructed the local Commission of Public Safety to subject him to "timely and discreet surveillance." Still, Moshè did his best to maintain contact with old friends and associates, with the families of Jews interned in several towns near his city, and with the neighboring Communities, making house calls to bring a Jewish word to parents and children.

On June 22, 1941, following a plan that had been settled for a while, Moshè went to Vercelli, where in the course of the afternoon he could comfortably visit the few families that still remained in this small Jewish center. It was a very hot day, sweltering. Having left the station, he was going toward the home of his ex-preschool teacher for a dutiful visit to pay his respects when he ran into a fellow Jew, rather advanced in years, an old acquaintance who brought up unending arguments every time Moshè went to give a talk in that Community. The fellow was a perfect Italian, quite fascist and, at the same time, liberal—as he loved to define himself—especially because he looked after his own interests by integrating himself more and more into the surrounding society. Not even the racial laws had restrained his ideas, convinced as he was that an Italian Israelite, honest and hardworking (as in reality he was), had nothing to fear. This difficult time, dictated by higher reasons of state, would certainly pass, sooner than one might think, and things would return to normal. In similar circumstances too, but especially in instances like these, you had to show that you kept your nerve and that you were obedient to the laws of the state, just as before or maybe more than before. He was so out of touch with the historical reality of those times that once he had even said this:

> You have to evaluate all the pros and cons with common sense. I, who took part in the First World War, and as an officer of the Alpine troops, now suffer, as you can easily understand, from not being able to serve my country under arms one more time. I've turned to my old comrades from the trenches so that they'll try to do something for me, and I'm still waiting for an answer, which I hope will be positive. My old and glorious uniform is always ready. And all of this is for the great love that I've always had for Italy, our beloved country, and especially now, so that it can't be said that with the excuse of these racial laws, the Jews are staying home while others are on the front lines, under enemy fire.

Moshè had greeted him and was about to continue on when the fellow came up to him and with a half-smile, asked, "Beh! What fair wind brings you here?"

Moshè, who had no intention of getting into an argument, limited himself to saying, "I came here to say hello to my old preschool teacher."

"Good, very good, a true mitzvah, and nothing else?"

"No, why?"

"I'm saying this because I know that you travel often and not only to visit old teachers. You know—excuse me if I repeat myself to you once again—that a bit of prudence and common sense would do you well and whoever you're around too."

Moshè, smiling, extended his hand and proceeded on his way, but without speaking. Sansonina, his teacher, received him with a maternal embrace and in spite of the suffocating, sultry day, wanted to offer him a hot coffee and some sweets that she herself had made. They talked about this and that, old memories, and of many dear persons who were gone. The present was ignored; Moshè did not want to break the peculiar atmosphere that reigned in that home, where even the furnishings took one back many years. He left, feeling a sense of tenderness for that woman, who lived entirely isolated from the present, meek, a voluntary prisoner of a past that by then was far away.

The heat was truly insufferable, and Moshè felt a burning thirst, now even more pronounced after the coffee and delicate sweets. He entered the first bar he saw, went to the counter, and ordered a glass of fresh-squeezed orange juice. While he was waiting to be served, he heard an animated discussion unfolding among the few customers present, interrupted by typical fascist exclamations and fists hitting the tables. Moshè wasn't able to restrain his curiosity to know more, and turning to the barman, he asked, "Would you mind telling me what's happening?"

"What? You don't know?"

"No."

"We've attacked Russia."

The answer was so unexpected that Moshè, without giving much thought to it, as he should have, completely happy and clapping his hands, exclaimed in a loud voice, "Oh! Finally! Now we'll see a few things!"

A glacial silence spread throughout the bar. The barman gave him a nasty look, and, with a tone of voice that did not promise anything good, asked, clipping his words, "And what does that mean? Would you like to explain yourself?"

Only at that moment did Moshè perceive that his attitude and his words were open to interpretations that might be a bit dangerous for him. But he recovered immediately, and in a solemn tone, he declared, "But of course we'll see a few things! It's time these dangerous subversives, these communists, start getting the lessons they've deserved for a long time. Now our victory is certain, and it's closer than before!"

"Bravo, mate!" was the unanimous response.

Moshè gulped down his drink as quickly as he could, and, making an obligatory, snappy salute after the fashion, he left the bar, which was well known to the townspeople of Vercelli as a center of fascism.

THE HEAD PHYSICIAN
AND THE BOATMAN

In October 1941, the chief rabbi was gravely ill. The family doctor, a fellow Jew and medical officer during World War I, ever proud of his professional skill, was once again hesitant about getting a second opinion, as proposed by the family. Unfortunately it wasn't necessary to be a student of Aesculapius to realize the gravity of the situation, and therefore the family members insisted. In the end, the doctor accepted reluctantly, with qualifications: "I repeat that I don't see the necessity, but if you insist, go ahead. I, however, won't initiate contact with anyone, although, as always, I'm available for discussion with anyone."

So it was that Moshè assumed the task of speaking with the city hospital's head physician. And who, if not Moshè, was best suited? Accordingly, after having phoned, he went to the home of the illustrious clinician. He was let in by a housemaid in a white apron, gloves, and a maidservant's cap. He halted, standing in the entranceway, and didn't go beyond, not then nor later. "Wait," he had been told. After a few minutes, the professor appeared. He was a man of about 40, elegantly dressed, sophisticated, hair oiled, his face carefully shaved, and thin. He saluted Moshè fascist style, in response to the respectful bow made by the visitor. The doctor looked Moshè over, from head to toe, holding his head high, eyes half-closed. It was a pose that did not change during that brief, incredible conversation. The doctor must also have suspected something from the moment he had heard the last name of the person who was now facing him on the telephone and whom he was examining with ill-concealed distrust and detachment: a young man, 25 years old, with a beard, but without a fascist emblem in the eyelet of his jacket. And, naturally, that was enough for him.

"So, you're the one who called me yesterday afternoon?"

He began, speaking slowly, as if every word cost him effort.

"Yes, professor."

"What is it about?"

"My father. He hasn't been well for some time, and things have gotten worse these last few days. We're worried about hemiplegia, at least from some of the symptoms, and the family doctor agrees—"

"What does your father do?" The question seemed, apparently, to have some bearing on hemiplegia.

"He's the Chief Rabbi of this Jewish Community."

"Ah!"

Silence. His misgivings had been confirmed, and there was no need for anything more. However, an answer that had a bit of a scientific flavor needed to be given. If not, what kind[1]—it's just the right circumstance in which to use that word—of professor would he have been? His hand, maybe unintentionally, passed over his badge, almost as though he wished to gain inspiration from that symbol, which, more than his actual professional skill, must have gotten him his position.

"You see, I have a cold." He sniffled the nothing that was in his nose to show exactly how it was. "And when I find myself in this condition, it's my practice not to go to the bedside of anyone who is sick . . ."

"Professor, I understand your legitimate concern, but it's a grave and urgent case and—"

With a brief wave of the hand he stopped his imprudent interlocutor.

"Look." He was rather slow in launching his discourse, as suited a head physician of his standing. "Look, in this condition I don't even make my rounds in the hospital to visit the sick." He continued with a certain effort to sniffle, as though to confirm that he had a cold, which didn't exist except in his mind. There was little point in going on. The young man remained like that, silent, giving the doctor a look of surprise and at the same time of supplication. But the head physician didn't lose time; he had spoken, made a quick, fascist salute, and went away, without adding a word, while the housemaid reappeared.

When Moshè, with the anger that had built up in his heart for such a shameful act, returned home, he found an unusual visitor at his father's bedside. Moshè's

---

1   The Italian word used here is actually *razza*, which means "type" or "kind" as well as "race." The English words *race*, *type*, or *kind* obviously can't carry the double meaning of *razza* that Segre intends here.

mother, taking him aside, explained to him who it was. When the brief visit came to an end, the young man, intrigued, accompanied the guest to the door, thinking to ask him some questions.

The person was Pinin, a boatman his father knew, and he asked Moshè, "You're the son, right? Good, it's a pleasure." He extended a calloused hand, that of an old man habituated to a great deal of manual labor. Shabbily dressed, he wore fustian. In his hand he held a battered old hat, dirty and frayed. His furrowed, sunken face was dominated by lively, blue eyes, full of wisdom.

"You wouldn't know me . . . many years have passed since I first met your father. You should know that we were schoolmates . . . something from the last century." He smiled, making a slight gesture with his hand. "I didn't go past first grade, studying was too hard for me, and then I had to learn how to earn a bit of bread right away. But your father, no; he always studied, and how! Very good at it! Now, you should know that we didn't see each other often in the course of our lives, only by chance on the bank of the river or at the market, where I was, and still am, a laborer.

"But your father was a great help to me in a particular instance. I went to prison, not willingly," he threw in, with a mischievous light in his eyes. "Oh, don't pay it any attention, nothing serious . . . a small business mess." And he smiled with an air of mystery. "Well then, your father, having known what had happened, came not only to visit me—he also was able to get me out. I've never forgotten his help. And yesterday, at the market, when I learned that our bishop of the Jews was very sick, I said to myself, 'If you don't go see him, you're a louse,' and so here I am to visit an old friend."

Right then, after the disastrous visit to the head physician, these simple words, spoken in dialect, took on a very personal feeling of great human kindness that moved Moshè. He hugged the old boatman and said to him, "Come back, Pinin. Papà and us will always be very happy to see you."

And Pinin returned, but on a day and at a moment that was the most feared and the saddest. Pinin came in smiling, with a basket in hand. He saw the young man's face lined with tears, and with a trembling voice, asked, "What's happened?"

"Papà . . . he's left us . . ."

The basket fell from Pinin's hand, and he took a large, colored handkerchief from his pocket, covered his face, and burst out sobbing, "I want to see him, I want to see him! Oh, what a brute I've been, what a brute! Look," and he pointed to the basket, "I've brought fresh fish, which is always good for you, but I was too late . . ."

A few months went by after the funeral, which Pinin had attended, dressed in his best and with a bunch of wildflowers. Moshè had become virtually enchanted by this old fisherman, poor and honest, illiterate but wise, and so one day he decided to go visit him. He ran into him while he was bustling about inside his small boat, between the iron bridge and the railroad bridge.

The visit was much appreciated by Pinin, who said, "I'm happy, my boy, that you came. It's as if I'm seeing your father, may God rest his soul; you look just like him. Aren't you afraid of poor devils like me? Watch out," and smiling mischievously, he made a broad sweep with his hand, "This is kind of a dangerous area."

"But what nonsense this is," the "boy" answered, putting a hand on his shoulder. "I'm the son of my father, and he was poor too, like me and like you—"

"But you're learned. I, instead, am a simple boatman, ignorant as a wood wedge."

"Are you going to keep talking nonsense? Did you already drink a lot today?"

"Ah, there's a good idea." Pinin stood up, drew in a line that was tied to the boat, and a bottle emerged from the water. "You know, wine stays cool in the water and besides, the fish . . . are teetotalers." He squinted his blue eyes, which shone with mischief.

Between one drink and another, imbibed directly from the bottle—which was offered to Moshè too—the old fisherman, stretched out on the riverbank, let himself share confidences. With a toss of his hand he had thrown his weatherbeaten old hat behind him. In his mouth he had a wooden match which, from time to time, he moved from one side of his lips to the other, as though he were slowly sucking licorice. He made a sweeping gesture toward the river, and, in perfect local dialect, began: "They say you have to pay attention to the waters of a river and stay as far away as possible. But I know these waters, I'm not a greenhorn. I think my mother gave birth to me, right here, in the water!" And he burst into a peal of laughter. "Actually, the river never betrays; it has its course, which doesn't change, it's always the same. Of course you have to know the river well and so, respect it, even when it doesn't burble because it's in spate. If you don't, one day or another, you'll pay, and pay dearly. You should never impose yourself on anyone with violence, not even a river. Mutual respect and then everything is OK . . ."

Pinin was silent, and, as a shrewd old man, he stole a glance at his young friend. Moshè understood that with that simple example from the vernacular level, Pinin was giving him a lesson of deep morality, about conduct in life and even politics. Thus Moshè said to him, "Of course, you're right. I understand everything you want to tell me, without a lot of words."

"It gives me pleasure. You know, I realized right away that with you I can say openly what I'm thinking, and today that isn't an everyday thing . . . You can see right away that you've never worn the 'bug' [the fascist insignia]. Bravo!"

"And then, you're a fine politician, too, with a good nose—"

"For heaven's sake, don't talk nonsense. Me, a politician? Are you making fun of me? Yes, I have a certain, intuitive common sense that moves me to think and act." Pinin stopped himself for an instant, uncertain, perhaps, whether or not to say what deep down he wanted to make known to a friend who was so exceptional to him. "You know, around here, all kinds of people have been seen in the past . . . they called them anarchists and subversives, but what can I tell you?" Here the tone was that of someone who deliberately wants to point out that he's saying things of scarce importance: "I wouldn't even know enough to give you an example. Except this. It was when we witnessed certain abuses of power, especially during the early years of this dirty regime, when they went from beatings with cudgels to castor oil to murder. Beh. Here, on the bank of this friend of ours, which the river is . . . here . . . in some cases . . . with the necessary precautions, of course . . . we settled some old and serious accounts . . . and the river never betrayed us."

The recollection of these two people, who Moshè, by chance, had met on the same day, at a particularly painful moment for him, never faded from his memory—two curious characters: one no less than the head physician of the city hospital and the other a simple boatman. There was an abyss between them in the level of their education, in the conventionally understood sense, but there was also a moral abyss between the one who in his candor as an illiterate, full of personal dignity, had never bowed to any command, had not accepted any compromise, and had stood up for himself in his own way, even if it was a basic way, and the one who, in order to have a career, had made himself conform, prostituting himself without second thoughts, in the unhappy fashion of the times.

WARTIME YOM KIPPUR, 1944

A year had already gone by since Moshè and his family, having left Asti precipitously, found refuge in the Langhe, evading the manhunt being carried out throughout the province by the Nazis and their fascist lackeys by what seemed a miracle. They had found a hiding place on an isolated farmstead. Even though it wasn't far from the road, it was a bit out of the way, as it was concealed by a dip in the land. It was ideal not just because of the location of the house. The owners were Piedmontese peasants of the old school, unpretentious, unpolished, honest, and always ready, in their own way but unfailingly, to give a helping hand to anyone who found themselves in trouble. And then there were the commercial and real estate relationships, in land and farmsteads, that the peasants had maintained over the course of several generations with the *abreu*[1] of Asti, and that had also established secure ties of friendship and great reciprocal respect. A firm handshake was all that was needed to conclude any kind of contract, even though afterward the participation of a notary was necessary for certain deeds. But it wasn't the stamped paper that gave official significance to the negotiations; actually, if a document hadn't been required by law, that handshake would have served to validate an agreement in the most complete and absolute way. The memory of good business relations, on the one hand, and the recent persecution of the *abreu* on the other, profoundly disturbed those good people, and help was always offered, with ready spontaneity and without hesitation. Years later, Moshè was readily able to contrast these, his by then old friends from the Langhe, with important

---

1   "Hebrews," that is, Jews, in Piedmontese dialect.

personages of various ranks to whom he had turned futilely on several occasions during those terribly troubled years. And then, near this farmstead, there also lived another family of peasants, who gave Moshè and his family all possible help. So it was that the head of the first family—Pinulìn with his son Lin—and the second—Carlìn—became more than friends for this fugitive *abreu*; they became true brothers. Carlìn had a brother who was a priest in Asti, and in spite of the roadblocks and the searches of objects and persons, carried out none too gently, Carlìn was always ready to go to the provincial capital to visit his brother when they needed to get supplies or to send news that was of interest to his friends in hiding. To get past these roadblocks, you also needed a certain courage, but Carlìn, equipped with exceptional intelligence and peasant shrewdness, always managed to get away with it. When he was on a mission, his friends, with some trepidation, thought about him often, and in the evening, in the stable, they waited impatiently for his return. His slow, steady pace, the stride of the Alpine troops, would suddenly alert us, softly, in the still of the night, becoming gradually more pronounced, until finally, sweaty, with a backpack filled with many things, he would appear in the doorway of the stable. After having rested a little, he would recount these encounters with the roadblock ogres to us, with that classic tone of sharp peasant humor, amusing himself first.

He said, "This time the *repubblichini*[2] stopped me again when I was walking to Asti, and right away they asked me, 'Bandits? Have you seen bandits?' And I, pointing my finger toward them and acting like I was frightened, made the sign of the cross, mumbling, 'Oh, oh, I'm so unlucky, I'll go back right away!' 'No, fool, *we're* not the bandits. You don't understand anything. We're asking you if you've run into any on your way. The reason we're here is to catch them and take them away. Calm down, imbecile!' And they split their sides laughing. Then I said, 'No, no, I haven't ever seen them, by the grace of God, I don't even know how we made it,' and I made the sign of the cross again . . . and so, without even asking me for my documents or the reason for my trip, they gave me a pat on the shoulders and let me by . . . the usual fools, like always."

---

2   *Repubblichini* referred, derogatorily, to the troops of the Republic of Salò, the puppet state Hitler created in North Italy with Mussolini as head of state after he had been rescued by Nazi paratroopers from house arrest. The Republic of Salò lasted from September 1943 to April 1945.

The "bandits" were obviously the partisans, and Carlìn knew many of them, partly because he collaborated with them actively.

A year had already passed, including, in 1943, a first wartime Yom Kippur, which Moshè had called "The Yom Kippur of the Resistance." But now the second wartime Yom Kippur war was getting close, and it looked as though it would be more difficult to observe because right then a rounding-up operation was being stepped up throughout the area. Thus the risk was greater, but it saddened everyone to think that such a solemnity would not be observed, even within the realm of the rather restricted possibilities. Moshè decided that we would keep watch by taking turns while the *tefillòth* (prayers) were going on, armed and positioned at what could be called a strategic point from which one could monitor part of the main road. Toward evening of that day, which is so sacred to all Jews, when the *tefillòth* were coming to an end, the guard shift fell to Moshè. Although he was sorry not to be present at the conclusion of the prayers, he went to take up his guard post, since he'd been chosen by lot. As the sun was already setting, his thoughts returned to his childhood days of Yom Kippur, so engaged and so tranquil, to his first fast, which he had completed with a certain amount of effort, and to his father, whose voice, warm and melodious, he seemed to hear just then. He was sitting on some large stones, his gaze turning restlessly toward the main road and the bottom of the valley. The first indistinct night shadows were descending when suddenly someone appeared there where the road took a sharp turn. The figure of a man was getting nearer. Moshè got up and, gun in hand, kept himself at the ready. But every fear quickly passed—it was one of his fellow partisans, just passing through. The encounter was, as always, quite genial, partly because many animated discussions had taken place between the two friends. The discussions had been on religious topics, which was unusual for those times and in those circumstances. Walter, that was his name, was Catholic but openly and, one could even say, ostentatiously, an atheist. Moshè had succeeded in silencing him only once. That was in response to his practically peremptory demand that Moshè—a Jew and thus religious and believing in God—prove to him that the Lord truly existed. While he went on chattering, Moshè had said to him, "Listen my good friend, your question shows once again that, regarding this issue, you really don't understand a single thing. Look, I, with my mere human capabilities, can't bring you any official documentation for what you are asking. God is infinitely above the simple human mind. Rather than proclaiming with such cockiness that you're sure God doesn't exist, give me proof of what you claim with all your might."

Walter, laughing, had put his hand over his mouth and had not added a word. Now, seeing his armed friend there at the observation point, he asked him, "What are you up to? Are you hunting for men or for women?"

Moshè informed him about what was happening at his house. Walter was lost in thought for a few seconds, and then, resolved, he said, "Listen, my dear *abreu*, this is what we'll do: You go pray to your God and ask him everything you want. I'll stand guard here until you've finished your litanies with the Most High. You can trust in me, as you know." And he put his hand on his chest.

This spontaneous offer from his friend moved Moshè deeply, and yet he didn't want to pass up the chance for one of his wisecracks: "I'm very grateful to you for what you've told me. Still, Walter, tell me the truth. Could this be a sign, even though a very faint one, of a healthy mending of your ways, of that greatly hoped for repentance for your spiritual future?"

Laughing wholeheartedly, Walter answered, "Calm down. Don't delude yourself with such useless hopes—atheist I am and atheist I'll remain. Go, don't lose more time. Your God is waiting for you!"

After Yom Kippur finished, Walter was invited to supper, and it's totally superfluous to add that even on that occasion, huge theological problems were discussed.

A VOICE TOLD HIM...

The war had ended in 1945 and life was returning to normal—somewhat for everyone, even for the Jews, relatively speaking, as always, given their long, complex history and the different sociopolitical worlds with which they came in contact.

The immediate postwar period presented an infinity of problems, one usually more difficult than the other, the solutions to which were achieved with a great deal of imagination and hope. The large and small Communities were slowly rising again from their physical and spiritual ruins. The walls of a synagogue could be reconstructed with greater ease than bringing people lacerated by so many tragedies back to the faith, energetic and responsible. The Jewish schools were reopened too, but with difficulty, because of the lack of rooms, teachers, students, and the necessity of relying on budgets that were still rather uncertain. Even after such a hard experience, or maybe precisely because of everything that had happened, families were still quite hesitant about sending their own children to attend a Jewish school. The young people, with youthful self-assurance and sometimes with a more pronounced indifference toward Jewish matters, tackled business or studies, falling again, automatically, one might say, into the vast, alluring stream of assimilation, as though they hadn't learned a thing from past experience. To be more precise, it should be said that something remained in their hearts, which is to say, a greater sensitivity and therefore a readiness to react to anything concerning anti-Semitism. Supporting mainly parties that at the time demonstrated a certain sensitivity to this problem, they protested whenever any cause for alarm was looming on the horizon. But, to assess things accurately, this attitude of theirs was in great part negative, inspired more as a matter of human dignity and by a sense of newly acquired freedom than by an authentic functioning Jewish consciousness. In fact, each time the danger was warded off, life took up its course again, and Jewish activities, genuinely religious or cultural, continued to be ignored. And that's not to mention Zionism, which, just as in the past, had disturbed the emancipationist dreams of their grandfathers, now returned once again to disturb the *italianità*, and this time even the "democracy" of the new generation. A few *hakhsharot* (training farms), which prepared whoever wanted to move to what was then Palestine, were reopened. But by and large they were small groups, made up either of those who hadn't been able to fulfill their dream because they were taken by surprise by the war, or of those who, scorched by the persecution, had learned how to rediscover the most authentic and natural path of Judaism. But they were few.

It has been noted that in chapter 12 of Genesis, it is written that the Lord said to Abram, "Go forth from your native land and from your father's house to the land that I will show you." Now, a scholar, or, better yet, a mystic, might ask himself whether such an order was ever repeated in the course of the centuries that followed. It is certainly not easy to give an answer, even a rough one, because when one's conscience hears these internal voices, it cherishes them modestly, with loving care, and they do not get recorded in ordinary documentation. And yet, even though it may seem strange, something like this happened right in the middle of the twentieth century, as even today those who were working in the offices of the Italian Zionist Federation, at Via Principe Amedeo 2, can testify.

Moshè had returned to Rome, and he carried out his activities in that very office. It happened one day that a fellow presented himself, a peasant—by his clothing and, by his way of speaking (his accent and vocabulary, which was more typical for a someone from the countryside)—and, furthermore, a southerner. In his hand he carried a big blue and white checkered handkerchief, which must have contained a bit of food for lunch. In fact, he had come directly from San Nicandro. He was part of that famous group, which years earlier had converted to Judaism. They had an utterly extraordinary faith, even though it was naive in some of its nuances. They also shared an uncommon collective courage for the dangers, which were not few, that they faced in town at the hands of just about all the other peasants and the upper crust of the place, not to mention the local priest, as well as those dangers they were subjected to during the German occupation. Regarding this minuscule new Community, emerging through a miracle, so to speak, in one of the southern areas of Italy that had gone for centuries without any Jewish presence, quite a bit has already been written, sometimes with a lot of imagination.[1]

Moshè had him sit down. Between the two was the big handkerchief, placed on the table, the corners of which framed a patriarchal face, suntanned and a little wrinkled. The guest spoke calmly, virtually dividing his words into syllables, sure of himself and of what he was saying. He spoke in a completely original style. He would refer to some detail, then suddenly stop, leaving the conversation hanging and searching Moshè's face to determine whether he was following him and whether Moshè had any doubts about what he was saying. For years the secretary of the Zionist Federation (Moshè) had known and been friends with many Sannicandresi, and thus he followed him with rapt attention, agreeing with what he was hearing with nods of his head. This reassured the peasant, who, after a long roundabout of words, came to the point: "Now then, listen to me." (His use of *tu*[2] was a sign of respect but also of a convergence of feelings and ideas.) "You need to know that about a month ago, I went to sleep as usual. But in the middle of the night I had a dream. I found myself at the door of the house, and I looked out at the countryside when, very clearly, without any doubt, I heard a voice, and I don't know where it came from, that said to me, 'Sell your house and your field and go to Eretz Yisrael.' This invitation, which seemed to me to arrive from above, was repeated three times, then the voice faded and disappeared. So, the next day, as soon as I was awake, I immediately told my family about this dream of mine, and all of them being in agreement, I set about getting my things in order as quickly as possible. In the end, after quite a few problems, which I'm not here to tell you about, I finished selling the house and the land, and now I'm here. Send me to Israel."

---

1   In the 1920s a small group of peasants in San Nicandro Garganico, a remote town in southern Italy, spontaneously converted to Judaism. Most members of this group immigrated to Israel soon after its foundation. For the most recent scholarship on the converts of San Nicandro, see John Anthony Davis, *The Jews of San Nicandro* (New Haven, CT: Yale University Press, 2010). Two early books are Phinn E. Lapide, *The Prophet of San Nicandro* (New York: Beechhurst, 1953); and Elena Cassin, *San Nicandro* (Philadelphia: Dufour, 1962). There is also a recent documentary, *The Mystery of San Nicandro*, inspired by Davis's book.

2   In Italian *tu* is the informal, second-person singular form of *you* and is accompanied by a correspondingly conjugated form of the appropriate verb. This distinction between formal and informal *you* (and accompanying verbs) is not used in contemporary English.

Moshè had listened calmly, relatively calmly that is, because at a certain point he felt himself getting worked up too, hearing these completely unaffected statements, made like someone recounting everyday events that happen in anyone's life. He had immediately thought of the well-known episode of Abram, even though the difference was obvious and considerable. God had spoken directly to Abram, whereas here it was a voice that was not clearly specified, and then—and here is a curious fact—he was immediately told to go to Israel, whereas Abram didn't yet know where he would go to live. But this last enigma could be explained, not as a privilege reserved for a peasant from San Nicandro but as due to a historical reality: the reality of the country of Israel, newly acquired from the conscience of humanity, after innumerable generations.

Naturally, the request was granted immediately, and the papers for the peasant and his family's trip were promptly completed.

Returning home that evening, Moshè couldn't help but think about his new friend from San Nicandro. To really understand this story, one also had to realize the importance of that house and those fields. Quite modest, they provided a narrow guarantee of life, harshly sweated-out by enormous efforts to cultivate that small bit of stingy land. In any case, the peasant is tied by tradition to the land of his ancestors, as the peasant from San Nicandro must have been. And yet he had no hesitation, and he had sold those "assets," which for years had meant life for him and his family. Continuing this train of thought, Moshè asked himself what would have happened if some wealthy businessman from the Eternal City or an industrialist or a professional had by chance had a dream similar to the dream of the Sannicandrese? He concluded, smiling, "One thing is certain, he wouldn't have come to me. At the most, he would have phoned the family doctor right away!"

YOUR NEIGHBOR

Concerning the celebrated saying of the Torah "Love your neighbor as yourself," as it is usually translated (which, more accurately, should be translated as, "Wish for your neighbor what you wish for yourself" [Leviticus 19:18]), the exegetical literature, from time immemorial, has always been vast and deep. Given the profound importance of the subject, the literature has also developed interminable theological discussions that sometimes move far afield from this all-important Jewish concept. A proverb says "Grammar is one thing, usage another" to point out that things are often simple only in theory. When one actually grapples with everyday life, the typology of the neighbor appears to be so varied, and sometimes even unexpected, that it is not always easy to figure out the most appropriate way, above all, to interpret the deep moral teachings, like the one cited above, for example. In fact, in the *Sayings of the Fathers (Pirkè Avoth)*,[1] it is said with the usual well-advised circumspection, "Don't judge others until you find yourself in their situation." This is an admonition that is valid for all times and that in essence means that it is difficult to judge another without knowing the reasons that prompted him to act in a particular way, and before condemning, one must ask oneself, "And I? If I found myself in his place, what would I have done?" All these teachings are undoubtedly at the highest level, and one must try to carry them out as well as possible. That does not mean that astonishment, when confronted with certain situations, may not be natural and humanly justified.

---

1   Alternative English translations of the title of this well-known and often-cited section from the Talmud are *Ethics of the Fathers* and *Chapters of the Fathers*.

Moshè had seen many "neighbors" pass before his desk at the Italian Zionist Federation, for whom he had always tried to do his best—not to acquire any special merit on earth or in heaven and not for careeristic goals either, but simply because he was sure he would be performing a mitzvah. From the many examples, here are a few, perhaps among the most curious and strange.

★ ★ ★

One day a young man with an extremely pale face, thin, and shabbily dressed, turned up, and Moshè had him sit down straightaway. The guest stared silently at the person facing him, and then, with the utmost calm, went straight to the point. He said, simply, "I am the Messiah."

Moshè looked at him more closely without saying a word, naturally surprised by that unexpected revelation.

And the other, in an unchanged tone of voice, said, "If you would like, I can also prove it to you."

At this point it was necessary to say something, and Moshè commenced: "I don't need any proof. A declaration of this kind is more than convincing, and so I believe you. But look, try to help me; an important person like you must also realize that a simple office worker like me, who has such modest tasks, which, unfortunately, are only worldly and which, besides, have to be completed at specific times, at a work pace that's very demanding—"

The Messiah interrupted him, with a tone that was already rather agitated: "So, in plain words, you don't want to listen to me, and . . ."

"No, no, for heaven's sake," Moshè hastened to say. "Nothing of the sort. Of course I would gladly listen to you, and it's also one of my specific duties. Just not today, because I have an important meeting in a little while, and I still have to prepare some pressing matters . . ."

"Come on, be honest," by then his voice was exasperated, "and say it to me: You're throwing me out—"

"No, no, I'm only asking you to set another appointment that's mutually agreeable, and—"

But he wasn't able to finish. The Messiah suddenly rose and without uttering a word headed toward the door. There he stopped, and turning toward Moshè, waved a hand with a gesture perhaps like the one that Father Cristoforo may have made when he said to Don Rodrigo, "Listen well to what I promise you. There will come a day . . ."[2] And he left.

Moshè no longer had the privilege of meeting with such an illustrious and rare personality; maybe he hadn't been able to recognize the exceptional favor reserved for him with that visit in time, and because of that he was no longer worthy of any heavenly disclosures.

★ ★ ★

A nun was at the door of his office, but she didn't enter. She said, "I'm here to collect donations for our poor . . ."

Moshè was silent and was thinking about where in the same agency he could direct the nun. He didn't deal with finances in any way. But the nun spoke up again immediately: "Don't forget," she said with a calculated and somewhat exaggerated, sugary smile. "Don't forget that during the war we helped you Jews a lot."

Moshè was still silent, but this time he was absorbed by other thoughts, and the nun, as though to excuse herself, went on: "Certainly not me, unfortunately. I wasn't yet old enough, but the Holy Father did."

At this point Moshè felt the need to clarify something immediately: "Look, Sister, if the Pope were present here at this moment, he wouldn't say what you are saying. The Pope has always done good for the sake of good, and he would not come here to extract compensation like you're doing right now. Is this your Christian charity?"

The nun turned red as a poppy, lowered her head, made a bow, and departed in silence.

★ ★ ★

Across from Moshè was an elderly person who in earlier times had also been involved in Jewish matters, and with a certain knowledge and skill. Then he went through hard times, physically and psychologically. There had also been many estrangements, because of familial and, later, ideological reasons. In due course, he had also been baptized, first as a Catholic and then as a Protestant. Moshè knew his entire story, and many years earlier he had even dealt with the man's case; but

---

2   The reference is to a passage in the classic nineteenth-century Italian novel *The Betrothed* (*I promessi sposi*) by Alessandro Manzoni, required reading in Italian schools.

the person who was facing him had never known that. He spoke slowly, letting his words trickle out, nearly whispering, forcing Moshè to pay the closest attention. As he spoke, he sometimes stopped himself, and it seemed almost as though he were being assailed by other thoughts at the same moment. It wasn't easy to understand what he wanted and, in particular whether it was a simple courtesy call, given their shared acquaintances, to be followed by a request for some book that the office had and loaned on request, or whether he wanted something more specific. Finally it came out, in words that were quite clear. He looked at Moshè for a long time, and then, enunciating each word, he said, "The Jews have had their day. You, why don't you get baptized?"

Did you come here on your own spontaneous initiative or did someone send you? Moshè thought. And right afterward, he said, "I don't agree with you. I'm convinced that the Jews, who have endured until now, still have things to do. Whoever has no purpose disappears—it's even a law of nature—but we Jews are still here. Me, I've never considered giving up on my responsibilities as a Jew in the course of my entire life, not even for a moment. And then there's dignity in declaring as much in the presence of everyone, and so I've stood up for my Jewish existence, always and in every circumstance."

Moshè would also have liked to add, *I've never betrayed my people*, but he didn't say that to his visitor out of politeness toward an elderly person and fondness for their shared acquaintances. The old professor was silent, seeming to concentrate on something, but he didn't add a word. He got up and took his leave, giving Moshè his hand.

★ ★ ★

Accompanied by a lady who was in a hurry to tell Moshè that she knew him quite well (but who Moshè didn't know at all), a fellow arrived in his office and was introduced as a professional dancer and director. Maybe. He wanted to be put in contact with an "Israelite" from Milan who managed an arts agency there. This lady, it clearly appeared, was struggling desperately, although with poor results, against the wrinkles of an already advanced old age and had hair that had been dyed time and time again. She began her introduction, which at the same time was a peroration, with a speech in a forced youthful tone. Her affected smiles underscored the heaviness of the years even more as she spoke, talking without saying anything, with vague, oily words. She spoke like someone who is worldly-wise, thanks to a rather adventurous life, and has learned that in many situations it's better only to give vague hints about certain things, deliberately avoiding explanations, as is the case in certain, specifically artistic circles like this one, or so it seemed. And, actually, she didn't hide the fact, not at all, and with a certain pride, that she spent her life comfortably in the midst of this noble society of art and fantasy.

But who could have sent her to me? Moshè asked himself fruitlessly in the meantime. Patiently, in keeping with his official duties, he continued to listen to her while with pen and paper he drew those scribbles that would delight certain psychoanalysts. Hoping finally to conclude this nonsensical conversation as quickly as possible, Moshè asked why they had come specifically to him, as he dealt only with Jewish education. The elegant, or quasi-elegant, lady looked at him completely surprised, as though she had been hearing absurdities, and said, "But it's well-known"—the tone was the tone of someone who knows what's what and thus won't be led by the nose easily—"but it's well-known, quite well-known, that whatever the Jews do: business, industry, even education"—she emphasized these last words—"very well-known"—and the tone this time was the tone that meant "come on, don't play dumb"—"that the Jews are always tightly connected to each other, ready for every eventuality, and when they want to," she said with a new, marked emphasis in her voice, "when they truly want to, they can find a solution, and without great difficulty, to whatever they want."

Moshè, who by then had lost his patience, remarked that at any rate it was better and much simpler to present oneself straightforwardly to the person one meant to meet with, with the appropriate personal credentials, when they actually existed, and never to use such convoluted and illogical ways. The two art guests looked at him with incredulous, ironic smiles. Maybe they thought this was the way Jews did things: First, they immediately say no, but then, as though it's a special favor, they always come to an agreement. It's well known, they must also have thought, that the Jews are quite clever and unsurpassed at this type of bargaining. But Moshè stood up to indicate the conversation was over and stated that he didn't know the lady from Milan and that he never dealt with matters that didn't relate to him. He extended his hand toward the two, who still remained seated. The odd guests then sprang up, at the same time, with faces composed in readily comprehensible expressions in which a sense of disdain toward that strange Jew suddenly seemed to prevail. With only a forced nod of the head, they went away, leaving Moshè with his hand still politely outstretched.

* * *

At a meeting restricted to managers and their assistants that took place in his office, Moshè clarified the theme that was to be discussed at meetings in various Italian cities: Jewish culture today in Israel and in the Diaspora. It was an old theme, he maintained, one that had always given rise to many debates, but almost always with little to show for it. As with so many other Jewish issues, it was about complex topics with different historical origins, which, in the case in point, produced new difficulties, represented by the return of the Jewish people to their ancient land and by the incredible growth of the Hebrew language and the attendant literature. At least one thing appeared to be abundantly clear: Faced with today's difficulties, the Jewish culture of the Diaspora couldn't help but be a secondhand culture. Another point not to be ignored: Culture can't be bought, or sold, or imposed (regarding the latter, such a possibility would only be a politicization of culture, which, however, is no longer truly culture). And it can't even be given away. You can give a book as a gift but not culture. Culture is born in the particular and forms and develops itself out of the direct experiences of life, even the everyday affairs of individuals and groups, who, as with so many other things, continually pose a series of questions of possible choices, of realizations, of alternatives, even if the solutions reached are always provisional. Actually, the life of a society is always in continual evolution. A small example of the enormous difference that exists between the Jewish culture of the Diaspora and of Israel might be this: When getting on a bus and buying a ticket that is written in Hebrew, a Jew from the Diaspora who has come to Israel for the first time also receives—from this small piece of paper that he struggles to succeed in deciphering—a clue as to what genuine culture is.

One of the participants observed that, now more than ever and especially in the Diaspora, one often heard insistent talk about culture, particularly from those who lacked any authentic basis in this field of study and experience. This point was also treated in depth by others who maintained that this was the way tendencies that deviate from true Jewish culture develop; those who present themselves as virtual experts on the subject matter are usually tied to cultures and politics that are not at all Jewish, and they are so influenced by these that they try to channel them into the Jewish domain. What we're dealing with, he concluded, is a windmill that wants to grind precisely what it lacks: the grain.

The last remark reminded Moshè of an old tale, with which he concluded the session. "Listen, friends," he said. "These last words remind me of a little story.

A Jew succeeded, all but miraculously, in fleeing the inferno of persecution in Europe during the Second World War, and he arrived in America. He even settled there, but he never failed to recall to friends and acquaintances, at every opportunity, all the suffering he had experienced during those sad years. In particular, the central theme of his stories was always hunger: the lack of bread, the atrocious hunger that gripped the stomach and clouded the mind for dearth of bread, the incredible effort to find even a single small piece, either by working or even by stealing, and so on. One day, one of his friends, who had heard him repeat all those stories to the point of boredom, said to him: 'Listen, by now we know, all of us, how atrocious your suffering was, but enough now with the bread. Don't you have anything else to tell us?'

"'And what for example?' he asked, virtually incredulous.

"'Talk to us, for example, about Jewish culture in the countries where you come from. It would undoubtedly be an extremely interesting subject for all of us.'

"'Why?' he asked, still hesitant. 'You're interested in culture?'

"'But of course. Always.'

"'I understand,' he replied, smiling. 'That's the way it always is: We always talk about what we don't have.'"

★ ★ ★

Telephone calls frequently constitute grounds for surprise too. As Moshè's father often used to say, wisely, "In this world there's no reason ever to be surprised by anything. Everything is possible—even the impossible!"

An unknown fellow telephoned to say that he was very, really very interested in the Kabbalah, which is something that is truly extraordinary, and to ask for some bibliographic references. Moshè, consulting a list of books subdivided by subjects, which he always kept within reach, referred him to some basic texts. The stranger thanked him heartily, but in his words Moshè immediately noticed a tone of uncertainty, and so he asked him, "Tell me, may I be of further service to you?"

From the other end of the line came a sigh of relief, and then, immediately, "Oh, yes, yes, many thanks. Actually, I wanted to ask you—could you explain to me, in a few words, what this Kabbalah is?"

★ ★ ★

The secretary of a well-known minister telephoned him.

"This is the secretary of Minister. His Excellency would like to know if there exist collections of Jewish jokes, in Italian, that appeared during the Fascist period."

Is there still anyone who would complain that high circles of government aren't interested in Jews?

★ ★ ★

On the phone again, an unknown female voice, varying greatly in pitch, but with the tone of someone asking about an ordinary administrative matter.

"Listen, I wanted to know—was Marìa, the mother of Jesus, Herod's lover?"

Moshè, quite put off by this question, responded, "I'm not qualified to provide any historical information about that. But at any rate, it would be a good idea to avoid the questionable fad of turning any event, remote or near, that concerns the life of your neighbor, into a science fiction film!"

And from the other end of the line, "And why are you taking it this way?"

★ ★ ★

The workday was over. Moshè was chatting in his office with several friends who were about to leave. Just then a fellow who spoke several languages very poorly introduced himself. Some doubt might have arisen as to whether his jumble of languages was genuine or planned, but the impression that he may have been a foreigner made them forget about questions of etiquette, like the man's intrusion in the office. The guest was given a seat and asked the reason for his visit. Moshè and his friends put forth all their good will, bringing out their linguistic knowledge as well as they could, but with scarce results. In the end, something became clear enough: After a long, meandering speech, maybe deliberately so, the request appeared to be rather obvious—financial help. Now the problem shifted. There was no longer anyone in the main office, but Moshè and his friends were ready to offer something from their own pockets. However, there was still a question to answer and that was whether this visitor was or was not a Jew. It was out of simple curiosity and would complete their judgment of him, his way of gesticulating, of speaking, and the characteristics of his rather hesitant face. Of course, this was not done to decide, on the basis of his response, to give or not to give him help, which, when necessary, had always been given, independently of religion or nationality.

He was simply asked if he was a Jew. Either he didn't understand the question or he pretended not to understand, and he looked around himself, silent. Then one of those who were present asked him, partly in German, mixed with English, "We want to know only this: Do you have the *milà* (circumcision)?"

The response, which came reluctantly and which, after a split second of silence made everyone burst out in resounding laughter, was, "Yes, of course, but I don't have it here with me. It's in my suitcase in storage at the train station."

"Your neighbor"—oftentimes a great mystery to grasp.

MIDRASHIM AT SEA

For many years Moshè and his family spent their vacation during the month of August at Porto Ercole. They had become friends with a large family of fishermen. Because of their customs (which were still a little old-fashioned), their unaffected, affectionate friendship, their ever ready and generous hospitality, and their sharp common sense, which was not without a sense of humor in facing life's difficulties, they often reminded him of his old friends from the Langhe during partisan times.

Thus it was more than once that Moshè and his son Dani were invited to go aboard their motor trawler and take part in the weekly fishing trip. They would leave Porto San Stefano on Sunday night and return on Thursday, toward evening. They sailed across the Tuscan archipelago, from the island of Giglio, along the coast of Pianosa, pushing on toward Capraia. In the evening they would drop anchor in a bay off the island of Montecristo, which, in the dark night, illuminated in an unearthly way by the moon, produced images from the contours of the landscape such as to excite the most unbridled fantasies.

After the nets had been cast into the sea, a long time would pass before they were hauled up. The time was spent chatting about this and that, playing cards, inventing diversions, always cheered by a glass of excellent Tuscan wine. Moshè had explained to the helmsman, Checco, which fish he could eat, according to his tradition. And the old fisherman understood the difference between permitted and prohibited fish perfectly. When, among the hundreds of fish that were flopping about in the great net that had just been pulled on board, Moshè pointed out to him a fish that he gladly would have chosen, Checco said to him, "No, you can't eat that one. See? It looks like it has scales, but actually they aren't." And he had Moshè verify what he had said.

Once they asked Moshè, during one of these long intervals between one casting of the net and another, if he would recount something for them, seeing as "you have studied a great deal, and we haven't." But what to tell, Moshè asked himself, and tell in a way that his friends would be able to follow with interest? After having excluded various possibilities, from history to literature, for different reasons, he thought of the Bible, and particularly the type of ancient Jewish literature that is based on the midrash—that is, a special mode of interpreting the biblical texts. The word *midrash* means "research," "study," "exegesis," and in particular it means that type of exegesis that aspires toward an ethical teaching by means of historical and legendary traditions. One of the characteristics of this type of literature is that in its golden simplicity it can be understood by everyone, and it often leaves behind a deep and abiding memory. Having made this choice, Moshè began to narrate the life of Abraham. Moshè told how, in particular, Abraham had succeeded in drawing close to the one God after a great deal of meditation garnered from the experiences of everyday life. Drawing close to God had also brought Abraham to struggle hard against King Nimrod and against all his gods, which were certainly incapable in any way of providing even a dim idea of God, made as they were of wood or metal, even if it was valuable. The fishermen, seated in a circle around Moshè on the main deck of the motor trawler, followed the story of these *midrashim* (plural of midrash) with the liveliest interest and often nudged each other in assent at the most important points.

One evening the anchor had already been dropped in the bay of the island of Montecristo, and it was late. Moshè thought therefore to suspend the story, saying that they could listen to the rest the next day.

Ofemio, Checco's son, said, clearly and firmly, "You must be joking. We won't let you go to sleep until you've finished the story like you should. Understood?"

Everyone else agreed unanimously. A new, two-liter bottle of wine was brought out, and the story continued for a long time more. Bear in mind that those fishermen usually set sail again when it was still dark. So that night their sleep was reduced to very little.

One day, while he was walking in town, Moshè was approached by one of his fishermen friends, who said to him, "Listen, Moshè. I tried to tell my family everything that you told us when we were sailing, but you know I'm uneducated, and I got a lot of things mixed up and at that point my wife said to me, 'Drop it! As usual you can't ever tell stories properly and in order.' I also wondered if maybe my wife thought that everything that I was talking about was only the fruit of my imagination. So . . ."

Here he stopped himself, smiling, but unsure if he should continue.

"So, what then? Tell me," Moshè pressed.

"Well, if it's not too troublesome for you, if you want to, and if you have the time, would you come to us this evening to recount a little something for us?"

So it was that that evening Moshè went to the house of his young friend and was welcomed not only by his close family members but also by many relatives, more than twenty people in all. That wasn't all—on the table there was an unending supply of sweets and drinks, from orange soda to white and red wine, to liquors, as though it was actually a grand reception. And Moshè recounted some of the episodes he had elaborated for his fishermen friends, which were listened to with the greatest attention and comprehension.

The visit he made that evening was not the only one during his stay that August in Porto Ercole. Before leaving again for Rome, Moshè went to other families, many of which were families of the fishermen who had embarked with him on the motor trawler.

Looking back after many years, Moshè no longer had any way of knowing how much of all that he had recounted remained in the memories of his friends, but there always persisted in him a very agreeable memory, a precious, one-of-a-kind experience. It was a confirmation of the value of midrashic tales for all times, tales that, at the folk level, both Jewish and non-Jewish, still knew the way to the minds and hearts of plain and honest people.

ISRAEL, 1948

In a meeting with the Rome Zionist Group, Moshè announced that in a few days
he would be leaving for Israel—to carry out tasks that had been entrusted to him
and to take stock of the situation, the war in progress, personally. Curiously, it
seemed to be following old patterns of Jewish history from the Bible on: Once
again a few lightly armed forces were facing many well-armed enemies determined to do anything. At the end of his talk, he recalled, in a laughing tone, something he had read some time earlier in a newspaper. In that article it was reported
that a Zionist leader had carried out his tasks scrupulously for many years but
had never visited Israel. So, without telling anyone he was going, he left and traveled throughout the country. Upon his return he organized a large meeting and
began his speech in the following fashion:

> Dear friends, you know that for years and years I've spoken to you about
> the Land of Israel. I've described to you how much is being done there, the
> resulting achievements, the efforts made by workers and farmers to restore
> the splendor of the past to the ancient land. But you also know that I had
> never been to Israel. Now, however, I've made a trip, and I've seen every-
> thing that is being done there, and I can finally say to you that everything I
> told you for many years tallies precisely with the truth.

Recalling this statement, Moshè added, "More or less the same thing has happened to me. You know that I've worked very actively in the Zionist field, but I've
never been to Israel. Now, finally, I can go there, and when I return I hope to be
able to tell you the same thing my Zionist colleague said."

The meeting having ended, Moshè was approached by several individuals who asked him many questions in private. Granted that one should give all possible support to our coreligionists in Israel, how was it that he had decided to go there, and right during the war? Whatever was he going to do there? And even if it was his own personal business, didn't he feel any responsibility toward his local Community, which might be annoyed when it was realized that a person like him, who was quite well known to the local authorities, went—him, an Italian—to a country in which a war that had nothing to do with Italy was being waged? And so on with other questions that Moshè responded to obliquely, not wanting to set off an argument with people who clearly were not very Zionist and who had attended that meeting more to nose around than for anything else.

The three-month stay in Israel went by in a flash. Although the country was in a state of war, Moshè had been furnished with a special pass, and he had toured from north to south, monitoring the dramatic events of those weeks from close by, sometimes almost at the front lines, which were really everywhere. Moshè would return to Italy with a more concrete vision of the local problems—a more genuine knowledge of the first steps of Zionism as they were being realized and of the movement in general as the persistence and evolution of an ancient idea and a biblical promise.

Moshè was traveling from Tel Aviv to Haifa, sitting near the driver. Behind him six other travelers had taken seats. A woman suddenly turned to the driver and asked something in German.

The response, harsh and quick, was, "Speak Hebrew!"

The woman kept at it, but the response was always the same. The driver struck up a conversation with Moshè and complained, "Really, should we listen to that language that reminds us of so many horrible things?"

"Maybe she doesn't know Hebrew."

"And what do I care?" he responded harshly. "I'm also a German speaker, but once I arrived here I forgot it, and I learned Hebrew."

"Maybe she needs something, and for you it would have been a simple act of courtesy to reply, and all the more so since you know German."

"You really don't know what you're saying." And he became silent, made gloomy by who knows what thoughts.

A few kilometers from Haifa a soldier signaled us to pull over and asked us to go down into a nearby shelter because there was an air raid warning in effect. The sound of airplanes was heard in the distance. The driver approached Moshè, whispering, all but embarrassed by what he was about to say to a stranger. But enunciating his words clearly, he said, "Don't think that I'm a boorish chauvinist. The fact is that I lost my parents and three brothers in the concentration camps." And he looked at Moshè with eyes misted over with tears. Moshè pressed his hand at length, in silence. Now everything was clear.

At the port of Haifa, it so happened that Moshè ran into [Chaim] Weizmann, the first president of the State of Israel, whom he had already met in Rome in 1935. Having gotten on board a ship of the Adriatic Line, Moshè settled in on the bridge, awaiting the departure. The first shadows of evening descended quickly, and a light mist veiled the intense red of the sunset. He was about to leave Israel, so it came naturally to mind to think over the trip he had made and the people he had visited, people from Italy with whom he had been occupied from 1938 to 1940. He felt joy and excitement at seeing again those youths, who by then were fully integrated in the life of the country, and he experienced strong feelings remembering, one at a time, that among them more than a few had fallen in combat during those months. There were families who had lost two children just a few weeks apart. All those youths, along with many others, had given their own lives to defend the threatened borders, so that Israel could continue to live, free and secure, on its own land.

Moshè, thinking about these latest tragic events, was led at the same time to make a kind of historical balance sheet, so to speak, of the vicissitudes of the small Italian Jewish world, from 1848 to 1948. There had been so many events in one century of history. There was the Emancipation, which, with its virtually sudden light of liberty, had blinded the Jews of the ghetto, many of whom lost every Jewish orientation, abandoning themselves to a galloping form of assimilation, without its own ideas and without dignity. And yet their feeling of being equal to everyone else, of being Italians like the others, was also a natural and honest impulse. In fact, they not only distinguished themselves, especially in the professions, which by then were open to them too, but in commerce, industry, and higher education, filling prominent positions in the public life of the country with great competence and exemplary dignity. There was not a single war of the Risorgimento in which Jews were not present, giving their lives without hesitation for the unity of Italy, and again, during World War I, when they were regularly distinguished for their ability and heroism. In the midst of this flowering of confidence in a life that by then would not have had other restrictions of any kind, one can understand, although not justify, the growing assimilation to Italian culture and politics over the course of several eras. And, as we know, there were even Jewish fascists and anti-Zionists, just like after World War II, when many of them ran to enroll themselves in the different parties that were emerging and that, in order to win Jewish support, were very generous (at the beginning) in making grand promises, even concerning international politics. Such choices can be judged only after taking into account how, in the face of this sudden surge of liberal—that is, assimilationist—ideas and initiatives, there was a serious lack of reliable Jewish organizations. The causes for this dearth of strong Jewish organizations need not be examined in detail here, except to say that it was the result of the small number of Jews in Italy, scattered in many communities and increasingly integrated with the great majority, and of the lack of a solid Jewish education among many of those who took on the great responsibility of educating the new generations. As he continued to examine the events of the years he had lived through and was still experiencing, Moshè thought about how less than a century after the glorious Emancipation all the rights that had been given to the Jews from King Carlo Alberto on had been taken away, and they had been driven back into a ghetto that was even crueler and more extreme. Hence the futile attempt at flight from that small Jewish world by many Italians of the Mosaic faith, and then, a short while later, the tragic deportation to the extermination camps. And so it was that after the end of this second World War, the Italian Jews, survivors of the Final Solution, found themselves once again facing huge problems, not the least of which was the reconstruction of a Jewish life in their country of origin, and the call, above all moral, to be present at the rebirth of the State of Israel.

Moshè, thinking again over all the vicissitudes of this small Jewish group and still maintaining his ideals unwaveringly and his plans unaltered, felt an almost acute sense of compassion for these Jews, who were few in number, morally and ideologically splintered, tossed about and repeatedly swept away by events they had been drawn into as Jews, yet not truly knowing what it meant to be Jews. And yet, in spite of this uncomfortable situation, the Jewish community in Italy had also been able to distinguish itself at the highest levels of Jewish learning, in this very century, and within the Zionist movement itself. And now, even in Israel, a handful of youths brought honor in the fields of war and in every other activity. It was a sort of labyrinth in which maybe not even the thread of Ariadne would have been very useful!

At Limassol, an Austrian Jew came aboard. He was the only coreligionist Moshè had the chance to meet on the ship. He even spoke Italian, and so the conversation took off quite quickly, and they became friends. He was middle-aged, distinguished for his manners and for experiences that were so numerous that they must have been acquired over the course of an adventurous life. He had fled in time when Hitler conquered Austria. He had wandered around Europe and then managed, barely in time, to find refuge in Cyprus, where he opened a commercial office, with good results. Now he was returning to Vienna to get news more directly, to discover what little he could learn about his parents, siblings, and aunts and uncles who had disappeared in the Nazi tragedy.

He concluded, saying, "I'm also going to try to take care of some business affairs. I had some possessions, houses, and a little money, but I'm doing this to get rid of every question, once and for all, because I won't get anything important from these things either and there won't be anything I can do about it."

And he laughed, surprising Moshè because of the equanimity of his entire story, as though he were narrating things that happened to others, not to him, things that were so personal, emotional, and financial.

Noting the astonishment of the young man, he added, "Excuse me—but are we or are we not Jews? And as such we always have to be ready for anything, the good as well as the bad. But none of that matters. What matters more is to always look to the future, to never give up, and to always go forward." And he sipped his glass of beer carefully and with pleasure.

Moshè realized that he completely agreed with his Austrian friend, and at the same time he was also very happy, because he seemed to have found an excellent commentary, maybe even a solution, to all the reflections that a few hours earlier had so intensely occupied and even oppressed him.

A RAILWAY PORTER IN VENICE

The ship arrived in Smyrna, where it would lay over for two days to load bales of cotton. Whoever had an Israel visa on their passport could not disembark because Turkey had not yet recognized the State of Israel. Moshè tried unsuccessfully to get permission to go ashore from the police who had come on board. Nothing could be done. The response was not only negative but also not very nice. The captain of the ship, who had listened to this fruitless discussion between Moshè and the police, approached Moshè, took him aside, and said to him, "Don't waste your time, it's useless. Enjoy this magnificent gulf from the ship. Even this is politics, what can you do?! See these bales of cotton we're already loading? I'm taking them to Venice, but everyone here knows that then, from Venice, I'll be taking them to Israel. You're not a businessman, that's obvious. If you were, I assure you that you would already be in town doing business."

To console Moshè, he offered him a glass of genuine Trieste grappa.

They sailed for Piraeus. A glorious sea, intensely blue. Islands here and there, everywhere, seemed to invite one to linger in the midst of their greenery, in a light that had a special allure. With a bit of imagination, which the extraordinary scenery prompted, perhaps one could better understand ancient Greek art and philosophy, that desire for beauty and perfection. Instead, the spectacle offered by Piraeus, then in the middle of a civil war, was distressing. Houses had been destroyed, stores were empty, few people were moving about. Policemen with many boxes of files came on board. Whoever wanted to go ashore had to undergo a thorough examination. Passengers were even asked whether they intended to spend any money. The obligatory exchange was between dollars and drachmas. For a few dollars they filled your hands with drachmas.

The several hours' layover allowed the travelers to disembark. They wandered around the city a little, but there wasn't much to see. Stores were closed or in ruins. Only one shop, featuring local sweets, was open. The travelers bought some and seated themselves at a small table in a bar a short way from the ship and surrounded by piles of rubble. While they were having a drink, some boys, dressed in rags and barefoot, emerged from the ruins and approached them to beg for coins. But at the same moment a guard also appeared, and with unheard-of violence, kicked those poor kids. The passengers sprang to their feet and ran to help. The guard was nearly attacked, and the kids fled. Now, however, came the reckoning with the defender of public safety, who wanted to take everyone to the station. Who knows how things would have turned out if the captain, watching the scene from the ship, had not rushed to the aid of his guests. Meanwhile, the sailors were doing a brisk business. They offered bags of rice weighing a few kilos each that had been prepared in advance and in return received magnificent suitcases made of real leather.

After a brief stop in Bari, the ship, in somewhat choppy seas, headed directly for Venice. The captain pointed out to Moshè that they were shifting toward the Yugoslavian coast.

"Why?" he asked.

"You know, the whole sea is still mined here."

"Oh, heaven help us!"

"No, no, don't worry. We're insured for such an eventuality too!" He broke into a resounding burst of laughter, but Moshè continued to worry.

The next morning the Venetian lagoon appeared, quite beautiful, even though the already advanced autumn, the fog, and a light drizzle gave a tinge of sadness to the nearly bare trees, the silent shores, and the few deserted houses. Wreckage of civilian and military ships appeared here and there, a cemetery of rusting iron recalling countless tragedies.

In Venice, Moshè made a short visit to the temple of the German[1] rite, the Scola Tedesca, where, in faraway 1904, his parents were married. He took a brief

---

1   Synagogue liturgies (*minhagim*), especially melodies, vary according to the places in the Diaspora where they developed over long periods of time. Thus the "German rite" (or Ashkenazic rite) developed

walk around the old and new ghettos,[2] which retain their own singular fascination, with memories that still seem to be chiseled into the stones. After crossing the Bridge of the Quattro Guglie,[3] he set off toward the station, to catch the train for Rome.

Moshè left his suitcases with the first porter he found waiting for clients near the checkroom, and, letting him know which train he would be taking, headed toward it. The porter, rather old but still vigorous, preceded him. Moshè saw that the porter was searching quite carefully, first for a car and then for a compartment, where he set about finding a place for the suitcases with the greatest care. Moshè was taking off his raincoat, and he was thinking that there were still porters who were scrupulous and meticulous in their service. But his astonishment knew no limits when he saw the porter move his fingers along the edge of the suitcases, and then to his eyes first and afterward to his mouth, to kiss them. In short, something like what happens in the synagogue when any of the faithful kiss the *Séfer Torà* (Scroll of the Torah).

More and more surprised, Moshè asked him, "May I know what you're doing?"

"What? Don't you see?" the old man asked, somewhat vexed. "Don't you see that it's Torah?"[4]

Moshè drew nearer and read. Written in Hebrew on the small tags glued to each suitcase, was simply, "Tel Aviv–Haifa!" He was speechless, he was moved. He reached out his hand.

"You're a Jew?"

---

in Germany and German Jews brought it with them to Venice when they immigrated there. However, there is not one German rite but different variations. The German synagogue (Scola Tedesca) in Venice that Segre refers to dates to 1528.

2   The ghetto of Venice, the world's first, actually contains three sections: the Ghetto Nuovo ("New Ghetto," created in 1516), the Ghetto Vecchio ("Old Ghetto," created in 1541), and the Ghetto Nuovissimo ("Newest Ghetto," created in 1633). The reason for the reverse order, the new ghetto being older than the new ghetto, is that the meaning of the word *ghetto* at that time was "foundry," and the site of the first ghetto was the "new foundry"; the site of the second ghetto (an extension of the first) was the "old foundry." By the time of the "Newest Ghetto" (a small extension of the Ghetto Nuovo), the word *ghetto* had acquired its modern meaning. For a recent discussion of the term's etymology, see Benjamin Ravid, "Ghetto: Etymology, Original Definition, Reality, and Diffusion," in Wendy Z. Goldman and Joe William Trotter Jr., eds., *The Ghetto in Global History: 1500 to the Present* (New York: Routledge, 2017), 23–39.

3   "Four spires," commonly known today simply as the Bridge of the Spires (Ponte delle Guglie). It is located on a main thoroughfare, at the entrance to the Ghetto Vecchio, and crosses a major canal.

4   The porter always responds in Venetian dialect.

"Both of us are." He had tears in his eyes.

"How much do I owe you?"

"Don't mention it! I've already had a great *simchà* (joy), and it's enough for me!"

A strong handshake, and the old porter descended the steps of the car with an almost youthful stride and soon disappeared into the fog that weighed heavily along the platform roof. Moshè, still hardly believing what he had seen, took another look at the tags. There wasn't any doubt: In bold, in Hebrew, it was written, simply, "Tel Aviv–Haifa."

MOSHÈ ON TELEVISION: 2 + 2 = 5

In the television offices on Via Teulada, work was underway on a project to make a major serialized film about Moses [Moshè].[1] Moshè was invited to contribute as an expert on Jewish matters. A first, introductory meeting took place with the well-known director [Gianfranco] De Bosio at the Hilton Residence. Picked up at home by a luxurious Mercedes, complete with a driver who opened the car door and ceremoniously greeted the illustrious guest, our expert thus made his first entrance into a world entirely unknown to him. Moshè was not only new to this kind of meeting, and at such a high level besides; he was also new to the kind of conversation that the renowned director set in motion, with great friendliness and warmth, as though it were a simple visit between old friends. The words were simple, for the sake of the nonexpert, but often fortified with technical expressions that, even though they were spoken informally, definitely did not facilitate the comprehension of certain ideas, at least not for Moshè. The tone of voice, which changed wonderfully according to the concepts expressed, sometimes hushed and mellow, sometimes more robust and incisive, often gave Moshè the sensation that he was no longer at the Hilton Residence but seated in the cinematographer's chair, intent on following the scenes of a film—so vivid and evocative were the director's descriptions. Yet following the thread of his argument wasn't always easy, partly because, in dealing with some topics, he equivocated, although with his usual, undiminished grace. His caution in proceeding on terrain

---

1   The six-part miniseries *Moses the Lawgiver*, starring Irene Papas and Burt Lancaster, was produced in 1974.

as difficult as that of the Bible can be accounted for by the fact that De Bosio knew who he was facing, and, with his great artistic sensibility, he was doubtlessly already perceiving how he might be able to realize certain themes, which perhaps were already taking on concrete form in his mind—so much so that sometimes he went almost inadvertently from simply talking to actually acting out some of the scenes as he imagined they might be done. Yet at the same time, not being perfectly familiar with Bible stories, he also feared that he might get off track. Hence he maneuvered with a great deal of shrewdness, like a true world-class diplomat. And besides, this film was intended for the major world markets. As for Moshè, beyond the immediate sensations that he felt, finding himself in an entirely new ambience, there was also something entirely unusual: For the first time he had to try to visualize, so to speak, events and people from the Bible, and it was not easy for someone who had known both only through the study of the Bible's pages.

This first meeting was then followed by others of a, let's say, collective character, in which various people participated. Among these people, sometimes, and unexpectedly, there was a fellow who must have been a television big shot, because ongoing discussions were interrupted and the utmost attention was given to the "new ideas" this fellow decided to suggest. And that it truly was only a matter of "new ideas," full of fantasy, was demonstrated by the fact that both the expert on Jewish matters and the expert on Christian matters, surprised by such nonsense, frequently looked at each other in silence, sometimes even open-mouthed in a shared, spontaneous gesture that underscored the total absurdity of what was blabbered out as though it were indisputable. This famous personage had no other distinguishing characteristics except for asking with a smile for cigarettes from everyone who smoked!

There was a new experiment, of special interest, that Moshè was slowly putting to the test. He noted how in those interminable meetings, they tried—with a great deal of imagination, ceaselessly, and with the utmost determination—to delve into passages from the Bible—not to derive authentic interpretations as much as to find something new, ingenious, and brilliant, something not in the text but which might also have been said. (Is that the typical kind of imagination that characterizes the world of cinema?) They tried to create episodes that "could be blended into the harmonious story of sacred scripture." Shrewd comments were heard, made even in a tone of considerable excitement, at the end of which the conclusion was, "Look, according to the text, it isn't like that, but it could work quite well because that way, in the end, it emphasizes . . ." In other words, whatever you want—but we were dealing with "creations" that do not show up in either Jewish or Christian fields. The attempt to insert modern themes, even if they forced the text without restraint, was completely clear. And, as everyone knows, this was not an isolated instance; these were the methods other classical texts had to undergo when they passed through the hands of film experts. During those meetings, Moshè also sought an example he could use to illustrate that the "modernization" of some things has an insuperable limit. In the end, believing he'd found one, he was able to talk privately with the director during a break in the meeting.

Moshè said to him, "Listening these days to so many learned remarks on the Bible"—his interlocutor looked at him smiling, encouraging him to proceed, such was his curiosity to know what his Jewish friend was about to tell him—"I came to think—by way of example, and only as an example, of course—of what might take place in a conversation between a young student, who is excited by the study of mathematics but who is also possessed of a prodigious imagination, and his teacher in this subject, which, as we know, is an exact science. Let's imagine this conversation: 'Professor, how much does 2 + 2 make?' The instructor looks at him, smiling, thinks it a joke but wants to respond as the question requires, so he says immediately, 'It's clear and rather simple: 2 + 2 = 4.' 'Good, splendid, superb. But if we'—the student presses—'were to say that 2 + 2 = 5, doesn't it seem to you we would have a more intriguing result, rich with surprises, stimulating, and one that, at the best, might even transpose psychological assessments through a transfer of calculated ratios onto a very different and entirely original plane?'"

De Bosio broke out in an open, candid burst of laughter; he had understood perfectly, but he was ready to play, and putting his hand on Moshè's shoulder in a friendly manner, making himself appear thoughtful, he said, "Well, as an idea, it's not bad. We'll have to think about it . . ."

THE JEWISH-CHRISTIAN DIALOGUE: STILL A LONG WAY TO GO

The Second Vatican Council, with its *Declaratio* of October 28, 1965, confirmed the profound change in relations between the Catholic Church and the Jews. The Council's text, even though overdue and in a form constrained by an excess of ecclesiastical caution, came to represent an act of reparative justice. In its initial intentions and original wording it was intended not only to remove, definitively, residual superstitions derived from theological misinterpretations but also to constitute a healthy and liberating self-critique, destined to be extended to all strata of Christianity. Nevertheless, although the *Declaratio* remains without doubt a foundation stone for the realization of human dignity, the Council's *procedure* reduced the document's innovative capacity notably, subjecting the aspirations that had justified it to subtle compromises expressed in the choice of a vocabulary that is not resolutely committed and in the acceptance of pressures coming from anti-Semitic circles of various kinds. The document, therefore, even with its great historical importance, represents a weakening of the original expectations and was destined to generate a great deal of hesitation regarding relations between Jews and Christians in certain circles. All this might explain how, even though on the one hand the Jewish-Christian dialogue developed and broadened in a positive way, thanks to minds that were honestly open to the Word of God, on the other hand, in one part of the Christian world, many hesitations and doubts continued to persist. Among the most closed circles confronted with what for them was an unexpected opening toward the Jews, a not inconsiderable residue of traditional religious anti-Semitism also persisted. Doubts were not lacking in the Jewish camp either, because history was still there to confirm the sometimes irrational alternation between periods of almost untroubled coexistence and other periods that were difficult and fully persecutory. These doubts, for that matter, also seem to have been amply corroborated by the fact that from October 28, 1965, the date of the promulgation of the declaration, ten years had to pass before the arrival of the document "Guidance and Suggestions for the Application of the Declaration *Nostra Aetate*" (January 3, 1975).

Moshè had greeted this avowed historical change of the Church positively. He was persuaded, even with the doubts that remained (and they were not few) and even though one of the fundamental features of the Church, missionary activity, remained unchanged. Cardinal Bea himself had frankly declared, "Christ is the way, the truth and the life, in which men must find the fullness of the religious life," clearly referring to the Church's missionary activity, which the Church would never have been able to renounce without failing in its primary existential purpose. Thus, even facing a new horizon, which was still far from cloudless, Moshè always sought to nourish and keep alive the dialogue between Jews and Christians. And that was true even before the historic *Declaratio* was promulgated in 1965. Moshè himself had organized meetings at various levels, had always complied with requests that were directed to him from different places, and had also formed sincere ties of friendship with several members of the clergy who demonstrated a fraternal concern regarding all these problems. Among these, always present in Moshè's heart and mind, was the noble figure of Father C. A. Rijk, from Holland, who had died prematurely many years earlier. He had always been ready to defend the Jewish people and their rights openly, not only in words but in deeds. Precisely because of his clear and unequivocal position regarding the Jews, Father Rijk himself was often marginalized in his own Christian milieu. This did not diminish his brotherly commitment and honorable cooperation in any way. Moshè often recalled to friends and in various conference publications what this *zaddìq* (righteous person) in the true traditional Hebrew sense, had once declared:

> The Church looks back to its origins, to the mystery of its nature; it is understandable that it must speak about the special bond that ties it to the line of Abraham, to the Jews, and that it must speak about the great spiritual patrimony shared between Christians and Jews. And all of a sudden

we discover that our neighbor, he whom we had seen from a distance and whom we had considered a stranger and often a malefactor, is revealed to be a brother with whom we are bound by close and profound ties. . . . Thus one can understand the reason why the Second Vatican Council Declaration begins with these words, "Searching the mystery of the Church, the Holy Council remembers the bond with which the people of the New Testament are spiritually tied to the line of Abraham." [As a direct consequence of the] great patrimony common to Christians and Jews, the Holy Council wishes to foster and to urge mutual knowledge and esteem between them. The renewal of the Church requests, or better still, requires a new encounter with the Jews in a spirit of impartial love and esteem, in a profound and religious exploration of the mysterious plan of God.

Another fine religious figure with whom Moshè maintained ties of sincere brotherly friendship was also a well-known Franciscan, Father Mariano, who often appeared on certain television programs. He was a remarkable person—for his educational and moral level, for the simplicity, humility, and extreme modesty of his behavior, and for the crystal clarity of his look and of his smile, which immediately won the esteem and affection of his interlocutors. He came from an old school of study and meditation, and even though he had been immediately and amply sensitized to the new orientations of the Church, nevertheless perhaps some qualms still remained in his unconscious, and he was unable to distance himself from them, even if it caused him a certain painful spiritual tension. There were numerous friendly, lively conversations between Moshè and Father Mariano, whether Moshè went to visit him on the Via Veneto or Father Mariano was a guest in Moshè's home. Such was the power of instant attraction that Father Mariano stirred in others that one time Moshè's daughter, a child of 4, a few minutes after having met Father Mariano during one of his visits, promptly brought him and gave him all her toys, arousing joyful astonishment in everyone and affecting the pious Franciscan deeply.

It happened one day that Moshè, after having watched one of Father Mariano's television programs, thought it worthwhile to write him a letter, to clarify some points that he thought were particularly important. Moshè reminded his friend that, in presenting the Ten Commandments, translated directly from the Hebrew text that had appeared, written on several panels, he had omitted the second commandment, which concerns the absolute prohibition of making images of any kind. Then, referring to another topic, that of loving one's neighbor, Moshè was specific:

> Referring to the quotations from Jesus, it would not have been superfluous had the passages from the original texts also appeared; but all that, I understand, is part of a convention that is not very praiseworthy even though it is quite widespread. Thus Jesus quotes those two passages, the first of which is a portion of the Shema, which Jews still recite today—and not, as you said, that the pious Israelite had to say. And the response of Jesus is perfectly in line with the Jewish tradition that ascribed a fundamental value to these two concepts; actually, it is an instance of a widely diffused Pharisaic interpretation. Essentially, then, historically speaking, Jesus doesn't say anything new but reaffirms a lofty Jewish teaching—"lofty," which is particularly obvious because it comes from God.
>
> Verse 18 of Leviticus, chapter 19, "Love your neighbor as yourself," then, is clearly understood by anyone who knows Hebrew—thus not only by Jews. In fact it does not refer to "Israelites only." That way of interpreting the words of the Torah is a way, used for centuries, of falsifying the translation. *Rea'* has the generic meaning of companion, friend, fellow human, neighbor, and even the Egyptian (Exodus 11:2), who was not of the same race or religion, was actually referred to with this word. That this love for one's neighbor also refers to non-Jews is readily apparent from what follows. In fact, one just has to browse through the text of the same chapter (19) of Leviticus to find verse 34, where this obligation is extended even to the stranger, of whom it is said, "And you shall love him as yourself." So, how does this play out? Didn't Jesus actually give this moral imperative the same significance that the Pharisees and other Jews, his brothers, gave it? Our ancient masters said, "Whoever cites the original author of a saying, brings about the redemption of the world."[1] Why not avail oneself of these simple opportunities to contribute to the true redemption of all humans? Certainly, true love of one's neighbor—which does not end in abstract statements but which turns to practical implementation through human action—would avoid many injustices, many false accusations, many errors, many misunderstandings, and besides, would teach us to have an even greater respect for that Bible that is equally sacred to Jews and to Christians.

---

1   This saying is found in *Pirke Avot* 6:5.

Father Mariano, thoughtful as always, responded to this letter shortly afterward with these words:

> I am truly sorry—believe me—for having distressed your noble heart, certainly not in bad faith, and neither, believe me, out of boorishness. I am definitely not a specialist in this material, just a student, sincere and serious. Regarding the enumeration of the Ten Commandments—on that occasion I didn't want to give a commentary but only to show a photograph of the Hebrew text. When I comment on the commandments, I will certainly bring the whole text. (God forbid that I would want to "delete" the words of the Holy Book!)
>
> Regarding my not having cited Deuteronomy 6:4–9 for the precept of love; this was a true omission, which I will remedy in the next broadcast of "In the Family," in which I continue (and will continue again at length) to speak about love. The precept is definitely divine, and it is there in the Old Testament. (God is the neighbor.) But Jesus, in *confirming it* (and drawing attention to its *centrality*), extended and transfigured it. What significance would the parable of the Good Samaritan have if not for the fact that at the time of Jesus, for all intents and purposes, many, many people saw only the children of Israel (and the Samaritans?) as their neighbor? (Apart from, of course, the noble exceptions that were not lacking even then and to which I alluded.) Jesus, in effect, extended and transfigured the precept, summoning everyone to see Him, the Man-God, in the countenance of every man. Even Christian forgiveness comes to be seen in this *new* light.
>
> I agree with you in recognizing that much of what Jesus said (apart from the mystery of the innermost life of Jesus: the Trinity) is there in the Old Testament; what is truly new is Him, who illuminates all the truths of the Old Testament with *new* light. The newness is His Person. Unfortunately we Christians don't live "His" command to love, precisely because we don't strive to see him in every person's face.
>
> Forgive my brevity, but this is the substance of what I think. I reaffirm to you my deep esteem and sincere friendship, thanking you also for the attention that you give to my modest programs. Shalom!

Even in this random letter we see all of the humane and lively personality of Father Mariano, constantly engaged in active educational and informational work, but the letter also makes one aware of the many difficulties of various kinds he had to face, as well as those doubts and spiritual tensions that undoubtedly must have tried him sorely and that he had already mentioned. His traditional greeting, "Peace and blessings to everyone," summed up his entire agenda of great human brotherhood.

We won't pause here to record those actions or those statements and episodes that were also part of this area of Moshè's activity and that related to those religious individuals who were still bound by perpetual bad faith to the old patterns of traditional religious anti-Semitism that reappeared in fiery form after the days of Vatican II in a thick, libelous pamphlet, *The Conspiracy Against the Church*, by a certain Maurice Pinay. These manifestations are not worth troubling over—they display such human meanness in their usually ponderous and offensive words, similar to what was customary in the depths of the Middle Ages. But, for the liveliness of Moshè's response, which he addressed to *L'Europeo* (December 8, 1978), it is worth reporting the text here. He was commenting, not without a certain sense of humor, on a pronouncement of typical spiritual illiteracy:

> The response of Father Colosio (*L'Europeo*, number 46), which judges Di Nola incompetent "to understand the Christian religion in a thorough and orthodox way, since he is, after all, of Jewish extraction," raises an obvious question. Apart from Jesus, who although being Jewish and circumcised, assumes a particular typology in the Christian tradition, there is no doubt that Peter, Paul, and the other apostles and many of those who were their contemporaries or who came after them in the immediately subsequent period, were certainly of Jewish extraction. And yet, in accordance with the history of the Church, doesn't this raise some doubt as to whether they had "understood the religion in a thorough and orthodox way?" Isn't that so?

Someone, maybe more subtly, might have added, "How can it be, on the other hand, that someone who is not of Jewish extraction, regards himself as extremely competent and capable of dealing with Jewish issues?" But it's not worth splitting hairs with someone who is an unsurpassed master in this genre of dialectical tricks.

★ ★ ★

Moshè had received a pamphlet titled *Ecumenical Council Vatican II, First Year: Pastoral for Lent 1967, to the Priests and the Faithful of the Diocese of Casale*, edited by the bishop of that city, His Excellency Giuseppe Angrisani, and published by Fratelli Tarditi Printing. Great was Moshè's surprise when he read these words:

> "How goodly are your pavilions, O Jacob, and your tents, O Israel. They stretch out like valleys, like gardens beside a river, like aloes planted by the Lord, like cedars beside waters!" (Numbers 24:5–6). These words were directed at the Jewish people, who were the people of God.
>
> But when that people showed itself to be obstinate in the face of warnings and constantly unfaithful, God disowned them and made preparations for his true people through Jesus Christ.

Moshè had known this bishop personally, and he had always appreciated his high moral and educational level, and thus it seemed almost impossible that he could have made such statements. So he decided to write him a letter in which, among other things, he said to him:

> Recently I had the occasion to read the Pastoral Letter that Your Excellency sent for Lent 1967, and I am taking the liberty of writing to you concerning it in order to submit some of my personal reflections to your courteous and benevolent attention.
>
> I must tell you that I was prompted to do so by a memory that dates back to now distant 1941, when it was that in Casale I lost my father, of blessed memory, chief rabbi in that city. On that sad occasion I was, with members of my family, surrounded by many kind expressions of condolence (which, of course, in those years of racial persecution took on a special significance), including the comfort of one of your personal letters, which I kept with the family correspondence, up to the moment in which my home in Asti was destroyed by the Fascists. It is this dear memory of an act of great goodness and affectionate brotherhood—for which I continue to be truly grateful to you—that induces me to write you. . . .
>
> At a certain point in this pastoral letter, speaking about the Jewish people, you say that "God disowned them." I ask myself, in sorrowful astonishment, how is it possible that even today one can hear this kind of statement from the authoritative voice of Princes of the Church?
>
> Is it permissible to think, I ask myself quite often, that the Lord, who is the God of Abraham and Moses, of Jesus and the Apostles, who is the celestial Father of everyone, would use double standards, as unfortunately

many humans often do? Could it ever be possible that the Lord would teach his creatures to discriminate? It can't possibly be so. Excellency, do you fully remember how many tears and how much blood has flowed from the age-old martyrdom of the Jews precisely because of this position which, many times over the centuries, the Church has taken toward them? . . .

And still I ask myself: Is it possible to understand how it could ever be that the teaching of Leviticus (19:18), "Love your neighbor as yourself," which the Lord taught to the Jews even before Jesus reaffirmed it, in keeping with the traditional Jewish system—could it ever be possible to understand how that most elevated lesson, first of the Torah, then of the Gospels, and then finally of the most conscientious humans—could be accepted and applied with such obvious or hidden discrimination? And I allow myself to say this to you because when you teach, speaking about the Jewish people, whom "God disowned," a good system for teaching your flock love for one's neighbor is certainly not being applied (excuse my words). Might this not be a mode of attributing to the Lord thoughts and sentiments that are merely human?

It is certainly not up to me, nor, believe me, would I presume to point out, especially to you, neither the words of Paul ("Has God perhaps turned his people away? That could never be. I too am an Israelite, of the seed of Abraham, of the tribe of Benjamin. God has not rejected his people who He knew beforehand as his people"),[2] nor the passage, "Regarding election, they are loved through their fathers, because the gifts and the call of God are irrevocable,"[3] and finally, not even the words that the Council of Vatican II used to emphasize the evangelical concept itself ("Jews should not be presented as rejected or accursed by God as if this followed from the Holy Scriptures"),[4] these being the words that the Council addressed to the entire Christian world. I certainly do not harbor this pretension, which could appear disrespectful, even if it definitely is not. . . . Why not try to realize, as far as our human possibilities allow, the Will of the Lord, who certainly does not want to reject any of His children but wishes them all united, who desires the unity of humanity in the unity of His infinite love for everyone?

---

2   Romans 11:1–2.

3   Romans 11:28–29.

4   "Iudei tamen neque ut a Deo reprobati neque ut maledicti exhibeatur, quasi hoc ex Sacris Litteris sequatur."

A few days later, by return of post, the response—clear, honest, and sincere—arrived:

> You have every reason to complain about my phrase, "God disowned them," referring to the Jewish people.
>
> As to my, at least partial, excuse, these two reasons apply: On the previous page I had quoted Saint Peter (I: 2, 9–10), who has a clear-cut reference to Hosea, where it says, "For you are no longer my people, and I am not your God" (Hosea 1:9). The second reason is of a general character: that is, since childhood we, unfortunately, have heard expression like the one you deplored. These phrases entered into our ordinary way of speaking without us paying them the attention they deserve, all the more so when they are unjust and offensive.
>
> What the Council approved was accepted by everyone and with complete sincerity. If at times we come up short, it is certainly not out of malice. It is somewhat like the phenomenon of certain "treaties" between two powers that have been signed but that from time to time, either because of an oversight or because of the carelessness of some official, are forgotten regarding some point.
>
> May you have faith in my sincerity and trust me always.
>
> Your most devoted.

Moshè, in turn, felt obligated to respond immediately, thanking the bishop for his courteous and thoughtful response and expressing all his gratitude for having rediscovered in him those sincere sentiments of friendship he had already admired in that distant 1941. He added that, of course, the road was still long and often difficult, but that with good will and reciprocal sincerity, they would be able to overcome successfully the many misunderstandings and reaffirm and consolidate good friendships. Beyond that, he allowed himself to add some observations regarding the prophet Hosea:

> Being a modest student of biblical studies, allow me, Excellency, to mention briefly something regarding the citation of Hosea of which you reminded me. The conjugal drama of Hosea, prophet of the eighth century BCE, whether it is real life or allegory, or also as it was intended, as prophetic drama, emphasizes the relationship between God and the people of Israel with the richness of very delicate familial nuances. God is Love

and Love is God never ceases, just as the love of a father who punishes his children so that they will mend their ways never ceases. The name of the second daughter of the prophet (*Lo ruchàma*, i.e., not loved) and that of the third son (*Lo ammì*, i.e., not my people) are symbolic names that indicate the sins of Israel, its idolatrous fornication. But after the punishments, the people of Israel—so says Hosea—would seek its first Bridegroom and the children would again find their Father. It is enough, in fact, to read the beginning of the second chapter of Hosea to realize this: Then the number of the children of Israel shall be like the sand of the sea, which cannot be measured nor numbered; instead of saying to them, "You are not my people," it shall be said to them, "children of the living God." The children of Judah and the children of Israel shall be gathered together, and they shall appoint over themselves one head; and they shall go up out of the land [of exile], for great shall be the day of Jezreel. Say to your brothers, "People of God" and to your sisters, "Beloved."

Apart from the small clarifications of an exegetical character, this exchange of correspondence—open, frank, and representing something new, particularly because it had developed not at an official, public level but between private individuals, and especially between a simple Jew and a high representative of the Church—could indeed appear to be a not insignificant sign of progress and positive evolution in relations between Jews and Christians. The experience acquired through the study of Jewish history and in relations between the people of Israel and the Church might suggest cautious expectations for the development of these relations. Moshè had also learned from texts and from his personal experience that oftentimes, along with principally religious questions that were theological in a broad sense, other problems of a completely different and seemingly odd character—since they were unconnected to true and proper biblical sources—were included. In the past, economic and political complications had left profound marks on these relations. Would these complications, which had held back the best of good intentions to establish brotherly relations between these two great religions, be renewed once again? That is what Moshè asked himself, with the lively hope that the new times would be able, however, to bring new and more durable solutions, eliminating the possibility of such quarrels, which were increasingly anachronistic and far from every form of authentic and operative morality, in a truly ecumenical sense.

ANTI-SEMITISM: INTERNAL AND EXTERNAL

Anti-Semitism is so old and widespread that even when—and it doesn't happen very often—you think a given environment has been civilized and decontaminated, here it comes again, in the most unexpected places, just like cockroaches. This illness usually turns up in the non-Jewish world but sometimes in the Jewish world itself as well, introduced there by people who declare themselves to be great friends of the Jews. Then there are also other cases—fortunately not numerous but still beyond dispute—in which this centuries-old venom is actually served up by Jews, Jews who are distant from Jewish involvement, sometimes even baptized, who think to justify this betrayal of theirs, practicing anti-Semitism of a completely traditional stamp. In other words, in such a case, if a person behaved in a certain way, it was because he had no choice because of all the iniquities the Jews had committed and were continuing to commit. Regarding these latter cases, there are some interesting examples, but it's better not to spend too much time on them; they are moral and intellectual drifters who arouse repugnance and pity at the same time because they will never find peace in their continual, irrational wavering between the most varied factions and positions. But concerning the other two types of anti-Semitism—one from the non-Jewish world and one introduced into the Jewish world by those who profess to be friends of the Jews—it may be worthwhile to bring forward two examples from among the many that might be suitable.

Let's begin with the second type, so as to follow the chronological sequence of the actions. Moshè often recalled the words that Theodor Herzl had written in his book *The Jewish State*, where he said, "And thus, paying close attention, one discovers that a great many ostensible philo-Semites are simply anti-Semites of Jewish origin who disguise themselves as benefactors."

Herzl's words came to mind when Moshè set about to prepare one of his speeches for a national meeting, at which he had been invited to address the theme "Old and New Aspects of Anti-Semitism: How to Recognize Them and How to Respond to Them." Moshè kept Herzl's idea in mind, of course, as a point of departure for an aspect of the problem that he wanted to examine, according it, however, the contemporary significance that was needed.

In his speech, Moshè observed among other things that regarding anti-Semitism, this ever delicate and complex subject, one must pay close attention and always be ready to speak up not only against the official anti-Semites but also against certain self-styled philo-Semites who manifest their friendship not on the natural basis of human relationships, true reciprocal esteem, affection, and the mutual need to work together to improve everyone, but on a vague current of philo-Semitism. Moshè added that although there is joy and comfort in having, among non-Jews, examples of real friends, nevertheless there are also painful examples of philo-Semites who are such in appearance only. It is an unhappy reality that should be kept in mind. Thus one should not assume that the non-Jewish antifascist is also automatically philo-Semitic, because sometimes it turns out that he defends the rights of Jews only with particular interests in mind—either personal or of the party to which he belongs.

These reflections—which are not at all far-fetched because they are corroborated, so to speak, by many examples—referred back precisely to Herzl's words, although certainly understood in a modern and relevant key, as has already been pointed out. All right, then, *what of it?* one might ask. Well, it was exactly these statements that brought about pandemonium throughout the Community in which this conference was held. It seemed, who knows why, that everyone, in one way or another, had been terribly and totally offended, from the simplest Jew or non-Jewish friend to the highest religious and cultural circles of the great Community where the conference took place. Moshè was greatly pained by these attitudes, which lasted for a long time and which attributed intentions to him he had never had. It was all the more distressing because it was absolutely not true that he had meant to refer directly to someone in the room—and this was something of which he was particularly and harshly accused. Who on earth had lit that blaze of slander and then had also fed it? Moshè had many suspicions, but he never had clear and absolute proof. What is certain is that he was placed in *chérem* (excommunication), so to speak, for a certain time, even by the one who solemnly tried to reassure Moshè that he wasn't with the others, that he was as close to Moshè as ever, and that, holding the position he held, he had done his best to fix everything. That was something that—as always, of course—he never did. That was one of the few times—like when a majority gangs up against a minority—in which different religious and cultural factions, both inside and outside Judaism, happily found themselves in accord, pleased perhaps by an event that offered them the possibility of emphasizing that all humans are essentially brothers. And would that it were so. The fact is that all the statements Moshè made, orally and in writing, had no effect, and this strange "influenza" lasted a long time, finally ending like so many things in community circles end, evaporating like mist in the sun, no one remembering even one detail of what had transpired.

Regarding the second type, there was a no-less-interesting experience that Moshè suddenly found himself undergoing a few months before his aliyah [immigration to Israel]. Being a member of a journalistic organization for religious inquiry, he participated with two non-Jewish friends and colleagues in a meeting on the theme of anti-Semitism. Among the numerous public attendees, there were other journalists, and among them were people who were completely unknown to Moshè. The topics dealt with were the usual ones, with some necessary connections made to the events of the day, among which was the reprinting of the notorious *Protocols*.[1]

A priest turned to Moshè: "You spoke about these 'Protocols.' In the end, I don't think they're much either. Nevertheless, I do think that the Jews have always had *plans*, and they still do."

---

1   *The Protocols of the Elders of Zion* was an anti-Semitic forgery from tsarist Russia that claimed to reveal a secret Jewish plan to conquer the world, then (the early 1900s) in its final stages. *The Protocols* was first published in Russian in 1903 and has since been reprinted many times in many languages worldwide. It is still popular in anti-Semitic and anti-Israel propaganda even today, although it has been shown to be completely false.

Moshè answered, "What you say is also not much in terms of originality, because it goes back to the case in point, which is the anti-Semitism that priests like you are always quick to unite with religious fervor."

A few days later, the December 17, 1978, issue of *Izvestia* published the following:

> In Italy, the Jews as a religious minority do not enjoy the fundamental rights of man, declared the head [!] of the Jewish religious community. Anti-Semitism in Italy, he added, keeps growing. In fact, fascist hooligans recently desecrated the Rome synagogue and the memorial of the Ardeatine Caves, where during the war, the Nazis shot Jews en masse. The Jews, and the direct descendants of those who eradicated the Jews during the war today protest new massacres of the Jews. The neo-fascists have circulated leaflets and inflammatory writings on the walls of houses. In the windows of the bookstores it is not unusual to see books that promote the crimes of the fascists and Nazis, with clearly anti-Semitic sympathies. The Jews in Italy are subjected to humiliation and persecution for religious reasons too. In spite of the Vatican's declarations on the equality of the Churches, writes the newspaper *Il Giorno*, religious sects, whose activities are based on an unrestrained anti-Semitism, have arisen in a succession of Italian cities.

Even though this report was rather peculiar, clearly written by some "special correspondent" who was incognito at the journalists' meeting, it should not have caused any amazement. It is actually well known, *urbi et orbi*, and for many years now (that is, since the Soviet regime has existed), that that type of government bases itself on lies and false fabrications—even at a scientific level—along with other characteristics that in truth are hardly democratic. This account, therefore, should have simply been archived together with many others of the same type, without even a line of commentary . . . but things hardly turned out that way!

Moshè, in fact, already busy with the activities relative to his aliyah, received a phone call from his former office, in which it was communicated to him that he had been urgently summoned to a discussion at the Ministry of the Interior. Surprised, Moshè asked to know the reason for such a summons, but he was told it concerned a topic too confidential to be dealt with by telephone. Shortly after the phone call the conversation was taken up again at Moshè's home, where the director of the Jewish Community office had kindly arrived with dispatch. At first the discussion started off rather vaguely—for example, had Moshè recently written something about Russia, something on the dissenters? "I've never done anything like that," Moshè declared, without any hesitation. Then the cat came out of the bag: *Izvestia* had printed, with a certain prominence, that Moshè had granted an interview with Tass in which it was stated that Jews in Italy did not enjoy civil rights, because of the government. Following this news, the Italian ambassador in Moscow had hastened to send a telegram to no less than the head of the Italian government to inform him immediately and properly regarding these grave allegations. The allegations also worried the head of state, and he turned to the relevant ministry to make inquiries about the case. That led to the summons for a conversation at the ministerial level *ad audiendum* ["for a hearing"] in a certain dedicated office of the Minister of the Interior.

To Moshè it seemed like he was dreaming. He understood right away that the misinterpretation—if it could be called that—emerged following his report on anti-Semitism at that meeting of the journalists, but he also immediately asked himself what kind of Italian ambassador was there in Moscow who had hastened to provoke such a tempest in a teapot. Being in Moscow and, in addition, being a diplomat, wasn't he able to understand straightaway that he was dealing with the umpteenth falsification, of which the Soviets were the unsurpassable masters? What's more, should he really have disturbed the head of the Italian government, who was occupied with much more serious matters? Couldn't he have immediately and officially denied this false news item, without needing to check it? Or did he, too, fear that there was something true in all this business and that he was unaware of it? Mysteries of diplomacy.

Moshè declared that if he was being accused of something specific, it should be done in writing, and then he would respond. He added that he was available and quite willing to speak with the head of the government himself, and he concluded, "Let's suppose, purely for the sake of argument, that I said everything that I'm accused of saying. What is the crime? A crime of opinion?" His interlocutor, seeming to find himself somewhat ill at ease facing these objections, was uncertain about what to say, but in the end he thought he had found a good solution that would allow him to fulfill the task he had received directly from the ministry. He observed that, in continuing to deal with an extremely confidential matter (and why extremely?), the best thing was actually to set up an appointment and discuss the matter with someone with the expertise to judge how things stood. He was convinced, he said, that everything would work out for the best, satisfactory to everyone. He ended, saying, "If you think about it, it's just a courtesy visit, which we can't forgo." So be it.

It was already December 31, and the discussion was set for the following January 2. One could readily see that there was no time to lose regarding a question of such importance.

Moshè, along with the person who had brought that fine news to his home, was immediately introduced to the director of the department. The director greeted him, thanking him for his promptness in responding to his invitation regarding a subject that was so important and "current." Straightaway Moshè reminded him that when dealing with subjects that are considered to be very important, good practice required that one put in writing what one was asking. Moshè again added that he would be willing to meet with the head of the government. Solicitous, the director immediately phoned the secretary of the head of the government and let him know the requests of his guest. After some "yes, yes, ok, thank you," he ended the call and said that a letter would be sent to Moshè, and then we would see. (The letter never arrived.) In the meantime, seeing as they were meeting, why not talk a little about this matter? And he smiled, inviting them to talk. For Moshè, doubts that the phone call to the secretary of the head of the government had actually been made arose instantly, but now there was nothing to do—he had to play the game. The person who accompanied him, respectfully asking permission to speak, stated that he regarded it his duty to clarify straightaway that everything the professor there present does is at always done in his own name (which meant, in other words, that the official Jewish organizations, in any event, were entirely irrelevant). Moshè once again found himself alone, but he was not surprised by what was happening in that rigid ministerial office. His long experience in the Jewish sphere had shown him far greater surprises. In any case, with that preliminary and official declaration it was as though that fellow had said, "We Israelites are good Italians, and we have nothing to object to regarding the way the government treats us, and therefore we don't have anything to do with this affair at all."

Moshè ignored this clarification. He would express his thoughts regarding it privately and frankly shortly after leaving the ministry. In the meantime, he began to expose the facts as they really were. He started by saying, quite candidly, that the first useful thing to do would be to recall the Italian ambassador, because from this rather tiny incident it seemed apparent that he wasn't fit to hold the position he occupied. He should have understood immediately that it wasn't a matter of anything other than lies (common lies, as usual) and not have bothered the head of the government. The director looked at him silently, without any expression on his face, and with a very slight movement of his hand signaled him to continue. Partly to reawaken the director a bit from his visible half-drowsiness and knowing that certain things in certain circles always have their effect, Moshè rattled off his various academic titles, his activities as a professor in university institutes, and his activities as a writer and journalist, with lots of details. One might say he presented his identity papers, which were quite useful on that occasion. And in fact, the illustrious director seemed to awaken from his apparent torpor, and from the expression on his face, now quite lively, it seemed clear that he was quite honored to have a conversation with such a personage. Moshè's discourse continued, with a great deal of decorum; he weighed his words and tone of voice because he knew—also from experience—that he who knows how to present his arguments well in police offices always creates a certain impression. As he was more convinced than ever that all the misunderstanding arose following his speech on anti-Semitism that was given at that meeting of the journalists, he informed his interlocutor in detail about everything he had said. Of course he'd spoken about anti-Semitism in Italy, which, unfortunately, still persisted at various levels, but, he also added, it had never occurred to him even for a moment to say anything about the Italian government as such, because it was quite well known to everyone how the government not only had nothing to do with such behavior but also how it had frequently interceded in defense of the Jewish Communities. He also emphasized to what extent anti-Semitism occurred in other countries, including Russia, where persecution in various forms against the Jews had not changed substantially from the way it was at the time of the tsar.

At this point the director's face lit up in a very personal way. He now smiled openly, he appeared to let go a great sigh of relief—and in all this maybe he was even sincere—and making a slight wave with his hand, he said, "Please excuse me, dear professor, if I allow myself to interrupt you. But tell me: then you're not a communist?"

"Me?" This time it was Moshè who was stunned. "Me, a communist? For heaven's sake, I've never been one. If you have the desire and the time, read some of my writing on these topics that we've just spoken about, and you'll readily see that I've always defended my people, that is, the Jews, openly, against anyone, and therefore also against the monstrosities of the Soviet dictatorship."

"All this," the director said immediately, revealing signs of sudden impatience, "all this gives me a great deal of pleasure. Let's break off this extremely interesting conversation of ours for just a few moments. Excuse me, but I want to get in contact with the president of the council right away." And Moshè believed that this time he really did it! "Hello? Hello, Dr.——of the Ministry of the Interior speaking. It's about an urgent matter. I would like to speak with His Excellency the Head of the Government immediately . . . How's that? He's busy in a meeting? Too bad . . . Well, patience, but at least let me speak with one of his secretaries—it's really an urgent matter . . ." A few seconds later: "Hello, ah, it's you, good. Listen, I have the honor of having here with me the professor— you know, the one who *Izvestia* recently spoke about. I strongly request that you reassure the head of the government that that news is devoid of any foundation, that what was printed in the newspaper is false, and that the professor who is present here has never been, and I'm completely certain of it"—and he stressed this word emphatically—"a communist."

Moshè left that office, deferentially accompanied to the elevator by the director himself, while the guards on duty in the long corridor were surprised by the unusual scene.

Yet the fact remains that a few days later this message from the Ministry of Internal Affairs arrived at Moshè's ex-office: "If the distinguished professor performs any other activities that might in any way interest us, we would be grateful if you would keep us informed."

A FAITHFUL ORDERLY

Almost ten years had passed since Moshè had the opportunity to see the letter of Priori Giusto, which is how it was signed.[1] In fact, the letter bore the date January 20, 1975. Thus it can't be ruled out that in the meantime, Priori may have once again rejoined his captain, Carlo Alberto Viterbo, of blessed memory, this time definitively.[2]

The reason that this text, edited here and there to facilitate reading, is being brought to light here is because of its elementary simplicity and hesitant writing, which quite often shows no awareness of grammar and spelling. It is a miniature record that, in a succinct and at the same time vivid way, describes a world rich in human feelings that are unpretentiously alive and expressive. That spare style is like a painting in which the painter, with a few basic strokes, reveals the most striking points of view. In a fascinating manner, Priori throws light on some aspects of World War I, on daily life in a small town like Rosignano

---

1   In other words it was signed surname first, formally, as in a roll call.

2   The phrase "of blessed memory" is actually indicated in Segre's text with the letters "z.l.," a traditional acronym for the Hebrew *zikhrono livrakha*, conventionally translated as "of blessed memory" or "may his memory be a blessing." Regarding Carlo Alberto Viterbo, Elizabeth Schachter writes, "Carlo Alberto Viterbo (1889–1974) made wide-ranging contributions over many years to the development and dissemination of Jewish heritage in Italy. . . . He was one of the leading figures of the 'Jewish Renaissance' based in Florence in the decades before the First World War; he was president of the Italian Zionist Federation in the 1930s; he was at the centre of the bitter divisions between fascist and anti-fascist Jews prior to the Racial Laws. In the period after the Second World War, he was one of the key players to reconstitute Jewish life in Italy, and editor, from 1944 to 1974, of *Israel*, the most influential Jewish journal of its time" (Elizabeth Schachter, "Carlo Alberto Viterbo: A Neglected Figure of Italian Judaism," *The Italianist* 33(3) (2013), 505–21, https://www.tandfonline.com/doi/full/10.1179/0261434013Z.00000000057 [accessed August 30, 2019]). His name is interesting too, because "Carlo Alberto" was the name of the king of Piedmont who granted Jews citizenship in 1848. (See Introduction.) It was typical for Jews in the post-ghetto era to name their children for members of the Italian royal family.

Marittimo (for example, his friendship with the pharmacist, a subscriber to the weekly *Israel*), and on the moving encounter between the orderly Priori Giusto and the captain, Carlo Alberto Viterbo, after some fifty-nine years. During those years no news had passed between the two of them. And then there was Priori's care in "asking to be remembered in memory of my captain." Here is a truly rare example of faithful friendship of a soldier for his captain, with whom he had shared the grave risks of World War I.

Here is the text:

> I, the undersigned Priori Giusto, of Rosignano Marittimo, Via Gramsci, number 21, Livorno.
>
> The 12th of September 1912 I enlisted in the 14th Light Cavalry Regiment at Lucca.
>
> The month of June 1915 (before leaving for the Front) I was selected as Orderly for Lieutenant Carlo Alberto Viterbo, born in Florence, Via Principe Amedeo 12.
>
> He sent me from Lucca to Florence to say goodbye to my family because we had to leave for the Front.
>
> We left from Lucca with two horses, his was named Torino, mine Silvano. On the 17th day we arrived at Tofane, which is also called the 5 Towers.
>
> After a long time we returned home.
>
> And for 59 years I didn't have any more news of you. It so happened that at Rosignano Marittimo our pharmacist had Your Newspaper. I looked at it by chance.
>
> And I saw that it was written that the lawyer Viterbo was Editor of Your Newspaper.
>
> Then I asked the pharmacist for the Newspaper, because he is one of Your Subscribers. I immediately wrote to Rome and Viterbo kindly responded to me, with a long letter that made me cry, partly because I felt grateful and affectionate toward (him).
>
> I responded to him that it would be a great pleasure to see him again. Then he wrote me again that the 12th of August 1974 he would go to the farm at Colle Val d'Elsa.
>
> That is how the day came that he invited me to his farm.
>
> I was so happy to see him again and to meet his entire family. I spent a truly unforgettable day, after 59 years.

His death has greatly saddened me, and I, too, want to contribute, sending you this small sum of 1,000 lire in order to be remembered in memory of my Captain, Carlo Alberto Viterbo.

My respects, Cavaliere of Vittorio Veneto

Priori Giusto

January 20, 1975

I am sending the 1,000 lire by money order, the 20th of January.

LA RASSEGNA MENSILE DI ISRAEL

In 1975, upon assuming the editorship of the *Rassegna*, Moshè wrote, among other things, the following:

> What can the *Rassegna* offer its readers? It has always offered culture. We certainly are not unaware of the objective difficulties of such an enterprise since we know that culture in its most authentic sense is an *internal* creation, never something that comes from the outside. In the Diaspora we are unable to have an alive, genuinely Jewish culture. That can happen and does happen only in its natural setting, in Eretz Yisrael. Culture actually wells up from those who speak, write, and live in the language of their people.
>
> Sokolow once spoke of Jewish culture as a "national industry," adding that it is the "quintessence of the spirit of our people. . . . It is our Torah."[1]
>
> Here, our Jewish culture cannot be anything other than secondhand. We often continue to believe that we can live off the revenue from capital, from the fruit of the labor and the learning of the preceding generations, while in reality what remains of this patrimony is being carelessly squandered, and by now is reduced to hardly anything. It is forgotten and badly managed, abandoned instead to be extinguished by a culture that is not specifically ours because it is Italian, Christian, and frequently anti-Semitic. . . . Speaking of which, here is another citation from Sokolow:

---

1   Nahum Sokolow (1859–1936) was a leading Zionist, journalist, and author. Among other roles, he served as president of the World Zionist Organization.

"Once," he writes, "it could not even be imagined that an ignorant Jew could be elected president of a Community. The wealthy who had no Jewish learning but felt the desire to have some honorable public charge supported yeshiva teachers and students."

. . . The *Rassegna* will also reach out to those Jews who, forgetful of their duties and their rights and immersed in a culture that has nothing Jewish about it, distance themselves from our Community, or, still worse, seek to pass off as Jewish, ideas that really have nothing to do with Judaism and that, on the contrary are often the most absolute negation of every Jewish ideology. We will not fail, therefore, to turn to those who are still under the illusion that through religious or political assimilation they will find the perfect solution to their problems, not realizing how sad and humiliating it is to seek acceptance in certain circles, paying as a price the renunciation of all those values that constitute the patrimony of Jewish ideas and Jewish life. True freedom consists in giving everyone the opportunity to live within the ambit of his own cultural and religious world, with equal rights and obligations for everyone. . . .

I am comforted in this enterprise by the example of everyone who in every part of the world works and struggles for the good cause of the Jewish people and by our brothers in Israel, who, in the face of enormous difficulties, continue with great courage and indomitable faith to defend and make their and our survival more secure. We will be at their side without hesitation, without second thoughts, without compromises, as history and our Jewish conscience as free people compel us.

From these brief quotations, it is quite clear how concerned Moshè was to make certain that the *Rassegna* would continue the approach toward Jewish culture and Zionism that had been the basic cornerstones of the teaching of those who had come before, especially Dante Lattes. For all intents and purposes, however, the general Jewish cultural situation had greatly worsened after 1945—from the time when Jews, having formally returned to freedom in Italy, had taken advantage of this situation to liberate themselves to the greatest possible extent from their responsibilities as conscientious Jews facing the non-Jewish world. The harsh experiences of the past, once again, were for naught. In the name of various political movements and the pseudo-cultural currents tied to them, which were often anti-Semitic, many Jews were ready to renounce not only all the traditions of Jewish life but also those Zionist ideals that for Israel were like the Italian irredentist ideals of many decades earlier. Hence Moshè had numerous concerns at the moment in which he assumed the editorship of the journal, which, for its honesty, its high level of learning, and its open defense of the Jews and now the State of Israel, was well known and esteemed even in the non-Jewish world, in Italy and abroad.

Moshè worked in accordance with these policies, often finding himself isolated in his work because more than a few of his coreligionists saw this journal as a tool that was quite dangerous for Italians of the Mosaic faith. Then there were those who, more or less openly, showed a certain antipathy toward this new editor who, after a hiatus of ten years following the death of Lattes, now returned faithfully to the approach of Dante Lattes. (During those ten years, under the guidance of the distinguished teacher Y. Colombo, the *Rassegna* had taken a more moderate line, especially regarding Zionism, and culturally speaking, had assumed a more philosophical voice.)[2] The regular feature "Problems and Polemics," which had been created by Lattes but had remained silent for those ten years, returned, appearing in the *Rassegna* every month and not particularly appreciated by many people, rabbis and presidents of Communities included. And, in fact, in the month of March, when Moshè left the *Rassegna* to move to Jerusalem, that column also disappeared from the pages of the journal, together with many other subjects traditionally accepted among those pages.

In his farewell to the journal's readers, Moshè once again reminded them of the goals for which the *Rassegna* had arisen and endured, hoping that these guidelines would be maintained in the future, too. His article concluded like this:

> Leaving the editorship of the *Rassegna*, I thought that, besides it being proper, it would also be useful to sketch in broad strokes some of the fundamental features that have justified the journal's reason for existence since its birth and represent the basis upon which it can continue to exist, following an authentic cultural tradition that has amply demonstrated itself to be still valuable and very relevant. This uninterrupted continuity and loyalty in standing up for and diffusing the Jewish idea has created a situation in which the *Rassegna* occupies a reputable position among Jewish publications—not only in Italy and not only in the Jewish world. Special credit for this important outcome is due, primarily, to Dante Lattes, the most significant personality of Italian Judaism in the twentieth century.

---

2   Yoseph Colombo (1897–1975) was an Italian educator.

Continuing this course, it will be possible not only to again honor the maestro with actions, and not just words, but at the same time to demonstrate the continuity of a teaching that has always given dignity to Jewish ideas in their true substance. I deeply hope that whoever carries on this work feels all the great responsibility that has been entrusted to him by this past.

Now, although he had left the editorship of the *Rassegna*, Moshè's worries certainly had not diminished, not even after the farewell article in which he had also clearly expressed his most warranted fears regarding the fate of the journal. And it was above all for these reasons that he wanted yet one more time to draw the attention of those leaders in charge of the fate of Italian Judaism to the great responsibility that they had undertaken in deciding who would be entrusted with the future fate of the *Rassegna*. Thus he decided, after more than a few doubts concerning the consequences, to write the following letter to the office of the president of the organization that represented the Jewish Communities:

I am writing following our conversation regarding the *Rassegna Mensile di Israel* to draw your kind attention to this journal, taking into account the rapidly approaching decisions that must be taken in order to assure the continuity and the distinguishing features that have given it a distinct, unmistakable presence from its beginnings until today.

The *Rassegna* was born October 15, 1925, through the initiative of Dante Lattes and Alfonso Pacifici, as a monthly supplement to the weekly *Israel*. The publications were forcibly suspended in 1938, but their normal rhythm was taken up again in 1948, when Lattes was director of the department of the Union of Italian Jewish Communities. Except for the period up to 1938, the *Rassegna* was under the authority of the Union, so that from 1948 on the Union provided for the attendant expenses, although with contributions first from the Claims Conference and then from the Memorial Foundation, contributions that gradually decreased. Regarding this subject, I am limiting myself to furnishing these few facts, since it is not my job, nor do I have the precise data with which to offer greater details about the assets of the *Rassegna* itself.

Concerning the distinguishing features of the *Rassegna*, I think it useful and interesting to re-read, at least in part, what was written, in chronological order, first by Attilio Milano in 1938 in the volume of the *Rassegna* dedicated to Lattes, *Writings in Honor of Dante Lattes*[3] (pp. 124–25) and then by Lattes himself in 1965, "For the 30th birthday of the *Rassegna*"[4] (p. 2 and following).

Attilio Milano wrote:

The agenda of this journal is vast and rigorous: within the boundaries of the "fundamental principles of the Jewish idea," its goal has been "to welcome all voices that can illuminate the thought and history of Israel and that intend to offer a contribution to the awareness of Israel's vicissitudes and its spiritual expressions." Within the compass of these noble programmatic guidelines, numerous studies on the Bible and the philosophical orientations of individual Jews, on the history of the Jews of Italy and other countries (foremost Palestine), on literature, art, and economics, have been perceptively developed in the journal. These studies are intertwined in a varied and agreeable harmony, in twelve large volumes with which, today, one can properly assess the value, the completeness, and the unity of the entire publication. . . . The thought and life of Israel are treated with strict scientific scrupulousness by gifted scholars. As a rule, these scholars are served by pens that seek, through a lively style, to make their writings broadly accessible, in order to reach more easily every place where the desire to know Hebrew in more than a dilettantish fashion exists.

Dante Lattes wrote:

A journal that is serious and open, in the vast world of the twentieth century in Italy, was and is a somewhat arduous undertaking. . . . In the *Rassegna* we have sought to present Judaism not only as a religious institution and a religion but also as a nation in all its forms, in all its views, ideals, struggling hopes, and all its duties and needs. For us Zionism has been a movement intended to reconstruct the nation of Israel as authentically

---

3   "Un secolo di stampa periodica ebraica in Italia," in *Scritti in onore di Dante Lattes*, special issue of *Rassegna Mensile di Israel* 12(2) (1938): 96–136.

4   "Per il 30° compleanno della *Rassegna*," *Rassegna Mensile di Israel* 31(10–11) (1965): 480–91.

and completely as possible, to carry on, and to champion its life and its history freely and in the homeland where Israel had lived at its origin and where it had created, upheld, and taught its ideals—where it had produced its prophets and its apostles, since the apostles of Christianity were also Jews. For Italian Jews and rabbis, Zionism was an . . . altruistic movement—carried out, that is, for their poor, unfree coreligionists of Eastern Europe. For us, instead, it has always been, since its beginnings, a movement of redemption and national revival. . . .

It is definitely not easy to overcome the obstacles and the difficulties in which the small, scattered, and uneducated population of the peninsula finds itself. Knowledge of the long and painful history of the Jews is relevant to all classes of the Jewish population. . . . What are the Communities doing for awareness and support of the ideology and history of Israel? What are the rabbis doing about the dissemination of Jewish ideas, of which they are the masters and the apostles? . . . I believe that it is their duty to study the means that are capable of spreading knowledge of Judaism not only among our own coreligionists but also among our fellow citizens of other religions. . . . Oftentimes I have sought to correct the false ideas, hostile opinions, and superstitions of the learned, of journalists, of philosophers, and of Catholic jurists regarding Judaism, as well as the straying of Jewish minds regarding what should have been their religion and their ideals, from Luigi Luzzatti to Benedetto Croce, and from Quasimodo to Ginzburg. . . .

Now, in a short while, I must leave this battlefield, this landscape of ancient and new groves to others (to whom?) to care for and cultivate, with love and with passion. However, the Jewish Communities, that is the Jews of Italy, must care for the *Rassegna*'s life, growth, and success as their own inheritance, as an exploit, and as a dear and precious possession. And they must strive so that the results of generations of Jewish thought will not be valued only as history, but so that they will arouse the esteem of Jews as well as their countrymen of other faiths and awaken the interest and the sympathy of others. . . . But the journal cannot do that by itself, nor live on manna that falls from heaven. The journal requires the loving, serious knowledge of

Jewish thought from Abraham up to his modern successors, the thinkers and writers of the twentieth century. Now I ask: Are there not men in Italy with a capacity for the support and thought of Israel, from the Bible to the rabbis, philosophers, thinkers, poets, and today's historians, and are there tools for their undertaking? Judaism is a living body, not a dead inheritance. . . .

I believe that the thirty years of the *Rassegna*, that is, the thirty volumes that constitute the results of its existence—with its hundreds of articles and its thousands of pages—are worthy of being appreciated and reread by the children of the new generation. . . . It is an inheritance fit not only to be preserved but also to be cultivated and appreciated by posterity, even though a present-day rabbi was induced to speak badly of it to please one of his Christian friends. In the pages of the journal one finds a little of everything: history and philosophy, ethics and poetry, politics and religion, theology and apologetics, literature and art, ancient and modern life, war and peace, dreams and afflictions, disappointments and fulfillment, the past and the future. What is principally reflected in the pages of the *Rassegna* is a remarkable era, perhaps unique in its events: It is the era of the Jewish rebirth after 2,000 years of exile, slavery, persecution, struggle, and dreams. . . . We who are the modest makers of these pages, or better, their compilers, humbly entrust them to our descendants, with the awareness of leaving them an inheritance that we did not construct or create but only gathered with our modest strength, with our honest efforts, and with the dispassionate collaboration of our friends.

From 1965, after the death of Lattes, to 1975, the editorship of the *Rassegna* passed to Yoseph Colombo, who in December of that same year, in a short polemical article, "The Duty to Continue" (p. 539 and following), wrote of

[the duty to continue] to work for the goals that were dear to him, continuing the work [of Lattes] in this journal, to which he gave the best of his labor as a writer and journalist every month for thirty years. . . . From his writings and from those of his teacher, Elia Benamozegh, and from their articles, we

regularly draw inspiration in rethinking the historical, ideological, and current problems of Judaism, problems to which
the *Rassegna* plans to continue giving its attention. We intend,
following what we know to have always been the desire of our
teacher, to make the journal an organ that can beneficially enter
every Jewish home in Italy, bringing the voice of that which is
usually called culture, which in our case is the voice of tradition,
of history, of the ideals of Judaism. . . . The *Rassegna* wishes to
continue to be a journal of high culture that publishes serious,
original contributions by competent specialists, just as it always
has been and as it is regarded by other circles of the Italian intel-
ligentsia as well.

To continue with Moshè's letter:

The opinions cited up to this point regarding the *Rassegna* emphasize the
cultural approach very clearly, partly because of the authority of those
who expressed them. It was the cultural approach for which the journal had emerged, struggled (even inside the Italian Jewish world itself),
and continued to exist, reaching the forty-fourth volume in 1979. The
Rassegna is a true and unique encyclopedia in the Italian language, regularly
consulted by university students.

Assuming the editorship of the *Rassegna* in 1975, as disciple, friend,
and direct assistant of Dante Lattes for many years, I sought not only to
maintain this approach, which had been followed until then, as well as I
could, but to restore to the journal that balance of variety, information,
and stimulus that Lattes had accomplished in a special way in peerless fashion. For me, too, it was a very demanding task. I didn't have any help in my
office even for the secondary but no less important jobs, for the manage-
ment of the *Rassegna*, and notably, for deciding the subject matter—both
in personal essays and when choosing from among the submitted or solic-
ited submissions, which in reality were always modest in number. As had
already happened with Lattes, I often ran out of any kind of contribution
from those who, given their background, there was reason to believe were
in a position, at least formally, to contribute. Instead, there was no lack
of critics, usually unctuous, because it is easy to understand that generally
speaking, people are not well disposed to hear words that touch on their
assimilation or their lack of Jewish literacy. Analogous observations could

have been made when themes regarding anti-Semitism were broached, this being a problem that frequently irritated not only non-Jews but quite often our coreligionists themselves, and in a pronounced manner. Similar phenomena occurred when questions of a political character were brought up. But even in these cases, I wasn't surprised. Having been at the breach for more than forty years, I bore in mind the ideological subtleties, and hence hues, that may vary yet remain substantially the same and therefore are profoundly corrupting to the vitality of authentic Judaism. Thus, serenely and stubbornly I continued down the path that Maestro Lattes had shown me, not taking any notice either of mafia-style silences (which were quite eloquent) or threats (which were not lacking). For my part, I was always concerned to provide authentic results accessible to everyone to the extent it was possible, yet still in keeping with the traditional dignity of the *Rassegna*. I did my work without regularly tackling scholarly arguments, even at the cost of causing some displeasure for the priests of abstract scholarship. The support and dissemination of Jewish ideas in their authenticity was carried out in such a way as to be able to reach an ever wider world, both Jewish and non-Jewish. This was done without ever indulging in the illiterate fantasies of an ever more rampant loss of culture, which is eroding even that small bit of homegrown Judaism that has remained.

The Zionist orientation of the *Rassegna* was a fundamental linchpin of Lattes's teaching from which I never strayed, mainly because it constituted and still constitutes a historical foundation and is therefore natural for a true Jewish culture. That is why Lattes, on many occasions, wrote that Zionism, even before being a return to Zion, is a return to Judaism. Such themes were too difficult for those coreligionists who were hasty and uninterested readers, mainly because once again they were busy seeking the exoticism of other cultures and other politics. In the article by Lattes quoted above, he also said, "In my rather long journalistic career, I continued to expose the deficiencies, the errors, and the negligence of those responsible for the moral and religious life of the Jews of Italy, but without any results. Mine has been a 'voice crying in the wilderness,'[5] in accordance with the phrase of the prophet Isaiah, to which neither the rabbis, nor the teachers, nor the heads of the Communities paid any attention." Because this indifference and lack of comprehension continues at various

---

5   Given in the text in Latin: "Vox clamantis in deserto" (Isaiah 40:3).

levels, it only reconfirms that the voice of the *Rassegna*, even if it is unique, is still extremely useful and necessary.

In a situation like this, it is my duty to call your kind attention and that of all the Union council members, to the dangers, which are easily foreseeable, should the *Rassegna* fall into inexperienced hands or those of someone who would want to change radically the approach that it has followed to this point. Everyone has to assume their proper responsibilities. In case such a thing should happen, it would be necessary for the *Rassegna* as such to cease publication and another be published with a different name in such a way so as not to create a deplorable muddle and misunderstanding. And this is worth saying, especially out of that respect that everyone ought to have, now and always, for Dante Lattes, the most important figure of the Italian Jewish world in the twentieth century.

Regarding myself more narrowly, you know that . . . I will make aliyah in April.

As I have already had occasion to tell you, I am always available, and not, of course, for personal gain (which I think I've fully demonstrated over the course of these four years) but because of the ideological and emotional bonds that tie me to Lattes and to his teaching.

The actual possibilities for my availability could be:

1. I would be able to continue the editorship of the *Rassegna* from Israel, maintaining contact in Rome with a trustworthy person. Such a solution is worth studying in its practical and feasible details.
2. Double editorship and two editorial staffs, one Israeli and one Italian. Keep in mind that in Israel I would be able to obtain more extensive assistance and it would be at a high level.

These two solutions raise technical problems regarding work and publication schedules and financial restructuring.

Having said that, it is clear that the Union can also decide not to avail itself of my assistance and can make all the decisions it considers to be best, taking into account, I strongly hope, all the considerations that I mentioned. If this is the case, I ask only that it might be possible, during the period that still remains of my residence in Italy, to be able to take part in a meeting devoted to this subject, since I believe my experience regarding this issue might, in any case, be useful on this occasion, too. . . .

Please excuse me for the long letter and accept my warm regards.

This letter bore the date of January 3, 1979. Moshè never received any response, either written or oral. It almost seemed as though this letter, which was so extensive and serious concerning a responsible, that is, Jewish, future of the *Rassegna*, either never reached its destination or had been sent on to the archives, the leaders of the organization itself not having deemed it worthy of their attention.

A few years went by, and one day a letter reached Moshè from Oxford, where an unknown reader of the *Rassegna*, a professor at that university and not a Jew, asked with open disappointment and clear bitterness why it was that the *Rassegna* no longer came out regularly as in the past and why it had inexplicably changed its policies. (Moshè never succeeded in discovering how the professor was able to find his address in Jerusalem.) In the detailed response that he gave that unusual person—not Italian, not Jewish, who nevertheless showed a definite interest in the *Rassegna*—Moshè told a little of the history of the *Rassegna* itself and informed the courteous correspondent about the efforts that had been made, in vain, to maintain the journal's traditional approach. Concluding his letter, Moshè wrote, "As I told you, this *Rassegna* was born October 15, 1925. For the history of the Jewish press in Italy, it can be stated that the *Rassegna* of Dante Lattes ceased publication March 31, 1979."

JACOB'S LADDER

The moment for great decisions had arrived for Moshè too. Since the time he was a new student at the University of Rome and had begun to take part in Jewish public life, many years had passed. Back then he had made a choice, difficult and extremely demanding, that most of the time forced him to face big problems and a sea of troubles, whether he turned to the inside of the Jewish world itself or sought connections with the outside world. To honor the truth, however, it should be added that more than once, on his own initiative, he had gone looking for trouble, even when life appeared to be passing by relatively serenely amid his coreligionists' sugar-coated assimilation and a formal absence of anti-Semitism. Rather obstinate in his ideas, he was almost always dissatisfied with what was happening around him in the Jewish world and in society in general. He had been educated since he was very young in a serious method of Jewish studies, and he continued this commitment unaltered. But, at the same time, he had been taught to live what he was learning. Judaism was not a simple religion that was mainly concerned with the salvation of souls in the world to come, fleeing life and seeking only to establish direct contact between heaven and earth. Rather, it was a discipline that guided one to move from the abstract to the concrete, to realize day by day in everyday life how much was to be learned from the traditional texts. He had learned that the observance of the mitzvahs (commandments) was not an end in itself but a precious means for learning to live in a sound way. One also found the most worthy, unerring way to link the world to heaven through the daily impact on life, public and private life, of living like this, in a sound way. Thus Jewish life, to be authentic, had to be harmonious in every one of its manifestations, large or small, and not fragmentary or qualified by easy compromises. This concept was also a not insignificant aspect of that monotheistic idea that had been the greatest and the definitive revolution in the field of ethics. Moshè had always had doubts and qualms, and he always asked himself to what extent he had acted justly according to these principles and to what extent he had erred in judgment. Hence Zionism, for him, had not been a free, incidental choice, as it might be for someone who joins a party or seeks to become part of a given political movement. Zionism was simply an integral part of his Jewish life, a modern solution for an ancient biblical plan.

When the news spread that Moshè had decided to move to Israel and that, without hesitating, he was leaving posts that were so diverse and important, the reactions were varied, which in any case was predictable. But sometimes they were also strange and not without a certain humor. Someone asked how it could be that a person who had so many responsibilities and a normal and secure life could renounce everything to move himself and his family to a country that was certainly dear to the religious tradition but rather troubled and insecure, thus exposing himself to chance. Others asked, more or less quietly, why on earth, and why precisely now, had he made this decision if, as he maintained, he had always been a Zionist? What could have happened? This last question almost seemed to hint at a true and proper flight, and who knows what the unmentionable reasons were . . . A distinguished prelate, whom Moshè had gone to visit to say goodbye, embracing him, had said, "I understand your praiseworthy religious fervor and your moving devotion to ancient traditions quite well. Is it that you, too, want to go to the Holy Land to be buried there when the time comes?" These and other questions were either made to him directly or arrived secondhand. But Moshè, who had already at least partly foreseen them—although some, as can be seen, exceeded his imagination—now delighted in giving vague answers, virtually as though he wanted to nourish this public and private inquiry even more. And that was mainly because, as it often happens, reality, which is simpler and obvious, often is ignored, and people prefer to indulge themselves in the most unbridled imaginings. For years Moshè's son had lived in Israel, where he was completely integrated. Now his daughter, having received her high school diploma, had decided to enroll at the University of Jerusalem. So it was a good time for the entire family to move to the ancient land of their ancestors. That was it.

The practical problems that Moshè had to face (and there were more than a few) were of two distinct kinds: taking care of all the paperwork connected to the departure and liquidating all the unfinished business relating to his residence in the city, and then, once they arrived in Israel, organizing a new life. As for the first group of matters that had to be settled, the tempo of work intensified with the passage of time and the approach of the departure date and kept everyone busy day and night so to speak. Nevertheless, regarding this, it should also be added that, as a result of completely fortuitous circumstances, many of these problems resolved themselves in the best way possible and in the course of a few minutes.

Moshè had gone to city hall, where he had to deal with several matters. There were a lot of people, and, although he had many other things to do, there was nothing else he could do but patiently wait his turn. However, since the expected waiting time had now gone on longer than foreseen, Moshè stood up, approached the attendant and asked him if he could speak with a manager, since he had urgent things to take care of. The attendant looked at him with an annoyed demeanor and didn't move or offer a word. When Moshè, staring, made him understand that he, too, knew how to reciprocate such courtesy, the man came around, stood up (barely), and asked, "Your first and last name?" Moshè said it. That fellow opened his eyes wide with surprise, stood almost at attention, and said, "I beg your forgiveness, sir; wait, I'll be back right away." Moshè sought, fruitlessly, to account for this instantaneous change. But he didn't have much time at his disposal because a member of the staff from the managerial level arrived, almost running, made a deferential bow, said, "I beg you, doctor, this way," and led him into his office. Here the manager immediately had Moshè sit down, apologized for the disorder on the desk, seated himself in turn, and with the warmest of smiles, said, "Listen, first of all, you are a relative of our comrade . . ."

Moshè began to understand something: His last name had been associated with that of a well-known communist leader. There weren't any kinship ties between them, but it would still be wise to take advantage of such an opportunity—if possible without telling any lies. So he responded, in the tone of voice of someone who would prefer not to go into the subject in depth: "You know, I've never in my life taken advantage of such things. Here, in front of you, I'm just another citizen and—"

"Fine, fine, I understand. What a magnificent thing. Would that many people would think in such a democratic way . . . I don't have to know anything more. Tell me how I can be of service to you . . ."

A quarter of an hour later, treated with great deference and accompanied to the elevator, Moshè left city hall with all the documents that he needed.

★ ★ ★

The specific rules that, according to the tradition, a Jew must observe to carry out the mitzvahs (commandments) are numerous, as is well known. There are no less than 613, of which 248 are "positive" (to do certain things)—the number, it is said, is equal to that of the parts of the human body—and 365 "negative" (which oblige one not to do certain things)—and which are equal, it is also said, to the number of days in the year. All the mitzvahs, in their totality, have a clear and precise reason: to make Israel the sanctified people, separate (*kadòsh*)—as the Lord is preeminently separate—and consecrated to the Lord. Only within these boundaries of a disciplined life should the life of the Jew who remains faithful to the Torah unfold. Any disobedience to the Torah is a violation of the pact of Sinai. It is also true that although the particular reasons for some of these mitzvahs are obvious and the special end for which they were instituted is clear, for others, on the contrary, such a clear and obvious interpretation is not always possible—which does not take anything away from the obligation to fulfill them, equally, with the others. That is what our Masters have always taught us, also observing that when dealing with the mitzvahs, one can never imagine, a priori, what infinite implications they contain and what influence, always positive and beneficial, they may have in the daily life of the Jew who remains faithful to the tradition. Among the numerous customs that regulate daily life, there is the one that prescribes that the Jew must always have his head covered, by a hat or by a skullcap (*kippà*). There is no need here to cite the varied interpretations that seek to provide an explanation that accounts for the custom. This is one of those cases in which it is not possible to supply a clear and definitive answer. But it is also true that even in this case one absolutely cannot foresee all the effects that the observance of this custom may have in store. As, in fact, once happened to Moshè . . .

Still organizing his affairs for his departure, he had gone to a city commission one day for a matter that concerned him personally. And he had chosen this commission mainly because in that same office he had twice been appointed juror. Thus he was welcomed with a great deal of warmth and was received almost immediately by the director of the office himself. The reason for his visit was explained, and the response was helpful and courteous: "There aren't any problems. Give me your identity document, and we can provide you with the document that you're interested in right away."

At this point, unexpectedly, matters became complicated. The only document that Moshè had was his passport, which was then at police headquarters for renewal. He then let the director know that at that moment he didn't have any document.

"I'm very sorry about this complication, but without an identity document I can't issue what you're requesting. How long will it take for you get your passport back?"

"In about ten days, not sooner."

"In that case, either wait to get your passport back, or else, since you're telling me that the requested document is urgent, come here with two witnesses. It's the same thing."

Now the situation had become truly complicated. He needed that document that he had requested urgently; he needed it that very morning. Setting out now to search for witnesses could take up valuable time. Believing that he had found a solution, Moshè pointed out that right there in that office he had twice received an appointment as juror and that therefore there could not be any doubts regarding his identity.

"Yes, fine, I agree," the director responded with a smile, "but your identity data that will also be transcribed on the document that you request can come only from an official document. The bureaucracy always has its requirements, and they have to observed. You understand, I could never put down, as an identity document, your appointment as a juror . . ." and he smiled in a friendly way.

By then Moshè was quite worried and he was about to get up when the director, who had been looking at him with particular attention for several minutes, even squinting his eyes to observe him better, motioned to him to remain seated, while he continued to look at him with even more concentration. At least one minute of complete silence passed by like that. Moshè asked himself what in the world was going on. Finally, as though his attentive scrutiny had furnished him with a definite answer, the director, with a wide smile, asked him, "Excuse me, but you're not that professor with the strange skullcap on his head who often talks on television in a broadcast about Jewish topics?"

"Yes," Moshè answered, also smiling and already thinking that in an unexpected way he had found a solution to his request. "Look," he said, "here is my strange identity card," and saying that he pulled the skullcap that he used in the broadcasts out of his pocket.

"Excellent!" the director exclaimed at this point. "Everything is in order." Saying that, he placed a finger on the buzzer. To the clerk who had been notified, he said, "Prepare me a document, thus and so, and regarding the identity, I'm signing as witness."

Shortly afterward, Moshè walked out of that office with the eagerly awaited document, and taking his *kippà* from his pocket, he studied it as though he had discovered something new. He walked on, thinking, "It's really true: The observance of certain mitzvahs constantly reveals new, unexpected meanings. Who would ever have imagined that a simple *kippà* like this could also be an excellent identity card?"

★ ★ ★

And more:

Among the various services that he had to discontinue there was the gas. Moshè took advantage of a visit of the gas company's agent who had come to take note of the data from the meter to ask him where he had to go to discontinue service. Surprised, the man asked him, "Why ever would you want to electrify everything? Look, it's not very economical, and gas is always better, believe me—"

"No, it's not for that. It's that I'm leaving this house."

"But you're going to stay in Rome, right?"

"No, I'm leaving the city too."

"What? What?" His surprise was great. "You're leaving this house and Rome, and with all that you still want to pay?"

"Exactly, that's right."

"I've never heard of such a thing . . . you must really be an honest person."

"But it's quite simple: I want to pay for what I've used and not leave unpaid bills, with the risk that others would then have to pay what they didn't owe."

"Oh, so that's the way it is. Well, it's your business, here's the address."

He shrugged his shoulders and went on his way, still incredulous at the enormity of what he'd heard.

★ ★ ★

And to finish on a note that I would describe as truly humorous:

A young board member of a Jewish institution, brilliant, with the gift of gab, which he used freely and which perhaps might even have given him the illusion that he understood many things in the field of Jewish studies, visited Moshè's office. He had written Moshè a letter regarding several inaccuracies that had been stated in the course of a television broadcast, which this young man had watched with great diligence. He began to speak at the tempo to which he was accustomed. He reminded Moshè that everyone has his own ideas (granted, but then can even ridiculous mistakes be defended?), and so each of us has his own autonomy, which must be respected by everyone. Thus even though some details of what Moshè wrote, but not all, you understand, had some truth in them, his words should be corrected at the right moment in a future broadcast. He then added that he would be very pleased if Moshè would return as one of the consultants for this program as he had been in the past.

Smiling, Moshè said, "I'm very sorry, but I've already, as they say, started putting the oars back in the boat. I've finished with everything that concerns our problems, and I'm leaving behind every Jewish activity for good."

The young man opened his eyes wide in surprise, and stammered, "But how, how can that be? Now you're going to tell me that you want to become a Christian?"

Moshè smiled and gestured with his arms, but he was silent. The other fellow pressed: "Come on, tell me, tell me. If it's like I said, why are you silent?"

"Look—you, as a good Roman Jew, still have the memory and the complex of a rabbi who years ago, here in the eternal city, was baptized. I'm simply making aliyah, I'm going to Israel. Do you understand?"

★ ★ ★

Israel. Moshè had already known it for many years, but it was one thing to arrive there as a tourist, curious to see ancient and modern things, and another to arrive there as an *'olé* (immigrant). When he landed at Ben Gurion Airport, it must be said, Moshè, to a great extent, still retained the spirit of the tourist. Nevertheless, with the passage of time, and truthfully it didn't take long, he got in touch with a completely different reality. This evolution is also worth recording.

Not that the reception by his old friends had been less warm than his previous visits—just the opposite. In some cases it was even more festive because it was sometimes accompanied by toasts and by well-wishing words, which, strangely, he then heard repeated even when he went to some office where he didn't know anyone. Such words were regularly addressed to him as soon as it became known that he was a new *'olé: barukh ha-ba* (welcome), *mazàl tov* (good luck), *be-hazlachà* (may you succeed). Simple words, but frequently spoken with warmth, which gave one the feeling of becoming part of a big family, where one had been awaited for a long time. And sometimes Moshè was even deeply moved. The Hebrew language, like all other languages, presents more than a few difficulties when one goes from the study of written texts to the spoken language, and the more one has the courage to *throw* oneself into speaking, without worrying about mistakes, the more readily the ear habituates itself and one learns many useful words even if afterward some are forgotten. But there were words that were impossible, under any circumstances, to forget. For example, the word *savlanùth* (patience). When paperwork dragged on at great length, even though the papers were in agreement with the precise information that he had gotten from the relevant agencies in Rome, and Moshè began to be surprised, the response to his pleas was always this: *savlanùth*. Little by little, this word kept acquiring an ever broader and pregnant meaning and one realized that one needed a good dose of *savlanùth* for practically everything, because this word meant, basically, "Dear friend, you have to learn that here everyone has to try to solve his problems on his own. Except in special cases, neither acquaintances nor friendships, even if they are tried and true, matter." At first, this discovery might even have shocked the new *olé* if, thinking about it after the first surprises, Moshè had not realized, thanks to his already long experience in Jewish matters, that all this process was simply normal and, after all, it was fair that it was this way. The fact that he was now living in the midst of a Jewish majority did not give him special rights in any way. What he was grappling with was a truly new form of life that spiritually and legally made him absolutely free. But it was still a life to be constructed, based entirely on his conscientious commitment, and not free of costs—or much less at the expense of others.

In other words, he had to realize, calmly and clearly, that he had not come to the ancient land of his ancestors to exercise rights he had acquired during all those years dedicated to Jewish matters outside Israel. What he had done in the Diaspora, as little or as much as it had been, was simply part of his duties as a Jew toward his people, and he had already received the reward by having had the opportunity to do what he had done. Now he had to engage in new duties toward himself and toward others if he wanted to rebuild a new life, as well as he was able, thus continuing an old custom, according to which the fulfillment of the Jewish ideal is always difficult, a continuous struggle. Overcoming what was incidental, the problems of the moment, and turning his gaze toward the future to work for tomorrow and not only for today, Moshè once more returned to the prophetic goal of being a prisoner of hope,[1] facing serious new difficulties of every kind that would be encountered. It was indispensable to remain faithful to this age-old hope that pushed one, day by day, to build a more positive future for everyone. Here, in the land of Israel, Moshè was aware of being immersed in the most complete way in the vast history of his people, of feeling that God was more present than ever in its millenary history and that the reciprocal collaboration between God and man should be still more concrete and active.

Among the many examples of *savlanùth* that Moshè had to face—sometimes, it has to be said, strange and incomprehensible—the one that we report here, is undoubtedly sensational:

The Bureaucracy—it is advisable always to write this word with a capital B— is a term that derives philologically from *bureau* (office) and from the Greek *kratòs* (power) and that means public administration considered in its systems, regulations, and mechanisms (in the disparaging sense, which everybody knows: hair-splitting, the pettiness typical of certain employees, and allegiance to the formalities). It is also worth noting that more than once this word has acquired meanings so rich in subtlety and unforeseen nuances that even the most expert constitutional rights judge could never succeed in interpreting the true meaning that "Bureaucracy" can take on in certain circumstances and environments.

It was the first time that Moshè had entered an Israeli ministry. Even though this visit had come about because of the necessity of producing a simple normal document and thus it was quite clear that on this occasion Moshè would meet with neither the minister, the person in charge of the ministry, nor with one of his directors but just with a clerk, he was still somewhat nervous because of the place to which he had come and because of his still hesitant Hebrew, which, at least he believed, would make him yet more uncomfortable in such an office. In a ministry, he thought, they undoubtedly spoke only a flawless Hebrew, and would he be capable of understanding and responding adequately?

---

1   For the personal importance and meaning of the phrase "prisoner of hope," see Augusto Segre, *Memories of Jewish Life: From Italy to Jerusalem, 1918–1960*, trans. Steve Siporin (Lincoln: University of Nebraska Press, 2008), 220–21. The phrase originates in the Bible, in Zechariah 9:12: "Return to the stronghold, you prisoners of hope; / This very day do I announce that I will restore double to you." H. Stuart Hughes used the phrase "prisoners of hope," borrowed from Segre's memoir, in the title of his groundbreaking book on twentieth-century Italian Jewish literature, *Prisoners of Hope: The Silver Age of Italian Jewry, 1924–1974* (Cambridge, MA: Harvard University Press, 1983).

He was directed to the second floor, which he ascended a bit fatigued because of the rather steep stairs, typical of the old Ottoman buildings. He had already noted the wide arches of the vaulting, and now as he went up, with a little imagination, his thoughts sought to reconstruct an earlier ambience, when the Jews, in the ancient land of their ancestors, went through different and difficult times. How many of his brothers might have climbed these worn stairs and in what state of mind? In their eternal silence of stone, these steps may have held pages of authentic history, which historians, even the most expert or imaginative, would never know how to voice. But now, fortunately for him, history had changed, and how! because the stairs that he climbed were nothing less than those of an Israeli ministry.

Moshè knocked lightly at a great, massive wood door that was partly open. There was no response. He knocked again and waited until, not right away, a rather hoarse female voice hissed, "Come in." He found himself in a wide, irregular room, virtually in semidarkness, where everything smelled musty, from the shelves—ancient and filled with paperwork in seemingly general disorder—to two broad desks next to each other, strewn with variously colored files that were rather faded. From a large, wide window, reflected light leaked in, in keeping with the surroundings. Behind one of these desks, the one nearest the window, a woman of rather ample figure and indecipherable age matched the somewhat sluggish atmosphere of the great room perfectly. She was slowly leafing through some papers. She didn't raise her head and silently continued in her work, which must have been very important, because she didn't so much as look up at the person who had entered and was now in front of her.

Several long minutes passed by like that. While waiting, Moshè looked around and noticed right away that no other employee was sitting at the second desk. He waited and waited, respectfully, in silence, repeating by heart the things that he would try to say in Hebrew. Suddenly, the woman, without raising her head, hissed a "Nu?" which is a syllable with different meanings, depending on the tone of voice in which it is pronounced. Moshè interpreted this concise sound as an invitation to speak and to explain the reason for his visit and his request. While he was talking, the woman glanced at him quickly a couple of times, without losing sight of the papers she had in front of her. When he finished, Moshè became silent, awaiting an answer. After a few seconds, the clerk, without offering a word, indicated the nearby desk with her left hand and continued her work. It was clear, Moshè thought right away, that his business must have been under the jurisdiction of the person who sat at the second desk and who was "out of the room" at that moment. So he remained patiently awaiting the clerical worker who was momentarily absent.

The minutes passed slowly, the woman tranquilly continued her work, and Moshè waited, on his feet. He was no longer deigned worthy of even a quick glance; it was as though he had left the room. At least ten minutes passed that way, in the most absolute silence, except for the light rustling of the papers that were being inspected and the sips of coffee or tea the woman drew from a large white cup. Afterward she slowly and carefully closed the file she had examined and scrupulously arranged it on top of a pile of other files she had to her right. Staring into space as though she were concentrating on something in particular, she finished sipping the coffee or tea from the great white cup and got up with difficulty. She gave a quick look at the visitor who was there, put the chair back precisely in its place, circled around her desk, passing close to Moshè, arrived at the second desk, and sat down. Crossing the chubby fingers of her hands—upon which she placed her fat chin—and, staring with an inquisitory, cold, professional, and maybe also a somewhat annoyed expression at the person who was facing her, she repeated, with a more resolute tone, an all but caustic "Nu?" which in this case could also have meant, "Come on, speak, hurry up, don't make me lose more time."

Moshè, after a few seconds of well-justified surprise and completely understandable perplexity, felt obligated to repeat, word for word, exactly what he had already said a few moments earlier.

The terse instructions furnished by the clerk were, for Moshè, rather vague, mainly because of the faltering Hebrew that the woman spoke. The document that he had shown her was, within a few seconds, filled with quick, broad deletions and added scribbles that later, in another office, turned out to be completely useless and in error. But all that, at this point, for this short history of ours, no longer has any importance. Moshè—this much is certain—left that office completely bewildered. Nor was he able to reconstruct, not even approximately and logically, the different phases of that strange encounter. Even considering the unlikely—was she a split personality?—he wasn't able to understand anything at all. And yet that is exactly the way things had happened; there was no doubt. The only thing that seemed clear to him was that not even a good knowledge of the Hebrew language would have been enough for him to understand the complexity of that ministerial office. Suddenly, walking along, he stopped, as though overcome by an idea that could be the key to that entire mystery: Everything that had happened had some relationship with *savlanùth* (forbearance, patience), with which, for that matter, he was already quite familiar. What, then, were the special secret rules? What if the richly imaginative actions that every clerk had to choose according to the case were carried out to determine whether each new *'olè* (immigrant) knew how to endure every eventuality worthily, thus rendering himself deserving of the right to live in the ancient Land of the Fathers?

Bureaucracy, always bureaucracy, more or less the same everywhere in the world.

★ ★ ★

Moshè presented himself at the gatehouse of the Ministry of Foreign Affairs and produced a request-to-appear paper in order to pick up a document. Behind a dark wooden desk, a middle-aged man with a large, black, drooping moustache that was perfectly framed on a nearly olive complexion, sat enthroned. As he spoke, his brilliantly white teeth shone. He examined the paper carefully and then said: "You"—in Israel one usually uses the informal *you*—"you are the professor."[2]

"Yes," Moshè responded.

"Wait." He lifted the receiver and dialed a number and asked for clarification. And then he said to Moshè, "All right, give me the number of your identity card."

"Just a moment," Moshè said and took the document out of his wallet.

The guard, surprised that a *professor* didn't know the number of his own identity card by heart, assuming an ironic tone of voice, said, "Oh, so you're a professor . . . and you don't even know the number of your identity card . . . unbelievable."

★ ★ ★

There were those—even friends—or some agency who took advantage of the word *savlanùth*. They did so for a variety of reasons (which could have been personal or bureaucratic) because they didn't want to commit themselves to doing what they could have done—to giving a hand, as they say, without straining their ideals, but simply being inspired to do for one's neighbor what one would want done for oneself. Well then, all this goes back to the typology of human attitudes that is easy to find in every country in the world. What mattered was that gradually, with the passage of time, as Moshè continued to orient himself, with

---

2   The Italian is *tu* (informal), which is what appears in the text, in contrast to *lei* (formal).

difficulty, to this new life, he also experienced a particular feeling of satisfaction, because everything he succeeded in accomplishing was almost completely due to his own work and that of his family. It was a new achievement, which stirred his abilities and his spirit of initiative. At times he even had the feeling that he, too, was a kind of *chalùz* (pioneer), even though he was in his 60s, comparable those who in past decades had been the true rebuilders of this country that had been abandoned and deserted for centuries. Nor could he forget that in the present he had many things available to him that the first authentic pioneers certainly did not find when they arrived in the Land of Israel.

One day, after he had a home, while he was admiring the splendid hills that encircle Jerusalem from a window, the famous passage of the Torah that speaks of Jacob's dream (Genesis 28:12) came to Moshè's mind:

> He had a dream in which he saw a ladder set up on the earth, with its top reaching the sky, and angels of God were ascending and descending on it. Then the Lord stood over him and said, "I am the Lord, the God of your father Abraham and of Isaac. The land on which you are lying, I am going to give to you and your descendants. Your descendants shall be like the dust on the ground; you shall spread to the west, to the east, to the north, and to the south, so that all the races of the earth will invoke blessings on one another through you and your descendants. I will be with you, and guard you wherever you go, and bring you back to this land; for I will never forsake you, until I have done what I have promised you." And Jacob awoke from his sleep.

It is well known that the strictly exegetical or midrashic commentaries on this passage are numerous and that, for that matter, the entire text of the Torah still continues to engage the studious, who search to penetrate the authentic significance of its teaching. Among other things, the following has been noted:

> What does that dream mean? That between him and heaven there was still a path, a direct means of communication, an understanding; the angels who rose on the ladder represented his faithful thoughts, his hopes, his prayers, and those who descended brought him support, the reassuring response of God. The one who calmed his fears, his anxieties, and his doubts was the same God of Abraham and Isaac; and that lonely strip of land in the infinite landscape and the soundless night was the land that one day would

be his. That is to say he felt, he desired, and he promised again to return there, to remain faithful to the mission entrusted to his grandfather and his father to fulfill the lofty task, the great message. He had faith in the immutable divine protection. He was secure that God would not abandon him, rather that he would be watched over and protected until His promise had been fulfilled. In Jacob's vision, as in Isaac's (Gen. 26:2–5), the feelings, intentions and hopes that engage and stir the spirit of the protagonist at a decisive moment are projected in heaven and then sent back or reflected on earth. (Dante Lattes, *Nuovo Commento alla Torà*, pp. 86–87)

This dream of the ladder, a midrash observes, was a sign that heaven's gate is always open to anyone who seeks to get closer to heaven and to feel the presence of God within, and that therefore whoever wants to is able to ascend it. This is an essentially theological interpretation, certainly not lacking an elevated lesson.

Among the commentators there are also those who seek to discover in the appearance of the ladder something more human—that is to say, had something new matured or was something maturing in Jacob's behavior? They observe that it was exactly at the moment when he had left his family and his homeland for the first time, weighed down by many uncertainties and justified worries about the unknown destiny he was going to meet—concerns not only for him but also regarding those who would be descended from him—exactly at that moment, through his vision, Jacob became aware of his responsibilities, not only for the immediate future but also for all time to come. It was certainly cause for great comfort for him to see in the angels an express guarantee, a sure sign of providential help, a clear proof that when one walks, within the realm of human possibility, on the Lord's path, one is never alone. But he also had to realize that, far away from his family, under only his own immediate responsibility, he would have to face a new life. This ladder could, in a certain sense, be considered a symbol of a future that was just as secure, even though it was projected centuries into the future, through his children and the long chain of the generations. At the same time it was a perpetual admonishment never to lose contact between heaven and earth. In fact, the indirect remembrance of this dream returns in Jacob's last words to Joseph (Genesis 48:3) and to all his sons reunited around him (49:1) to whom he tells what will happen at the end of days. The ladder thus remains an image of sincere and constant faith, of a future guaranteed for all generations to come.

It is important to know that Moshè had been a passionate student of midrashic studies for many years and that he dedicated a large part of his free time to them. He knew quite well that such studies weren't appreciated by everyone, and more than once he had found himself dealing with purists who interpreted biblical texts strictly scientifically and who, in response to some of his observations about certain passages, had said to him with an air of condescension, "But what you're saying is a simple midrash and with midrash, you know, you can say whatever you want." Maybe, but maybe not—not only because the midrash frequently offers authentic interpretations but above all because it knows how to find the direct and immediate path to the heart and can be understood by everyone, without distinction. Moshè's great interest in this genre of studies, even though it was vast and covered many centuries of ancient Hebrew literature, had sometimes even spurred him on to invent new, modern contemporary midrashim. They definitely were not lacking in imagination, but they were always connected to the biblical text in some way. On the other hand, the midrashic imagination, one can easily say, knows no limits.

Now one must ask oneself why in the world Moshè had thought specifically about that Torah passage on that day. The reason might have been quite simple: He had accomplished part of his agenda as an *'olè* and was making a preliminary final balance, so to speak, regarding how much had been brought to conclusion, even in the midst of countless problems. The matter of Jacob had been a dream, but how many times had Moshè also dreamed about *ascending* to Israel? He was certain, then, that the words that had been delivered in that far-off time to the patriarch, "and I will bring you back to this land," were valid even for him, a rather distant descendant of Jacob. Thus, almost spontaneously, that dream came back to mind—because the ladder that led to heaven could also appear to Moshè to be a ladder that brought him home, hence a particular comparison, one that was not without a great deal of imagination. Continuing this curious line of reasoning of his and developing it, Moshè then asked himself who all those angels who went up and down that famous ladder could possibly be. And, smiling for the unexpected idea that flashed through his mind, he had the audacity to make this comment:

Jacob, as the third patriarch, undoubtedly also had notable prophetic abilities. Abraham had already been called a prophet (Gen. 20:7). Now it cannot be excluded a priori that in that dream of his that was so complex and full of significance, there could even be this: In his prophetic vision projected centuries into the future, Jacob also saw, in those angels, unassuming 'olìm (immigrants) who, with infinite patience, with *savlanùth*, went continuously up and down the staircase of the *Sokhnùth* (the Jewish Agency) and many other offices in order to get their paperwork in order. And why on earth should these immigrants have the image of angels? Because only by reaching this high level would it have been possible to understand *savlanùth* properly and to realize that even settling in the ancient land of the ancestors is not a free gift; you have to be able to earn it.

HEBREW, THE HOLY TONGUE

Language is that complex of words and expressions a people uses to express, communicate, and exchange thoughts and feelings. Every people has its own language ("every people, according to its language," Esther 1:22)—original or derived, at least partly, from others—that characterizes it, and also vice versa. Between a people and a language there is, one could say, a phenomenon of osmosis through which certain words and phonetic sounds reflect a particular way of behaving or a certain way of thinking and at the same time condition the structure of the language.

The Jews are also a people and therefore have their own language. But the history of this singular language, like that of its people, has, in the course of the centuries, taken many complicated turns, especially because the people who spoke it have not always been in their ancient land but have traveled the earth far and wide, learning an incredible number of other languages. It can be reckoned that there is no other people like the Jews who over the course of generations have learned so many languages. Today, for example, whoever strolls along Ben Yehuda Street in central Jerusalem hears Hebrew spoken *also*, while hearing languages from the four corners of the earth. And it's not just a question of tourists—although as always they come here in great numbers—but of people who have been settled in the country for a long time. Goethe claimed that he who does not know foreign languages knows nothing of his own. Maybe so, but it's a fact that the Jews, having had to learn foreign languages, often ended up forgetting their own. And maybe the Hebrew language would have become a dead language, like ancient Greek and Latin, if the people who spoke it had disappeared and if this strange Semitic language had not also been different from other languages, just like the Jews distinguish themselves from other peoples. Sometimes, even today, you hear someone who says, "I would like to learn Hebrew, but of course the modern version." Such a person forgets, or never knew, that even though Hebrew, like every language, has evolved, the fact is that the language of the Bible (and later, that of the Mishna) in its fundamental grammatical and philological structures, has remained exactly what it was in ancient times. Today, someone who spoke the Hebrew of the Bible and the Mishnah would certainly not create the same sensation in Israel as someone who spoke the language of Dante in Italy. Maybe an explanation for this philological mystery can be found by referring to the most ancient traditions. From these one learns that this language of the Jews is the same one the Lord used to create the world and later to promulgate the Torah from Sinai. If these are the origins of this language, it's no surprise that we are talking about a language that is completely special, and in fact it is called *leshòn ha-kòdesh*, "the holy tongue." Besides the Torah, all the other biblical books later came to be written in this same language. If someone were to ask, "In what language did the lofty conversations between the Lord and Moses take place?" the prompt response would be, "But of course, in *leshòn ha-kòdesh*, in the holy tongue," that is, in Hebrew. If, then, it is true that this language, one of a kind, is always expressed in a way that everyone can understand—*Dibberà Torà kilshòn benè adàm* (the Torah speaks a human language)—that is simply due to the fact that back when the Lord, Blessed be He, spoke from Sinai in *leshòn ha-kòdesh*, every one of his words was simultaneously translated into seventy languages.

When one sets out to study it, this sacred language presents more than a few problems: It is a language of twenty-two letters, all consonants; one has to guess the vowels, which is not always easy; one writes from right to left; and its pronunciation is not the same in every country. For Moshè this was not a minor problem, especially when he tried to understand the Ashkenazic or the Yemenite pronunciation. One time when he was in an office with a friend, he was talking with someone who was also waiting to deal with a matter. When they left that office, Moshè felt the need to say to his friend, "Well, I've finally found someone who speaks excellent Hebrew."

But Moshè heard the response with great surprise: "But that was an Arab! Quite often Arabs speak excellent Hebrew."

Moshè, born and educated in the Diaspora, had gotten used to hearing only synagogue Hebrew, not spoken Hebrew. For centuries even European Jews had lost the use of the spoken language, save for the rare exceptions among highly educated persons and except for dialect forms, which, however, were only a mixture of corrupted Hebrew and local dialect. Hebrew, gone from the street and markets, had remained intact in the synagogues and in the centers where the Torah was studied. Under the guidance of a teacher, who was often nervous and without much pedagogical training—his salary was generally an act of *zedakà* (charity), as one said—Moshè, too, had learned how to pronounce those strange symbols. He did so with a certain amount of difficulty and with a certain sense of reverential fear. And then, woe to anyone who began reading with his head uncovered. The teacher's black rod would begin to whir menacingly around the head of that careless and irresponsible boy, and he would have to suffer the usual rebuke: "Don't approach our language with your head uncovered like some *goy* (non-Jew)." In Moshè's case the menace was even weightier, because there was always the danger that his deplorable lapses of memory would be reported to the chief rabbi, who was Moshè's father.

Hebrew, although by then reduced to a language of the synagogue, continued to constitute an important spiritual bond among all the faithful who frequented the synagogue. It can't be said that most of them understood the words, which were usually sung in unison. Nevertheless, those words never failed to arouse strong emotions in their souls. This response to Hebrew was another great proof of faith and a confirmation of the mysterious power of this ancient language that came from the Orient, apparently still carrying the echo of distant events, from the ancient patriarchs onward. Knowing only the fundamental facts about the occasion a particular prayer commemorated or recounted from the summary descriptions of the text in Italian that they held in their hands, congregants were affected and cried during the sacred services of the Holy Temple, both in joy and in pain, depending on the event. Thus on the Ninth of Av, the date that memorializes the destruction of the First and Second Temples, they sang passages related to the sad events by the light of candles as a sign of mourning, and then the tears of the faithful fell on the old pages of the holy texts that in the past had already gathered many other similar proofs of great faith. When they celebrated the holiday of Purim, they knew it was a great festival for the victory that had been achieved thanks to a few against a cruel tyrant, and everyone, praying, smiled and winked at his friend next to him on the bench, even if he didn't understand what was written in the prayer book and sung so well in the beautiful baritone voice of a *chazàn* (cantor). But the memory of a victory, though distant, always gave a great deal of pleasure and hope, even if those songs were performed in times of dictators, filled with dangers for the entire Jewish community. With the prayers finished, the book that contained the text of the prayers, the characters of that language that was so ancient ("Now the whole earth used only one language," Genesis 11:1), was put again into its drawer, after having been kissed many times.

Moshè had had the advantage of sometimes hearing this language spoken at home, even though not very often, because his father, rabbi of the Community, knew Hebrew well and received house guests who came from Austria and Hungary to see him. On these occasions, Moshè tried to catch some of the words he had noted in the prayer books or the Bible. This undertaking was always demanding. When Moshè began to attend high school, his father dedicated several hours a week to teaching him some grammar, reading, and the translation of classic literary texts, ancient and modern. Even when, with a certain effort, he began to babble his first sentences in Hebrew, and also later, in Rome, when he continued to study the Hebrew language under the guidance of distinguished teachers, there always remained a sense of special reverential awe in him toward this language that he now began to use as a spoken language. It always reminded him that those same sounds had rung out at the moment of Creation and on Sinai, thus taking on the typology of a sacred tongue. Isn't it written, maybe in an ancient text, that he who lives in Israel, eats foods cleared of every tax to the priests, speaks the holy tongue, and recites the Shema ("Hear O Israel," the beginning of a daily prayer, Deuteronomy 6:4) morning and evening, is already assured of the world to come? There was not any doubt that the holy language had extraordinary effects on this world and the world to come.

It took time before he was free from these and other language anxieties. He experienced a first big surprise in 1948 when he disembarked from the ship in Haifa on the occasion of his first trip to Israel, which served to show him that the holy language had made great strides forward in the ancient land of the ancestors, because—there could not be any doubt—it was already the language that was commonly spoken by almost everyone. At the police checkpoint, there was a young man in front of him who started speaking a good Hebrew, at least in Moshè's judgment. The policeman, who had to deal with a lot of things and didn't have time to lose, interrupted him after his first words, saying, "Ok, you're a teacher and you come from Morocco." Easy, no? For the policeman, certainly, but not for Moshè.

People who had been living in Israel for a while had by then acquired an ear for all the nuances of the language and for the ways in which it was pronounced, but that is not to say that they always succeeded in guessing correctly. Thus, for example, when Moshè spoke Hebrew, he was often asked, "Are you from Argentina?" After a few years, Moshè, too, had become polished in this practice of listening. In fact, not long ago, he found himself at the Hebrew University of Jerusalem where the centenary of Umberto Cassuto's birth was being celebrated. When a professor began to speak, Moshè turned to his wife and asked, "What do you think? Is he from Livorno or Pisa?"[1] He was from Pisa . . . But we can forgive Moshè's childish, happy surprise during the first weeks of his stay in Israel in 1948 when, walking through the streets of Haifa, and then Tel Aviv, he saw business signs, advertisements for various products, and posters, all of them written with the same characters in which nothing less than the Torah had been written. He then asked himself repeatedly, "Maybe this is the reason why the Orthodox don't want to recognize the State of Israel and continue to speak Yiddish among themselves?"

More recently, even after he had already been residing in Israel for several years and had grown accustomed to many things that were more or less agreeable, Moshè always felt a certain sense of discomfort and even disgust when, passing by certain bookshop windows, he saw books on display that were undoubtedly pornographic, yet written, nevertheless, in that holy language, or in the evening when he watched television broadcasts of films, spoken in Hebrew—the same eternal holy language—that dealt with topics that were hardly edifying from a moral point of view.

In the language that echoes today through the streets of Israel, returned to new life like so many other activities, born so to speak from nothing, there are many words that are derived from other European languages and words with roots of Greek and Latin origin. They have become integrated into this tumultuous flowering of neologisms. This is a phenomenon that is common to many other languages. You give and you receive, even in the field of philology. Thus there is nothing unusual—except for a certain humorous flavor—about the use that is sometimes made of certain words that has nothing to do with their original meaning. These words are employed by those who want to draw attention to themselves

---

1   Livorno and Pisa are only 17 miles apart.

as cultured persons (attaining just the opposite result instead). Thus, among the many examples, the word *philosophy* gets used—in so many ways. Recently this sentence was heard: "From the philosophical point of view, sport is conformist." Which philosophy is involved? And then the word *psychology* gets used a lot too. Moshè heard one day that a neighbor had said to the gas service man that he didn't use gas for heating because he was afraid that something might happen. And the technician said, "I understand. I understand that it's a psychological problem."

In spite of the perplexities of speaking, the search for the right word, and the gross errors one hears not only from the people but also from deputies when they speak in the Knesset (Parliament) and even professors at the university, Hebrew, and thus that eternal, holy Hebrew language, has found here in Israel the soil best suited for its rebirth yet again to a new, flourishing life. Today there is no subject matter in everyday life, regarding not only education but every other industrial, commercial, scientific, and literary activity, that has not found its suitable vocabulary. The days of the *Golà* (Diaspora) in the countries where Moshè had lived until a few years earlier and where he occasionally returned, were already distant—when, that is to say, the holy language was far removed from the reality of life and was often neglected even by those who as teachers (that is, certain rabbis) were supposed to teach it to others. Moshè amused himself recalling episodes he had experienced or telling stories he had learned from his father and from other old relatives and friends.

Thus it once happened that Moshè had to give a lecture in a synagogue in the presence of the local rabbi. Following tradition, he turned to the rabbi and said, in Hebrew, "Birshùth ha-Rav," which means simply, "With the permission of the rabbi." This is simply a proper act of courtesy by whoever is to speak in a place like the *beth kenèseth* where the local rabbi usually speaks. Hearing those words, the rabbi extended his arm toward the young lecturer, making a gesture with his hand that meant, "Could you explain to me better what you want?" Thus Moshè was reminded of a little story that his father had told him as true and that referred to an event that had actually happened, and at which Moshè's grandfather himself had been present. Here is the story:

One day two Jews, awaiting evening prayers, were chatting at the entrance to the synagogue. Now, two Jews waiting to form a *miniàn* (the minimum number of persons—ten—prescribed for certain liturgical services), what could they be doing if not speaking ill of their coreligionists and maybe even of the rabbi himself? At just that moment here comes the rabbi himself, in person. Well then, one of the two whispers to his friend, "Nedabbér 'ivrith kedé sheha-rav lo javìn" ("Let's speak Hebrew so that the rabbi won't understand")!!

In this paradoxical quip—in which, as in so many other anecdotes, the Jew is always amused to make fun of himself—there is information, nonetheless, that reminds us that during the times in which Hebrew language study was limited to just a few, there were not only rabbis (among whom there were those who did not know how to speak Hebrew) but also private coreligionists who dedicated themselves seriously to the study of the holy tongue. And that, the story apart, corresponds to the truth.

WHO IS A JEW?

Once again this question, Who is a Jew? suddenly came back in fashion in the newspapers, on radio, and on television, with particular reference to the groups of Jews arriving in Israel from Ethiopia, and then it was even discussed in the Knesset (Parliament). Moshè felt a painful sense of surprise, as when there had been so much discussion about the Bené Israèl, Jews who had come to Israel from India. That it was not a new issue but one that seemed to return every so often to the forefront of interminable discussions can be justified, to a certain extent, if one takes the history of the Jewish people into account. Among no other people who has lived in its own territory for centuries would one confront such subject matter at the juridical and religious level, and sometimes with a great deal of obstinacy too. But the Jews, as is known, are spread all over the world, and certain groups have also remained isolated from the rest of their brothers for many centuries. This is an indisputable fact that can raise many doubts about their authenticity as Jews. But beginning with this principle, why not extend this doubt to all the Jews of the Diaspora, whether they are preparing to immigrate to Israel or remain in their communities? The Jewish people, after all, should be preserved in its integrity. And who can declare with absolute certainty that the birth certificates of many rabbis who have intervened so furiously in the dispute are immune to doubt?

These are the first notes that Moshè put in writing, wishing, so to speak, to secure his thoughts, with the intention of later writing a fine letter to the highest rabbinic authorities to present them with his ideas on the subject. And, taken by this topic with an unusual sense of commitment, Moshè set down his ideas on paper, exactly as they presented themselves to his mind, helter-skelter, without any intention of confronting the subject systematically from a juridical and/or religious point of view. The documentation of our friend's spiritual travail is reproduced here just as it was given to us. After the initial comments made by him, which we have reported above, Moshè continued, even numbering his thoughts:

II. (Number I has already been noted, as reported above.) Dear rabbis, were the Nazis so nitpicking in establishing who was or who wasn't of the Jewish race? Of the 6 million Jews murdered, is it possible to say with certainty that all of them were truly Jewish, or could it be that persons who only had some vague family ties with other Jews were considered Jewish?

III. Don't forget several interesting passages from the Bible, which are truly ecumenical, *ante litteram*,[1] as for example:

a. "Then the Lord thought, 'Shall I hide what I am about to do from Abraham, seeing that Abraham is bound to become a great and powerful nation, and through him all the nations of the earth will invoke blessings on one another? No, I will make it known to him, in order that he may give instructions to his sons and his family after him, to keep to the way of the Lord by doing what is good and right, so that the Lord may fulfill for Abraham what He promised him'" (Genesis 18:17–19). Now we have to ask ourselves: Do today's rabbis, who are also descendants of Abraham, our Father, act with humanity and justice with their declarations?

b. "The stranger that sojourneth with you shall be unto you as the home-born among you, and thou shalt love him as thyself; for ye were stranger's in the land of Egypt" (Leviticus 19:34). Isn't today's generation, which underwent the dreadful Nazi persecution, capable of drawing a new lesson from these great words, a lesson also inspired by humanity and justice for everyone (and all the more so for Jews, even if there might be some doubt regarding their authenticity)?

c. "Moreover concerning the resident alien who is not of Thy people Israel, but comes from a far country for Thy name's sake (for they shall hear of Thy great name, and Thy mighty hand, and Thine

---

1   Latin, "before it's time," literally "before the letter."

outstretched arm), when he shall come and pray toward this house, then hear Thou in the heavens Thy dwelling place and do just as the alien petitions of Thee, that all the peoples of the earth may know Thy name, to fear Thee, as do Thy people Israel, and that they may know that this house which I have built is called by Thy name" (I Kings 8:41–43). Is it just to give such care and kindness to the stranger without it being understood that at least equal treatment should be given to fellow Jews, even when there may be some doubt as to their authenticity?

    d. "It shall come to pass in days to come, that the mountain of the Lord's house will be established as the highest mountain, and elevated above the hills. All the nations will come and say: 'Come, let us go up to the mount of the Lord, to the house of the God of Jacob; that He may instruct us in His ways, and that we may walk in His paths; for from Zion goes forth instruction, and the word of the Lord from Jerusalem.' Then shall He judge between the nations, and arbitrate for many peoples; and they shall beat their swords into plowshares, and their spears into pruning hooks. Nation shall not lift up sword against nation, nor shall they learn war anymore" (Isaiah 2:2–4). Regarding this passage, the historian Renan wrote, "Glory to the Jewish genius who longed for the end of evil, invoking that desire with unequaled intensity and saw rising on the horizon, in the midst of the terrible darkness of the Assyrian world, that sun of justice, which alone can make war between men cease." Are the rabbis who are saying what they've said about the Ethiopian Jews convinced that, acting like this, they too will become actively involved in this grand utopia of peace sung by Isaiah?

IV. Judaism is not exclusively religious, and it is not exclusively national. But it can be said that these two factors complete each other if one bears in mind that Judaism is a system of life that engages the individual in every act of his life. Elia S. Artom wrote:

> It's not unusual for a Jew to forget his Judaism and repudiate it, arriving at a point of officially adhering to religious ideas and practices that are incompatible with Judaism. If that happens, he completely or partially loses his rights as a Jew. He may no longer

be considered a Jew by others, and may not even consider himself a Jew, but he will always be a Jew: a degenerate Jew, an assimilated Jew, a renegade Jew, but always a Jew, and always subject to all his Jewish obligations. And a simple act of will, accompanied by those external forms that give him validity in the eyes of others, may, at any moment, allow him to reacquire what he had lost.

The rabbis of the Holy City, in their decisions, are also aware of these standards which are well known to everyone as well.

V. Isolation, which has already been mentioned, certainly poses various serious problems, including that of *mamzerùth*, the situation of the child born of adultery or incest. Of course, this problem may exist, but if it arises for groups of the Benè Israèl and Ethiopian Jews, why, in their scrupulous diligence as tireless defenders of the Jewish tradition, have the great rabbis not raised the same issue for the Jews who came from the Soviet Union, who were cut off from every vestige of Jewish life for many years? Have these great spiritual leaders of ours realized the absolute illiteracy regarding Jewish matters from which the new generations coming from Russia suffer? And since standards of such heavy rigor weigh on *mamzerùth*, why isn't this problem also raised regarding Jews who come from Europe, from cities large and small, where the rabbinic presence has always been inadequate, and, as is well known, very easygoing? And why, then, be worried specifically about this problem only for those who come to settle in Israel? Shouldn't Jews who live in the Diaspora also follow Jewish standards scrupulously? Has the Israeli rabbinate ever concerned itself with this problem too? One could comment that their task is limited to Eretz Yisrael. But hasn't the Jewish people always been ONE, wherever, dispersed, it finds itself? And doesn't purity need to be attended to for all generations of Jews wherever they may be found?

VI. In 1935, together with a small group of people—Moshè wrote down—when Mussolini began the war of conquest against Ethiopia, I quickly became involved with my fellow Jews from that country, who were now threatened with grave dangers under fascist rule. Good results were achieved, and for decades, even after the end of World War II, no one knew anything about it.

"In those now distant times," Moshè wrote at the end, "what mattered to us was to be able to save people who we considered, without quibbling, our brothers. Nor did we try to get special credit. Hence, the discretion of our action . . . hence, my interest and my current concern for these brothers of ours."

Whether or not these modest notes were put in order at a level acceptable for submission to the offices of the Israeli rabbinate and then were actually sent by Moshè, we don't know. The only thing still recalled is that together with those hasty notations, which above all revealed Moshè's state of alarm over the treatment reserved for these brothers, a piece of paper with a few memories of his childhood in his small Community of origin was also found. It is certain, from its contents, that this last "memorandum" would not have been sent to the highest rabbinic authorities (partly because the authorities weren't capable of understanding the Jewish-Piedmontese dialect). It is almost certain instead that these memories surfaced in his mind while he was intent on examining this important issue of who is a Jew and that he had made these notes in order to cheer up his troubled heart with some humor.

Moshè wrote:

> I remember that this issue was never addressed in our Community. Yes, words like *mamzér* and *samdà* circulated, but with completely different meanings. *Mamzér* was used to mean "wicked person," "cunning person," "a cheat," "a bad guy"; *samdà*, a convert, with derogatory connotations, meant a Jew who converted and was looked down on for that in the Community. It was a word that also became associated with wine when it wasn't genuine: *vin samdà*, that is, "watered-down wine."
>
> With people whom one didn't know, there was a certain system for finding out if they were or weren't Jews. A system, of course, that was not scientific, nor inspired by the usual rabbinic acumen but by that simple common sense of the people that more than once resolved so many ostensibly complicated questions in the best possible way. To illustrate this curious manner of identification there is a story: One day the local rabbi had sent his own son to the station to welcome a guest—naturally a Jew, but one whom that boy had not yet met. When he asked his father how he would be able to identity him, he heard his father say, "There are only a few passengers arriving on this train. As soon as they leave the station,

follow behind them and in a soft voice but in such a way that you can be understood, sing, in any tune, 'Lekà dodì liqrath kallà se l'é un judì si volterà,' that is, 'Come, my friend, to meet the bride (the Sabbath).'[2] If he is a Jew, he'll turn around . . . You can't go wrong. You'll find our man!"[3]

---

2   The first words of a well-known acrostic hymn that is sung Friday evening, composed by Shlomo Alcabez of Safed (1500–1580). [Segre's note.]
3   See the Introduction for more on this rhyme.

GLOSSARY

This glossary combines Augusto Segre's glosses in the original Italian version of *Stories of Jewish Life* with additional glosses by the translator. Italian conventions of Hebrew transliteration are followed.

ABREU (Jewish-Piedmontese dialect): Hebrews, that is, Jews.

'ALIYÀ: Literally "going up," and meaning "immigration" (to Israel).

'AM HAÁREZ: Ignoramus.

APICOÌRES: Heretic.

ARÈL (Jewish-Piedmontese dialect): Uncircumcised male, that is, a Christian.

ARON HA-KÒDESH: Holy Ark, which contains the scrolls of the Torah.

'ARVÌTH: Evening prayers.

BAR MIZWÀ (English: bar mitzvah): Rite of passage for males at the age of 13 marking the attainment of "religious majority." Literally "son of the commandment."

BARUKH HA-BA: Welcome.

BE-HAZLACHÀ: May you succeed.

BENÈ ISRAÈL: Literally "children of Israel." Here it refers to the Jewish immigrant group from India.

BERAKHÀ: Blessing.

BETH KENÈSETH: Synagogue, literally "house of assembly."

BIRCAT COHANÌM: Blessing of the priests.

CHALÒM (pl. *chalomòth*): Dream.

CHALÙZ: Pioneer.

CHAMÒR: Donkey.

CHARÀNNA (Jewish-Piedmontese dialect): From far away, referring to Charàn (Haran), a place where Abraham lived before he began his journey to Canaan.

CHASÌD: Pious person.

CHAZÀN (pl. *chazanim*): Cantor, officiant. Also spelled here as *hazàn* (pl. *hazanim*).

CHAZÈR: Courtyard, court, ghetto.

CHAZÌR: Pig.

CHÉREM: Excommunication.

CHERPÀ (Jewish-Piedmontese dialect): Shame.

COÉN (English: Cohen): "Priest." In English the word is usually spelled Cohen and is a common Jewish family name. Jews who are Cohens, in other words, "priests" (with or without the surname), are descendants of Moses's brother Aaron and members of the tribe of Levi. Their ancestors were once the priests of the Temple in Jerusalem. Today, as descendants of priests, they perform several minor, although special roles in rituals, but they are not otherwise distinguished from other Jews and are not to be confused with the fulltime professional priests of other contemporary religious traditions.

DUCAN: A raised platform in the synagogue where the prayers are recited.

ETROGHÌM: Citrons, an essential ritual object for the festival of Sukkot.

GOI or GOY (pl. *goìm*): The nation, non-Jew, and therefore also Christian in Jewish-Piedmontese dialect.

GOLÀ: Diaspora.

HAKHSHAROT: Training farms. Centers for professional agricultural training before immigration to Israel.

HATIKVÀ: "The Hope," a poem by Naftali Herz Imber (1856–1909). "Hatikvà" was the anthem of the Zionist movement and today is the national anthem of Israel.

HAVDALÀ: Separation. The ceremony and prayers that are recited at the end of the Sabbath in particular.

HAZAN: See *Chazàn*.

IESCIVÒTH: Academies of sacred studies.

KADÒSH: Separate, holy.

KASHRUT: Jewish laws regarding mainly food.

KEDUSHÀ: Holiness.

KETUBBÀ: Wedding contract. A legal document, often decorated, stating the obligations of the husband toward his wife and the date of the wedding.

KIPPÀ: Skullcap, cap.

KNESSET: Parliament.

LEKÀ DODÌ: "Come, my friend," the beginning of an acrostic poem in honor of the Sabbath composed by Shlomo Alkabetz Halevy, kabbalist of Tzfat (1500–1570), and recited each Friday evening.

LESHÒN HA-KÒDESH: The holy tongue, that is, Hebrew.

LIMMUDÌM: Academies of sacred studies.

LULAVÌM: Palm leaves, an essential ritual object for the festival of Sukkot.

MAMZÈR (pl. *mamzerìm*): Bastard, born out of wedlock, born of incest. Also used to mean "wicked person," "cunning person," "a cheat," "a bad guy."

MAMZERÙTH: Illegitimate birth.

MÀZAL TOV: Congratulations. *Mazàl* (Hebrew) literally means "star" or "fortune," and *tov* (Hebrew) means "good."

MELDA (Jewish-Piedmontese dialect): Pray.

MIDRÀSH (pl. *midrashìm*): Study, exegesis. A particular mode for interpreting biblical texts. When the exposition entails a teaching with a legal character, one has a *halakhic midràsh*; and if it concerns an ethical or religious teaching, one has a *haggadic midràsh*, which interprets the texts through historical and legendary traditions.

MILÀ: Circumcision.

MINCHÀ: Afternoon prayers.

MINIÀN (English: minyan): Quorum, number; the minimum number of men (ten) prescribed for particular prayers. Boys who are 13 years old "enter the *miniàn*," that is, they achieve religious majority and are bound by the observance of the precepts. (See *bar mizwà*.) Women are counted in minyanim today in many congregations, but they were not counted in Italy during the period Segre is writing about.

MINIANÌSTA: One who participates regularly in a *miniàn*. *Minianìsta* is a Jewish-Italian term derived from *miniàn*. In some Italian Jewish communities, *minianiste* were paid a minimal "salary," part of a welfare system for the poorest members, which ensured a daily prayer quorum and some income to the unemployed.

MISHNÀ: Repetition, study. A collection of traditional Jewish doctrine, especially the legal portion, as well as the study of this doctrine. The definitive arrangement was compiled by Rabbi Jehudà ha-Nasì (the Patriarch), 165–210 CE.

MIZVÀ (pl. *mizwòth*; English: mitzvah): Commandment, precept, norm, good deed.

NER TAMÌD: Eternal light. A flame or electric light at the front of every synagogue that is always lit.

NIGGÙN (pl. *niggunìm*): Musical motif. The traditional melodies of religious music.

NONNA: Grandmother.

'OLÉ (pl. *'olìm*): Immigrant.

PARASHÀ (pl. *parashòth*): The particular passage of the Torah (Pentateuch) that is read on a given Sabbath.

PARÒKHETH: The curtain at the front of the Holy Ark that holds the Torah scrolls.

PEÒTH (sing. *peà*): Side curls, that is, the curled locks of hair worn mainly by Hasidic Jewish men at the "corners" (the literal meaning of the word) of the beard.

PURÌM: Lots, fate. Also the holiday Purim, the Festival of Lots, which recalls the events narrated in the book of Esther. On this occasion the *Meghillath Ester* (Scroll of Esther) is read.

RECHIZÀ: The ritual washing of the deceased.

SAMDÀ (Jewish-Piedmontese dialect): Apostate, convert, excommunicated. *Samdà* has derogatory connotations, meaning a Jew who converted and was looked down upon by the Community because of their conversion. *Samdà* also became associated with wine when it wasn't genuine: *vin samdà*, that is, watered-down wine.

SAVLANÙTH: Patience, forbearance.

SCIAMMASC (pl. *sciammascìm*) or SHAMMÀSH (pl. *shammashim*): Synagogue attendant, beadle.

SCIOHAT (pl. *sciohatìm*) or SHOCHÈTH (pl. *schochetim*): Ritual slaughterer.

SCOLA: Synagogue or temple, but literally "school" (*scuola*), because the synagogue is the center of study as well as prayer.

SÈFER TORÀ: Scroll of the Torah, literally "book of the Torah." The scroll is written on animal hide and has conserved its form since ancient times, when the public reading of the Torah was instituted. It contains the Pentateuch (Five Books of Moses), written by hand.

SHAMMÀSH: See *Sciammasc*.

SHEMÀ': Listen, hear. The beginning (and name) of a daily prayer that is considered the central prayer of Judaism (Deuteronomy 6:4).

SIMCHÀ: Joy.

SOKHENÙTH: Agency, specifically the Jewish Agency, which acted in many ways as a government before the founding of the State of Israel.

SONÈ JUDÌ (pl. *sonè judìm*) (Jewish-Piedmontese dialect): Literally "Jew hater," that is, anti-Semite.

SUCCÒTH (also Sukkot): The Festival of Tabernacles, the autumn harvest festival during which temporary huts are built.

SUR MURENU: Literally "Signor our teacher," that is, the rabbi. *Murenu* is a Jewish-Piedmontese term based on a Hebrew root for teacher.

TAJARÌN (Piedmontese dialect): Tagliatelle (a kind of pasta).

TALLÈTH (English: tallith or tallis): Mantle, prayer shawl. A *tallèth* is worn during certain prayer services.

TALMÙD TORÀ: Study of the Torah. School in which one studies the Torah and Jewish material in general, that is, a Jewish boys elementary school.

TEFILLÀ (pl. *tefillòth*): Prayer.

TEFILLÀTH SHACHRÌTH: Morning prayer service.

TEVÀ: Ark, which contains the scrolls of the Torah. In Italian Jewish dialects, *tevà* becomes the word for the entire area in front of the ark, including the pulpit. Segre uses a phrase common to several Italian Jewish dialects, *va in tevà*, literally "go to the ark," which is what one does as a bar mitzvah, in order to read from the Torah to the congregation for the first time. Thus *va in tevà* is another way of saying "become bar mitzvah." For more on the word and phrase, see Umberto Fortis, *La parlata degli ebrei di Venezia e le parlate giudeo-italiane*, s.v. *Tevà* (Florence: Giuntina, 2006).

TIQQÙN CHAZÒTH: Prayers in memory of the destruction of the Temple in Jerusalem recited at midnight.

TORÀ: Torah, teaching, law, usually meaning the Pentateuch, the Five Books of Moses.

TZEDAKAH: See *Zedakà*.

ZADDÌQ: Righteous person.

ZEDAKÀ: Charity, literally "righteousness" or "justice."

NOTES

A NOTE ON THE TRANSLATION

1. But for the historical Jewish Italian dialects, the languages spoken among Jews when they lived in ghettos, the opposite was the case. *Giudeo* was the normal in-group term that Jews used to refer to themselves. Umberto Fortis identifies the Jewish Venetian variant *iudì* as "the most widespread word [among Venetian Jews] to indicate the Jew" (Umberto Fortis, *La parlata degli ebrei di Venezia e le parlate giudeo-italiane* [Florence: Giuntina, 2006], 290). Fortis also identifies other variants, such as *judìo* and *judà*, for twelve other Jewish Italian dialects (291–92).

2. Collected from Bruno Calimani, September 23, 1978. Signor Calimani recalled it as an anti-Jewish taunt he heard sung before World War I: *Ebreo, Giudeo, cadite il capeo. Che passa il Signor stanotte, ti muor* ("Hebrew, Jew, Your hat is falling down. When the Lord passes by tonight, you will die").

3. Professor Dario Calimani, personal communication, March 2019.

4. Segre may sometimes be using the term *Israelite* ironically as well as descriptively, as in the title of the chapter "Fifty Years of Israelite Journalism" (*Cinquant'anni di giornalismo israelitico*), which reports critically on the Italian Jewish newspaper *The Israelite Banner* (*Il Vessillo Israelitico*).

5. Ephraim Nissan, "The Paradox of the Italian Jewish Experience in 1990–2010," article 66, Jerusalem Center for Public Affairs, February 24, 2011, http://jcpa.org/article/the-paradox-of-the-italian-jewish-experience-in-1990-2010/ (accessed March 21, 2017); emphasis mine.

6. Nissan, "Paradox of the Italian Jewish Experience."

7. Oxford online dictionary, https://en.oxforddictionaries.com/definition/congregation (accessed March 13, 2018).

INTRODUCTION

1. In English, see, for instance, Cristina M. Bettin, *Italian Jews from Emancipation to the Racial Laws* (New York: Palgrave Macmillan, 2010); Renzo De Felice, *The Jews in Fascist Italy: A History* (New York: Enigma, 2001 [1961]); David Kertzer, *The Kidnapping of Edgardo Mortara* (New York: Knopf, 1997); Shira Klein, *Italy's Jews from Emancipation to Fascism* (Cambridge, UK: Cambridge University Press, 2018); Michele Sarfatti, *The Jews in Mussolini's Italy: From Equality to Persecution* (Madison: University of Wisconsin Press, 2006); Elizabeth Schächter, *The Jews of Italy, 1848–1915: Between Tradition and Transformation* (London: Valentine Mitchell, 2011); Alexander Stille, *Benevolence and Betrayal: Five Italian Jewish Families Under Fascism* (New York: Summit, 1991); and Susan Zuccotti, *The Italians and the Holocaust: Persecution, Rescue, Survival* (New York: Basic Books, 1987).

2. Cecil Roth, *The History of the Jews of Italy* (Philadelphia: Jewish Publication Society, 1946), 61. Isaiah 2:3 reads, "For instruction will go forth from Zion and the word of the Eternal from Jerusalem."

3. The standard general histories of Italian Jewry, though dated, are Roth, *History of the Jews of Italy*; and Attilio Milano, *Storia degli ebrei in Italia* (Torino: Einaudi, 1992 [1963]). I have drawn mainly on these two works for this brief survey. For a learned and personal synthesis, see Arnaldo Momigliano, "The Jews of Italy," in Arnoldo Momigliano, *On Pagans, Jews, and Christians* (Middletown, CT: Wesleyan University Press, 1987), 238–53.

4. According to Della Pergola, in 1500 the Jewish population of Italy is estimated to have been 120,000, or 1.14% of the total. Sergio Della Pergola, *Anatomia dell'Ebraismo Italiano: Caratteristiche demografiche economiche, sociali, religiose, e politche di una minoranza* (Rome: Carucci, 1976). Compare this number with a Jewish population of only 30,000 today, composing 0.05% of the Italian population. https://www .worldjewishcongress.org/en/about/communities/it (accessed May 17, 2019).

5. Attilio Milano, "Un secolo di stampa periodica in Italia," in Guido Bedarida, ed., *Scritti in onore di Dante Lattes*, special issue of *La Rassegna Mensile di Israel*, 12 (1938): 96–97.

6. Gino Luzzato, "Un'anagrafe degli Ebrei di Venezia del Settembre 1797," in Umberto Nahon, ed., *Scritti in memoria di Sally Mayer* (Jerusalem: Fondazione Sally Mayer, and Milan: Scuola Superiore di Studi Ebraici, 1956), 195–96.

7. Sarfatti, *Jews in Mussolini's Italy*, 40, as cited in Klein, *Italy's Jews*, 37.

8. Augusto Segre, *Memories of Jewish Life: From Italy to Jerusalem, 1918–1960*, trans. Steve Siporin (Lincoln: University of Nebraska Press, 2008), 39.

9. Andrew Canepa, "Emancipazione, integrazione, e antisemitismo liberale in Italia: Il caso Pasqualigo," *Comunità* 29(174) (1975): 196, as cited in Schächter, *Jews of Italy*, 20.

10. Segre, *Memories of Jewish Life*, 61. Historian Cecil Roth confirms the event: Rabbi Olper "kissed a crucifix at a public meeting in the Piazza San Marco" during the short-lived revolutionary Republic of Venice of 1848–1849. Roth, *History of the Jews of Italy*, 493. Some recent scholarship argues that the decline in the observance of Jewish religious customs such as synagogue attendance did not mean the *assimilation* of Italian Jews but rather their *acculturation*. The claim is that Italian Jews performed their Jewishness in different ways than they had in the past. See, especially, Klein, *Italy's Jews*. This revision goes against the consensus of scholarship on Italian Jewry, including Augusto Segre's assessment and his lived experience.

11. See "The Philosopher of the Po" in this book.

12. Manfred Gerstenfeld, "The Roles of the Jews in Italian Society," interview with Dan Vittorio Segre, Jerusalem Center for Public Affairs, article 53, January 17, 2010, http://jcpa.org/article/the-roles-of-the-jews-in-italian-society/ (accessed May 17, 2019).

13. For more on Augusto Segre's place among Italian Jewish literary authors, see Steve Siporin, "The Shop at the Edge of the Ghetto," *Rassegna Mensile di Israel* 82 (2016): 153–78.

14. I. L. Peretz, "Bontsha the Silent," in Irving Howe and Eliezer Greenberg, eds., *A Treasury of Yiddish Stories* (London: Andre Deutch, 1955), 223–30.

15. Benjamin of Tudela, *The Itinerary of Benjamin of Tudela: Travels in the Middle Ages*, trans. Marcus Nathan Adler (Malibu, CA: Joseph Simon/Pangloss Press, 1993 [1907]).

16. For example, Jachetu comes from the Hebrew Ya'akov (Jacob).

17. The porter always responds in Venetian dialect.

18. Augusto Segre, *Memorie di vita ebraica: Casale Monferrato–Roma–Gerusalemme, 1918–1960* (Rome: Bonacci Editore, 1979). The English edition is Augusto Segre, *Memories of Jewish Life: From Italy to Jerusalem, 1918–1960*, trans. Steve Siporin (Lincoln: University of Nebraska Press, 2008).

19. My discussion of life review is based mainly on Mary Hufford, Marjorie Hunt, and Steven Zeitlin, *The Grand Generation: Memory, Mastery, Legacy* (Seattle: University of Washington Press, 1987). Other important contributions to the concept of life review include Simon Bronner, *The Carver's Art: Crafting Meaning from Wood* (Lexington: University Press of Kentucky, 1996); Robert Butler, "Successful Aging and the Role of the Life Review," *Journal of American Geriatric Society* 22 (1974): 529–35; Sharon R. Kaufman, *The Ageless Self: Sources of Meaning in Late Life* (Madison: University of Wisconsin Press, 1986); and Jon Kay, *Folk Art and Aging: Life-Story Objects and Their Makers* (Bloomington: Indiana University Press, 2016).

20. Mayer Kirshenblatt and Barbara Kirshenblatt-Gimblett, *They Called Me Mayer July: Painted Memories of a Jewish Childhood in Poland Before the Holocaust* (Berkeley: University of California Press, 2007).

21. See Segre, *Memories of Jewish Life*, 293–342.

22. Segre articulated the same idea and feelings in *Memories of Jewish Life*: "From a simple, old peasant, who's drawn his experience solely from the hard labor of the fields, who through his good fortune hasn't been corrupted by any form of education nor been influenced by self-interest and political expediency, I've learned a lesson of high human kindness, of an ancient human kindness, simple and great, biblical in flavor, as in the age of Boaz and Ruth" (307–8).

23. In the 1920s a small group of peasants in San Nicandro Garganico, a remote town in southern Italy, converted to Judaism. Most members of this group immigrated to Israel soon after its foundation. For the most recent scholarship on the converts of San Nicandro, see John Anthony Davis, *The Jews of San Nicandro* (New Haven, CT: Yale University Press, 2010). Two early books are Phinn E. Lapide, *The Prophet of San Nicandro* (New York: Beechhurst, 1953); and Elena Cassin, *San Nicandro* (Philadelphia: Dufour, 1962). Davis's book was the inspiration for the recent documentary *The Mystery of San Nicandro* (directed by Roger Pyke, Matter of Fact Media, 2012).

24. Segre's footnote in the story reads, "The first words of a well-known acrostic hymn that is sung Friday evening, composed by Shlomo Halevi Alcabez of Safed (1500–1580)." Compare Segre's text with one I collected in Venice, in Venetian dialect, from Anna Campos, October 22, 1978. Segre's text, naturally, is in Hebrew and Piedmontese dialect, whereas Anna Campos's text is in Hebrew and Venetian:

Segre's text	Campos's text	
Lek'à dodí	*Lecha dodí*	Come, my friend,
Liqràth kallá	*Likrat kalá*	To meet the Bride
Se l'é un judì	*Se el xe judì*	If he is a Jew
Si volterà	*El se voltarà*	He'll turn around!

Umberto Fortis, in *La parlata degli ebrei di Venezia e le parlate giudeo-italiane* (Florence: Giuntina, 2006), 292, also reports the same rhyme from Venice as *Lehà dodì / Likràd calà / Se el zé ebreo / El se voltarà!*

CPSIA information can be obtained
at www.ICGtesting.com
Printed in the USA
BVHW080729190620
581569BV00007B/15